IDENTITIES
IN TRANSITION

MESOLITHIC STRATEGIES
IN THE SWEDISH PROVINCE
OF ÖSTERGÖTLAND

Edited by Göran Gruber

Riksantikvarieämbetet

Riksantikvarieämbetet
Box 5405, SE-114 84 Stockholm, Sweden
Phone +46 (0)8-5191 8000
www.raa.se

Riksantikvarieämbetet UV
Internet bookstore customer service:
Phone +(46) (0)31-334 29 05
Phone +(46) (0)31-334 29 04
Fax + (46) (0)31-334 29 01
kundservice@arkeologibocker.se
www.arkeologibocker.se

Editor Göran Gruber

Translation Alan Crozier

Production and layout Britt Lundberg

Graphics Dag Hammar, Lars Östlin

Drawing Anette Olsson (Bohusläns museum), Leif Karlenby, Anna Molin,
Fredrik Molin, Roger Wikell (Societas Archaeologica Upsaliensis)

Photography Bohusläns Museum, RAÄ UV Öst, Jan Norrman

National Land Survey maps © Lantmäteriverket, S-801 82 Gävle. Dnr L 1999/3

Printed by LTAB Linköpings Tryckeri AB 2005.860

Preface

The title of this collection of articles, **Identities in Transition – Mesolithic Strategies in the Swedish Province of Östergötland**, *has been chosen to stress our view that identity is constantly undergoing changes and transitions into something different. This applies as much to our own identity in the present day – as archaeologists and interpreters of the time we call the Mesolithic – as it does to the people who lived in this early period of the Stone Age. Sometimes these changes are seen very clearly, reflected in material culture. We thereby have an opportunity to interpret changes in social conditions and mentality as well. In other contexts the changes are more diffuse and elusive. Transition is a major theme which the articles in this volume take as a point of departure. Although the difference in time between us and the people of the Mesolithic is difficult to grasp, the study of changing identities can serve as a bridge over time. The changes of identity that took place in the Mesolithic are not essentially different from those in our own time. Our own identities have been created as a part of the constantly ongoing transition process of which the Mesolithic people were a part.*

In this book we have focused on the geographical area that constitutes the Swedish province of Östergötland. The province is bounded to the east by the Baltic Sea and to the west by Sweden's second largest lake, Vättern. The province of Östergötland as a cultural and political unit is not attested earlier than the Middle Ages and is therefore not strictly relevant for a Mesolithic study. The geographical area that is today called Östergötland has nevertheless functioned throughout history as a transition zone between rather different geographical environments and has proved to be a landscape space with good potential for studies of cultural variation and cultural encounters. Particularly when it comes to studies of Mesolithic society, Östergötland is able to display sites which shed partly new light on problems connected with this. They are sites that differ considerably in character.

Fig. 1. The Swedish province of Östergötland is bounded to the east by the Baltic Sea and to the west by the country's second largest lake, Vättern. Graphics: Lars Östlin.

We believe that it is important to get away from universal explanations of prehistoric phenomena and instead show the many regional variations that have occurred. These are often variations on a theme, which in turn demonstrate that cultural identity is something that develops and interacts on several levels. In traditional Swedish archaeological research, Östergötland is included in the larger geographical area that is usually called eastern central Sweden (or eastern middle Sweden), which is a rather misleading name for an area that is geographically in south-eastern Sweden. The name eastern central Sweden reflects the political significance of the area, in that the capital of Sweden is located here. The designation eastern central Sweden is at all events a theoretical construction. In archaeological terms it also reflects to some extent territorial thinking between Swedish academic environments in different regions, with the creation of appropriate geographical landscape spaces for studies within easy geographic range of each university. Unfortunately, this has resulted, for example, in distribution maps of finds in which Lake Vättern is divided from north to south to create a boundary between constructed culture areas – as if Mesolithic people in these parts were not able to maintain contact with the people on the opposite shore, just 20 kilometres away.

The fact that the focus of this publication is nevertheless on Östergötland is also due to the organization of archaeological excavations in Sweden today. Östergötland is the area covered by the institution where the majority of the authors work. The Eastern Archaeological Excavations Division (UV Öst) of the National Heritage Board (Riksantikvarieämbetet, RAÄ), has Östergötland and certain other parts of south-east Sweden as its main sphere of operation. The National Heritage Board's Archaeological Excavations Department, the country's leading institution for contract archaeology, has regional offices for excavations at different places in Sweden. UV Öst, which is the biggest actor involved in field archaeology in Östergötland, has conducted excavations since the late 1980s in connection with, for example, major infrastructure projects. It is in connection with these that most of the province's Mesolithic sites have been discovered and also in several cases excavated. In the last fifteen years our knowledge of the Mesolithic period in Östergötland has grown tremendously, both qualitatively and quantitatively, and with it our understanding of Mesolithic society and its varied identities. With this book we want to assemble and present the current state of research, for the first time and for an international audience. At the same time, we want to give readers a perspective on the history of research and a historiography of the work of some earlier scholars.

The content of this volume rests on two foundations. One is represented by the extensive surveys conducted in recent decades, above all in the eastern parts of the province. The other is the excavations of a number of small Early Mesolithic sites, and the large-scale excavation of the Middle and Late Mesolithic settlement site in Motala, beside the river called Motala Ström. The Motala excavation took place between 2000 and 2003 in connection with a major project in contract archaeology occasioned by railway construction. Among other things it has yielded a body of organic material that is unique for Östergötland, including a large number of leister points of antler.

Identities in Transition begins with a presentation of Mesolithic research, finds, excavations, and so on in Östergötland up to the present day, in an article by Tom Carlsson, Göran Gruber, and Fredrik Molin, all three of whom work as archaeologists at UV Öst. Professor Lars Larsson of Lund University then places the Östergötland material, in particular the Motala excavation, in a broader inter-regional context. Thomas Bergstrand, a marine archaeologist working at Bohuslän Museum, devotes his article to a study of leister fishing, based on the discovery of leister points and the fishing place investigated by the underwater investigations in Motala Ström. Joakim Åberg, also an archaeologist at Bohuslän Museum, deals with the large amount of bone from the Motala site, in an analysis that provides opportunities for a renewed discussion of economy, site selection, and settlement patterns. The lithic materials, flint and quartz, from the same site are discussed in texts by the archaeologist Nicklas Eriksson, UV Öst, and the archaeologist Roger Wikell, Societas Archaeologica Upsaliensis. In the article "Home Sweet Home", Tom Carlsson performs a spatial analysis of the settlement site, based on the idea that it cannot be viewed as random; there was regularity and active thought behind it. A more sweeping view of the part played by the Motala site in Mesolithic research, and the kind of society reflected by the site, is presented by Magnus Rolöf in his article "A More Human Society".

Associate Professor Anders Kaliff, of the National Heritage Board's Archaeological Excavations Division and Uppsala University, interprets the Early Mesolithic site of Mörby, in Hogstad parish in western Östergötland. The site was excavated in 1996 and revealed the hitherto earliest dated traces of human activity in the province. The volume concludes with three articles based on the field surveys conducted in Östergötland in recent years. Fredrik Molin presents a number of coastal Mesolithic sites from the Ancylus period in the neighbourhood of Motala, in western Östergötland. Roger Wikell discusses surveying strategies in the eastern parts of the province, where newly discovered material shows that the whole archipelago of eastern central Sweden was claimed, as land uplift made sites accessible. Finally, Roger Wikell and the archaeologist Alf Ericsson, UV Öst, identify in their article a number of settlements along the Littorina shore in south-east Östergötland, viewing them as parts of a socio-economic system around the large axe site of Ämtöholm in Valdemarsvik.

With this publication we wish to give both international and Swedish readers a deeper insight into the extensive new material that has emerged in Östergötland and the exciting interpretations stimulated by it. The majority of the material treated in the book has been discovered in the last few years and is the subject of ongoing research. We hope that the book will spread a knowledge of this research and thus open the door to a broader interpretation of regional and local variations during the Mesolithic in Northern Europe.

Linköping, March 2005

Lars Z. Larsson   Anders Kaliff   Göran Gruber
Head of Division   *Project Manager*   *Editor*

The Mesolithic in Östergötland
An introduction

Tom Carlsson, Göran Gruber, and Fredrik Molin

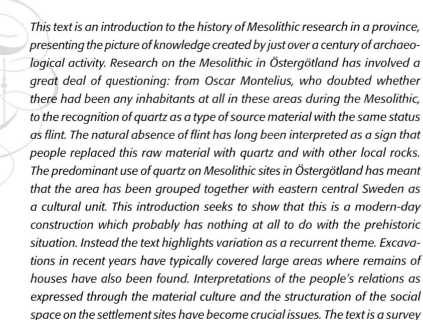

This text is an introduction to the history of Mesolithic research in a province, presenting the picture of knowledge created by just over a century of archaeological activity. Research on the Mesolithic in Östergötland has involved a great deal of questioning: from Oscar Montelius, who doubted whether there had been any inhabitants at all in these areas during the Mesolithic, to the recognition of quartz as a type of source material with the same status as flint. The natural absence of flint has long been interpreted as a sign that people replaced this raw material with quartz and with other local rocks. The predominant use of quartz on Mesolithic sites in Östergötland has meant that the area has been grouped together with eastern central Sweden as a cultural unit. This introduction seeks to show that this is a modern-day construction which probably has nothing at all to do with the prehistoric situation. Instead the text highlights variation as a recurrent theme. Excavations in recent years have typically covered large areas where remains of houses have also been found. Interpretations of the people's relations as expressed through the material culture and the structuration of the social space on the settlement sites have become crucial issues. The text is a survey of research hitherto but simultaneously a starting point for future excavating research which allows the prehistoric people to be present.

Östergötland is a province which has been defined since the Middle Ages as a demarcated area *vis-à-vis* its neighbours, partly through the promulgation of a medieval law code. We do not know, however, at what point in time the people of Östergötland and the neighbours around them began to link this identity to a spatial concept. Since the Middle Ages the province has varied considerably in extent depending on the vicissitudes of power politics. To try to sum up a region on the basis of the earliest archaeological remains within a territorially constructed area may therefore appear somewhat meaningless or else seem like regional centrism.

There are nevertheless several reasons for summing up the more than hundred years of archaeological experience of the Mesolithic in the province. Our knowledge of the Mesolithic in Östergötland has been radically changed since the 1990s as a result of a large number of excavations in connection with large-scale infrastructure investments. What has inspired us to try to give an account of the shared features in the archaeological evidence is the existence of several recurrent expressions, both in the material culture and in the mode of spatial organization. Rather paradoxically, it may be said that it is precisely the mixture that is specific. In the way people express themselves through their material culture, a constant flow of cultural contacts are made visible. Direct and indirect contacts from several geographical quarters shaped the cultural mix that makes up the specific character. If material culture is not only a passive reflection of a society's economic adaptation to its surroundings, the objects are just as much a medium for expressing social and cultural identity. People belonged to more or less formalized associations in which material culture actively communicated between users and observers.

Our aim is to try to describe the state of research and what has shaped the state of our knowledge in Östergötland. We can assure our readers, however, that research and publication are not intended to strengthen any modern regional patriotism, but rather to counter any such tendencies. This introduction provides a background to the texts in the publication. The aim is not to delimit but rather to tie things together.

A brief history of research

In preparation for the international congress of archaeology in Stockholm in 1874, Oscar Montelius studied the collections at the Museum of National Antiquities. His aim was to discuss whether or not there had been a Stone Age population in central Sweden. Montelius had noticed a Stone Age culture that distinguished itself from the previously known ones, and he presented these new findings at the congress (Montelius 1870–1873). Among the stray finds in the museum there was nothing striking that could give its name to any new cultural group. The lack of flint made classification impossible, so the finds could not be linked to known chronologies. The collections mainly consisted of simple greenstone axes.

Quartz had not yet attracted any attention as a raw material. Settlement sites with nothing but quartz were first noticed in the 1930s (Engström 1932b). Sten Florin worked with the waterside locations of quartz settlement sites and their dating (Florin 1948). A hundred years after Montelius' discovery of a Stone Age population in eastern central Sweden, the next attempt was made to divide the material chronologically. Stig Welinder suggested the name "flint and quartz group" after having conducted several small-scale studies in the 1970s (Welinder 1973b, 1977). The few flint artefacts were still necessary for imposing order on the material.

The difficulty of finding distinct types in the pieces of quartz still colours the view of this regional tradition. An attitude like "seeing is believing" impedes archaeological research. Quartz was for a long time ignored in surveys, and only the occurrence of flint was taken as evidence of human presence. Flint was synonymous with the Stone Age.

In the last few decades, however, archaeology has accepted quartz as source material. Through increased knowledge of the significance of quartz for Mesolithic people, archaeologists have once again been able to fill the earliest Stone Age of eastern central Sweden with people (Åkerlund 2003). Two worlds, one of flint and one of quartz, thus stand out in Scandinavia. The world of flint is linked to a Western European technological and material community. Areas with quartz as raw material reflect a different community, another lithic culture. In the border zone between these two worlds there are regions with contacts in both directions.

Stray finds and sites

The Mesolithic environment in Östergötland followed the well-known post–Ice Age environmental developments, characterized by dense tundra forests in the Preboreal time to the deep Atlantic forests, shallow bird lakes, and in particular the proximity to the sea. In the Late Mesolithic the Baltic Sea was saltier than it is today, with the Littorina Sea about 40 m higher than the present sea level. Two bays cut deep into Östergötland, forming a narrow inner archipelago with large and small islands. In many respects the landscape resembled the outer Mesolithic archipelago, with a varied environment of skerries and forests. Lake Vättern today is perceived as a barrier marking the boundary between the eastern and western provinces of Götaland. Until recently it was claimed that there were no Mesolithic settlement sites around Vättern because the nutrient-poor lake was not considered equally as attractive for settlement as the more nutrient-rich lakes of the plains (e.g. Kindgren 1991:51ff.). It has now become obvious that this picture is mistaken, particularly since two lacustrine Mesolithic settlement sites were recently found north of Motala (Helander & Zetterlund 1998; Roger Wikell pers. com.). Along the whole former shore of Vättern there are a great many stray finds of both pecked axes and the typically western Swedish Lihult axes. In the light of the newly discovered sites, these may be assumed to represent settlements that are unknown today.

The Late Mesolithic settlement site at the place where Motala Ström flows into Motala still has no counterpart in Östergötland. A very large and varied body of organic and lithic finds gives us opportunities for renewed discussions about, for example, settlement patterns and cultural influences. Finds of more than 50 leisters of bone/antler, decorated antler artefacts, house remains, axe manufacture, skeletal parts of humans, and the more than 180,000 stone artefacts suggest a settlement site of more complex and sedentary character than anything previously found north of Denmark/Skåne (see Bergstrand, Carlsson, Eriksson et al., this volume).

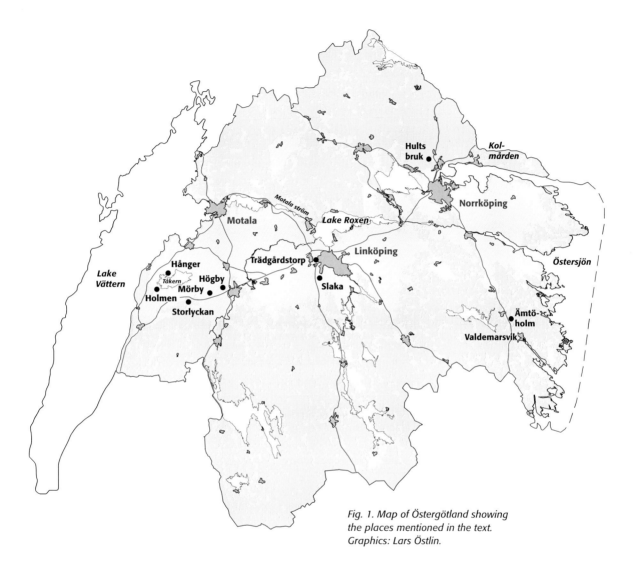

Fig. 1. Map of Östergötland showing
the places mentioned in the text.
Graphics: Lars Östlin.

Around Lake Tåkern there are about 30 registered sites from the Mesolithic and the Neolithic, with finds including flake axes and core axes (Arne 1905; Browall 1999). The site at Holmen stands out as one of the most interesting. Among the finds were pecked axes and Lihult axes and a number of antler tools, including a decorated chisel (Browall 1980:48ff.; Browall 1999:297ff.). The antler tools have led to the interpretation of the site as a probable Mesolithic burial (Browall 1999:301; Browall 2003:21ff.; Molin 2000:34). From Holmen we also have a blade of Cambrian flint. Isolated microblades of Cambrian flint have been found at Högby.

Östergötland belonged to both the flint world and the quartz world by virtue of its geographical location in a border zone. The archaeological research tradition, however, has focused chiefly on flint. We still do not know, for example, how large a proportion of quartz there is in the material around Tåkern. Many quartz settlement sites have been discovered in recent years in eastern Östergötland (Åkerlund 1996a; Ericsson *et al.*, manuscript in preparation). Only a few of these have been excavated, however; an example is Leverstad (Lindgren 1991).

A large number of pecked axes show the location of Late Mesolithic settlements (around the city of Linköping) probably on the shores of the Littorina Sea. Among the finds there are also a few axes of western Swedish Lihult type (Damell 1976:14f.). On the outskirts of the city there are also known settlement sites with worked quartz and microblades of flint (Molin 2000:35). Of great significance is the recently discovered settlement site at Trädgårdstorp, where several well-preserved Mesolithic settlement remains have been documented. Together with the large extent of the site, we glimpse an area of possible semi-permanent character. The finds consists of both quartz and flint, with microblades of both materials (Molin in prep.). Along the whole coast as it was in the Mesolithic, several similar find spots have been documented. These consist overwhelmingly of quartz and axes of both pecked and Lihult type. The majority of the sites give the impression of short-term seasonal use. Certain sites distinguish themselves in this respect, however: Borgsmon or Hults Bruk outside Norrköping, where both occupation layers and about a hundred axes have been documented (Nordén 1932; Engström 1936:5ff.).

Between quartz and flint

In general terms, the Swedish Mesolithic can be divided into different *raw material regions*. Flint totally dominates in the southern and western parts, while quartz is mainly found in eastern central Sweden and to the north. From this broad perspective, the regional availability of suitable raw materials stands out as a crucial factor (Åkerlund 1996a). Geographically and culturally, Östergötland lies between a world of flint to the southwest and a world of quartz to the north-east.

In the world of flint in Scandinavia there are several different Mesolithic cultures named after archaeological find spots, for example, Maglemose and Kongemose. For the Late Mesolithic we know of the Ertebølle culture from southern Scandinavia and Lihult on the west coast of Sweden. In Norway the corresponding culture is called the Nøstvet. The landscape on the west coast at this time was an archipelago with many islands. In this part of Scandinavia, Mesolithic people saw the sun setting in the sea. Flint dominates the raw material, and the material culture displays both similarities and differences with respect to the areas to the south. The toolkit consists of several recognizable flint objects which, to the archaeologist's relief, can be divided into different types: core axes, blade

Fig. 2. Aerial photograph of the plains of western Östergötland. Photo: National Heritage Board.

scrapers, and borers are guiding artefacts. Microblades were manufactured from handle cores. The culture also has a greenstone axe (the Lihult axe) characterized by coarse scars left by the manufacture. It is primarily polished at the edge and it often has a triangular cross-section.

The world of flint ranges from the coast on the west towards the interior. On the eastern shore of the large Lake Vänern is Kinnekulle, a high mountain with the only known source of Cambrian flint. Mesolithic people were not slow to use this source. Cambrian flint has its physical limitations, however. It is not suitable for the manufacture of large objects and seems to have been mostly used for making microblades (Kindgren 1991). At many places in eastern central Sweden there are microblades of Cambrian flint. None of these sites, however, shows such a raw-material mix and such high numbers and proportions of Cambrian flint among the total flint as the Motala site (Carlsson *et al.* 2003; Molin 2000). Nor do we find any traces of the manufacture of these micro-blades anywhere else. The microblades at the other sites were probably mounted in finished tools. The distribution of these artefacts testifies to broad contact networks.

To the east and north of Lake Vättern, the world of flint comes to an end. Unlike western and southern Sweden, quartz and other local rock types dominate the sites here. In eastern Sweden some 90–100% of the finds are of quartz. The quartz was for a long time incomprehensible, since retouched pieces occur very rarely, and hence no tools can be registered. It has proved fruitless to try to find or translate defined tool forms of flint from different cultures in southern Scandinavia. This was pointed out back in the 1930s by Engström, who was one of the first to realize the significance of quartz at sites with-out pottery (Engström 1932b). The anonymity of quartz meant that no type site was identified at an early stage of research – which in turn increased the anonymity. If any of the sites known today had been published a hundred years ago, we would probably now be finding concepts like "the Paradiset culture" in the literature (Hammar & Wikell 1994). For the Late Mesolithic, perhaps one of Engström's sites would have given rise to a name, for example, "the Hult culture" (Engström 1936).

The meaning-bearing elements in material culture are found at a different level than in the raw material or the purely technical aspect. There has been criticism of the inter-pretations of mass material in terms of typical objects and flint flakes (Knutsson 1998; Lindgren 1998). Similar criticism has long been heard in Finland (Siiriäinen 1969, 1975). Quartz, together with other locally occurring rocks, behaves in a way that corresponds to its nature and thus leaves different traces from flint. Any artefacts were shaped according to the special properties embedded within the material.

People used quartz, working it into suitable artefacts within the framework of tradition and custom. The Mesolithic societies in the world of quartz appear to have had a passive and pragmatic view of lithic technology (Knutsson 1998). An opposition to this relation between man and object as passive, and perhaps a more fruitful view, is that societies were not opportunistic at all but rather "takers of opportunities" (Whittle 1996:367). By man-to-man contacts or by hearing, people knew what was behind the next hill. They knew of different ways to cope with the nature of making tools. If flint had been essen-tial to any part of life, economic or cosmological, flint would have been accessed.

Archaeologically investigated quartz sites are mainly found in the former eastern outer archipelago (Knutsson *et al.* 1999). The landscape was characterized by tens of thousands of islands and skerries. There were eskers running north–south for distances of tens of kilometres, with light-coloured sandy beaches. Pine was a common tree on the poor soils, while mixed oak woods dominated the inland and the valleys on the larger islands. The settlements left by fishermen and seal hunters, who saw the sun rise in the sea, tended to face south on sandy beaches. This was an extremely rich environment with good opportunities for providing a livelihood. Many places were visited and used by the canoe-borne population, and all these places contain worked quartz. A widespread system of small campsites and larger assembly places can be discerned through the varying quantities of quartz and the size of the habitation areas. At the campsites there may be only a handful of flakes while the assembly places, such as Eklundshov at Södertörn, just south of Stockholm, may have hundreds of thousands of pieces of quartz (Lindgren 1996a). The quartz was picked up as nodules along the beaches or sometimes even quarried from the veins that run through the Precambrian rock. The cores were mainly worked with hammerstones in three reduction methods: platform technique, anvil technique, and bipolar technique (Callahan 1987). The stone axes are mainly pecked axes of rock which were pounded into a round shape, but there are also polished, almost square axes. A special find group from the archipelago consists of knives of different types of rock.

The use of microblades links the Late Mesolithic societies in much of Europe. We find the manufacture of microblades on the west coast of Sweden and in the interior, but not in the outer archipelago on the east coast. This difference is probably not only due to ecological factors; it is also a cultural expression. These material traces have been interpreted as reflecting two socially distinct groups (Lindgren 1997; Åkerlund 2000).

People most probably did not feel the absence of flint. Quartz was not necessarily a replacement for flint. The regional groups have to be studied on their own terms, naturally bearing the neighbouring areas in mind. In central Sweden, in the area between quartz and flint, there are a number of settlement sites with great similarities to the Motala site. Quartz predominates, but there are also cores of quartzite and flint (Lindgren 1997:31). In Motala there are handle cores of both raw materials. This shows that the site was closely associated with the world of flint but that the choice of raw material also linked it to the world of quartz. The absence in eastern central Sweden of other indicative Mesolithic artefacts, such as microliths, shows that something in the "European Mesolithic community" stops at the boundary between quartz and flint. At any rate, this applies to the lithic tradition.

Huts and the organization of social space

Excavations chiefly in western Östergötland have recorded a pattern of small, early inland settlement sites datable to 8300–6500 BC (c. 9000–7500 BP). These places are characterized by their location beside watercourses and shallow lakes in the process of being filled with vegetation. On several sites remains of post-built huts and occupation layers have been found. The oldest dated hut remains were excavated on the site at Mörby, and together with the hut remains from Högby these are among the oldest dated traces of settlement from Sweden.

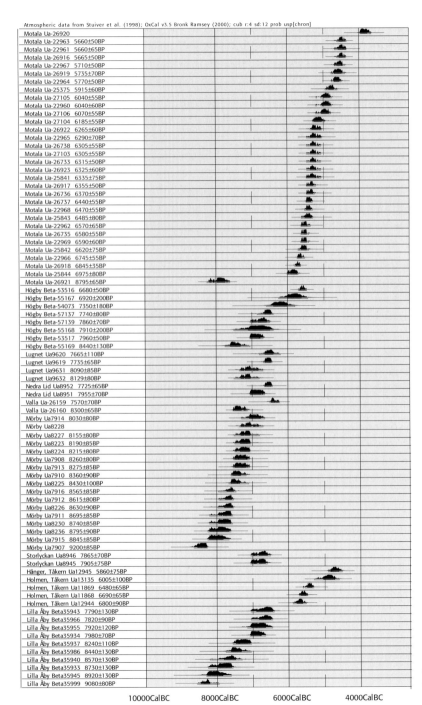

Table 1. A selection of datings of Mesolithic sites in Östergötland.

It is extremely unusual to be able to identify such early houses or huts, which puts the remains from Östergötland in special perspective. In southern Scandinavia there have been excavations of a small number of settlement sites with traces of huts from the Early Mesolithic. They are typically small sites with small hut structures, often in a location beside an in-filling lake or a bog. Examples of such places are Ageröd in Skåne, Ulkestrup and Lundby II on Sjælland, and Duvensee in Schleswig-Holstein (Larsson L. 1975; Larsson L. 1978b; Bille Henriksen 1976; Bokelmann 1981). These places display a fairly similar pattern with small huts located beside open water. Excavated Danish sites from the Maglemose period show huts of much the same appearance as those from Östergötland, that is, with round-oval or semi-oval to rectangular structures. The degree of preservation cannot be compared, however, and the Danish huts also tend to be bigger (Blankholm 1985, 1995; Grøn 1995).

The remains of the hut excavated in 1997 at the Storlyckan site show what is for Östergötland and the rest of south and central Sweden a very interesting spatial connection to a chronologically well demarcated assemblage of finds, consisting chiefly of quartz and flint. The relation between find distribution and hut is fully comparable, for example, to the majority of Danish Maglemose sites (e.g. Grøn 1995). In contrast, other excavated hut remains, from the settlement sites at Högby and Mörby, show a weak link between structure and finds. It is clear that the relative spatial organization of the sites and the structures is different.

The lithic material from the settlement site at Storlyckan comprises a large proportion of flint, which means that Storlyckan differs significantly from the settlement sites in central Sweden. On the other hand, the distribution agrees with that of the relatively nearby settlement site at Högby. By far the majority of the flint consists of blades and blade fragments, with the distribution virtually confined to the hut. Based on the distribution of the flint, it was possible to demonstrate that flint had been worked at the opening of the hut. The microblades of flint displayed an almost total coverage inside the hut, with a large concentration in the middle. Here is it obvious that the material was deposited in connection with a specific activity in the room itself (Molin & Larsson M. 1999:17f.; Larsson M. & Molin 2000; Larsson M. 2003).

The recently excavated house remains from the site at Trädgårdstorp likewise show a striking spatial connection to the finds from the site. In one of the structures there was an evident division in the deposition of the worked raw material, as flint had been knapped solely along one of the short sides of the house, and quartz at the other end of the house. As in the hut at Storlyckan, the majority of the finds in the middle of the house consisted of finished artefacts in the form of scrapers and microblades (Molin in prep.).

Fig. 3. Palaeogeographical map illustrating the relation between land and water in Östergötland during the Ancylus period. The shore of the Ancylus Lake on the map is at 75 metres above today's sea level. Map by Dag Hammar.

Man and landscape

The Early Mesolithic sites in Östergötland have the character of small seasonal sites to which people returned in a repetitive cyclical pattern. These recurrent moves probably created the picture of the chronological and stratigraphical layers that have been documented at the majority of the settlement sites. Datings with a span of up to 1,500 years are not uncommon. A couple of settlement sites also show clear overlayering in the form of wind-blown material. The oldest certain traces of human activities can be dated to the transition between the Preboreal and Boreal periods, around 8300–7500 BC. The period is characterized by the transformation of the Baltic Sea from the Ancylus Lake to the Littorina Sea. The earlier Yoldia Sea covered the plans in Östergötland as far as the Tåkern area. The Ancylus Lake likewise covered much of the province, forming a wide bay that cut in towards Lake Vättern, which frames the western plans. This geographical region was also bounded to the south and north by elevated areas of forest. It seems that the first establishment of human settlement in this part of Östergötland took place during the Ancylus stage.

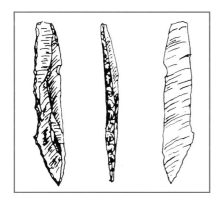

Fig. 4. Harpoon barb of flint found by the excavation of the settlement site at Lilla Åby, just south of Linköping. Drawing: Leif Karlenby.

The majority of the excavated settlement sites have their chronological centre of gravity in the period 7500–6500 BC, which may indicate a more intense phase of colonization. However, there are no large sites from this time which could have served as collective dwelling sites for large groups of people. It is a problem to discover these sites today. As yet we cannot be sure that they exist. According to the prevailing models of Mesolithic settlement patterns, we should look for these places along the coast as it was then. The only excavated settlement sites lying close to the coast of the Ancylus Lake are Lilla Åby and Trädgårdstorp in the central part of the province. These sites, however, are not right on the coast but a couple of kilometres inland. These places too give the impression of small settlement site structures. It is perfectly possible that the pattern of large settlement sites along the coast did not develop until the Middle–Late Mesolithic in Östergötland.

The location of settlement sites influences how the local surroundings were used and how material and artefacts flowed between these sites and between regions. The density and placing of the settlement sites affected all the different aspects of life. An important factor to discuss is the colonization of a new territory, which may be regarded as the opening of new spatial and social relations (Gosden 1994:24; Boaz 1999:138f.; Larsson M. & Molin 2000).

Much of today's archaeological research focuses on how people shaped the landscape for different activities which may be of both sacral and secular character. The landscape is viewed as an active part of people's lives, and even after death, and thus is a meaning-bearing medium. People's active participation in the landscape, for example, through places for extracting stone, manipulating the forest, making paths, and so on, is an important component of the discussion (Edmonds 1999). The Mesolithic world was a world created by kinship and forefathers, and time and place had a special meaning. Richard Bradley (1998:24f.) has discussed whether there was a "Mesolithic world-view". Similarities over large areas in mortuary practice and material culture would seem to support the possibility. The meaning of time for social and spatial changes, that is, how people shape a world filled with meaning over time, is an interesting and relevant point of departure. This is something discussed in recent years by Christopher Gosden (1994), who sees the significance of time for how changes in settlement and spatial perception can be interpreted. What we call settlement sites are places in the landscape where repeated activities take place (Gosden 1994:35). The perceived landscape, with its tapestry of interwoven elements, may be viewed as an important part of the Mesolithic person's view of his place in the world. "The interpretation of place is a struggle for position within the meaningful world" (Thomas 1996:91). The different parts of the landscape are woven together into a whole that people can understand. Those who moved in the landscape during what we call the Mesolithic created names, places, and myths, a structure that can be described as a history of the landscape (Thomas 1993:81).

Recurrent visits to the same places or areas can thereby be seen as the creation of a cultural and mental landscape which was ordered according to the group's view of the world around them. Seasonal moves should not just be viewed as an adaptive process. The landscape had a meaning-bearing function for the people who lived and moved there. Traditions and stories about the landscape were linked together. By repeatedly performing certain actions, such as movements between different sites, patterns are formed which become a cyclic history (e.g. Lindholm & Vogel 1996; Hodder 1999:194).

Material culture and social interaction

What united the Mesolithic societies was a material culture that enabled social relations with other groups and with their landscape. Similarities in material culture can thus be viewed as a way to structure and order the surrounding world (Gosden 1994:127). By changing parts of their material culture, the Mesolithic groups could create an identity of their own. This enabled both differentiation and union between different social groups.

During the Mesolithic Östergötland occupied an intermediate position between south-west Scandinavia and central Sweden, where artefacts such as flake axes, bone/antler harpoons, Limhamn axes, barbed points, handle cores, and microblades indicate influences and contacts with southern and western Sweden. The large quantity of quartz found on the settlement sites, on the other hand, is fully in keeping with the almost totally quartz-based culture along the Baltic coasts in eastern central Sweden. This dualism was pointed out by Stig Welinder (1977). The flint group that he was able to distinguish is associated with the west Swedish Lihult culture when its characteristic axe type is found at the group's settlement sites, while the quartz group's settlement sites are dominated by pecked axes (Welinder 1977:49ff.). Several other features in the material from Östergötland likewise corroborate east-west connections, including the find of a west Swedish barbed point. The Mesolithic in southern Scandinavia has traditionally been divided into several different culture groups, each of them characterized by a distinct material culture, such as the Maglemose, Hensbacka, and the Flint Group (e.g. Welinder 1977; Larsson L. 1990; Verhart 1990). The geographical boundaries are fluid, and various attempts have been made to define them more exactly and to study the paths of contact between the different groups. Studies of the distribution of pecked axes and Lihult axes suggest rather clearly demarcated regions, but with contacts between them (Kindgren 1991:58ff.).

In a major work on the Mesolithic in north-west Europe, Peter Gendel (1984:162) claimed to be able to distinguish different social territories characterized by a differentiated stock of microliths. According to him, differences in material culture are largely due to social and economic stress, which is noticeable above all in the latter part of the Mesolithic in Europe. A similar study, although based on bone/antler points, has been conducted by Leo Verhart (1990:139ff.). His basic assumption is that the most appropriate way to study and distinguish social territories is to proceed from the lithic material. The problem is that it can often be difficult to determine the exact provenance of this material. From his studies of bone/antler points, Verhart nevertheless claims to be able to discern several distinct social territories. It is interesting that the size of these territories decreased over time (Verhart 1990:149). In recent years economic stress as an explanatory model has been toned down in the discussion, and factors such as contacts between people and prestige have been put forward (Verhart & Waansleben 1997). This can also be seen in a study of the Mesolithic in southern and central Sweden, where regional differences in the form of variations in projectile points and axes have been observed (Larsson M. *et al.* 1997:47ff.). These variations have been interpreted in terms of an idea about the meaning-bearing function of material culture. Relations of exchange emerge between different regions, in which material culture reinforces the social identity of a group.

If we return once again to the Mesolithic in Östergötland, the discussion about social territories can also be applied here. Many of the tool forms mentioned above hint at the paths of contact that existed between different social groups in south and west Sweden at this time. There are also obvious features distinguishing, say, Östergötland from southern Sweden. The most striking difference is that microliths are almost totally absent (Browall 2003) and that Mesolithic transverse arrowheads are also extremely rare in the province. We have clear evidence that, for example, microblades and different types of bone/antler harpoons were used, types that indicate a shared material culture. An interesting thing in connection with this discussion is the observations made in recent years in northern Skåne and southern Småland (Karsten & Knarrström 1996). In this area it is possible to see how people in the course of the Early Mesolithic increasingly replaced flint with local raw materials. Here the dualism in the choice of raw material – whether quartz or flint – is highly interesting for Östergötland. Parts of the material culture seem by all appearances to be shared, for example, microblades, while others, such as microliths, can be regarded as distinguishing attributes. Differences in material culture can thus indicate the emergence of regionally developed social groups.

Living in a transitional area

Owing to academic research traditions, the Mesolithic in Östergötland has chiefly been discussed from an east coast perspective. Research from western Sweden has primarily focused on the areas west of Lake Vättern. The distribution maps of finds and settlement sites reflect this situation clearly (see e.g. Kindgren 1991). Regional academic territories have had the effect that the large Lake Vättern has very rarely been regarded as a central unifying factor in a regional system of prehistoric relations. Vättern is usually divided with a line into one side belonging to Västergötland and one belonging to Östergötland.

The term eastern central Sweden is often used to define a demarcated archaeological region to which Östergötland is usually assigned (Welinder 1977; Åkerlund 1996a). The most frequently applied criteria has been the occurrence of quartz as raw material and pecked and greenstone axes. The geographical extent of this term is unclear, however, varying significantly from one scholar to another. The area has shown distinct tendencies to grow in size since the 1970s (see Lindgren 2004:53). The problems of finding unambiguous artefacts of quartz and the wealth of variation in the form and appearance of greenstone axes have had the result that this spatial demarcation is rarely defined in terms of archaeological variables. Eastern central Sweden is defined by Christina Lindgren as an area with a marine economy, the use of quartz, and the occurrence of greenstone axes earlier here than in adjacent areas. The northern boundary is palpable in that the microblade tradition ceases from the Late Mesolithic, giving way to the much longer macroblades (Knutsson 1994). The differences between the archipelago, with its thousands of islands extending for miles, and the thick forests in the inland or on the shores of large lakes, make the circumstances very different.

One must perhaps ask *why* definitions of regions are interesting at all. Why has it been an important part of archaeological research to separate people according to the tools they owned? What do similarities and differences in material culture mean? Of course, it is an important part of all scientific work to define one's area of investigation. The object of study must have a limit. For archaeology, attempts at clear chronological and spatial limits have often meant creating static concepts rather than analytical apparatus. The definitions have become an obstacle rather than a tool. Researchers studying, for example, the Neolithic, rarely consider the Mesolithic as well, except perhaps as a background against which to see the differences and the development. The same phenomena are often interpreted in completely different ways, for the Mesolithic usually against an economic background (Whittle 1996). The geography is likewise mostly perceived as a necessity for the relevance of the comparisons. Perhaps it is just as much a matter of the identity of archaeology, in the form of systematization

An interested person who has read the text in order to find a definition of *what* distinguished Mesolithic people in Östergötland may perhaps feel a certain disappointment that it is the mixture that is the specific. A constant flow of cultural contacts is visible in the way people expressed themselves through their material culture. Direct and indirect contacts from several geographical quarters shaped the cultural mix that constitutes the specific character. Border zones like Östergötland reveal the possibilities that people either had to accept or reject parts of a geographically extensive common Mesolithic material culture. Individuals belonging to social groupings made conscious choices from the material expressions found in the flow of contacts. People were not opportunists but rather takers of opportunities. And their intention was probably not to demarcate but to unite.

From blank spot to focal point
An eastern Swedish site from a south Scandinavian perspective

Lars Larsson

Based on information and interpretations presented in this volume, this article contributes some views and comments from a southern Scandinavian perspective. This includes a brief history of the physical conditions and the mental barriers which had the effect that research on the Mesolithic in eastern Sweden did not really get under way until the 1990s. The text discusses the localization of the Motala site and the conditions for social structures of special character, linked to the immediate surroundings. The finds and the time of settlement are also considered from a southern Scandinavian perspective.

Facing the unforeseen

From a north European perspective, Mesolithic research in Sweden has chiefly concentrated on finds and sites in the southernmost part of the country. Good preservation conditions in a significant number of bogs, former lakes, and lagoons, here had the effect that objects of bone and antler survived, and sometimes wood as well. The west coast of Sweden attracted attention slightly later, mainly because shoreline displacement processes facilitated the dating of coastal settlement. In both areas the lithic material was primarily of flint, which was a well-known phenomenon with an early-developed typology and familiar terminology.

It was not until the 1970s that Mesolithic settlement was the subject of attention in central and northern Sweden (Welinder 1973b; Broadbent 1979). The majority of the material consisted of quartz, which was perceived as being much harder raw material to work than flint. In these archaeological stances there was not only a practical but also a mental obstacle. Quartz has partly different splitting properties from flint, and therefore in certain cases it can be difficult to shape objects of the kind known in flint. The translucent surface of quartz makes it more difficult to judge objects from a quick ocular inspection than in the case of most artefacts of flint. The mental obstacles are connected to a more or less conscious evaluation of raw material, as quartz is deemed to be second-rate material for tool manufacture – a substitute for flint. Although intensive studies of quartz have been pursued in the last few decades, there is still a classification structure for quartz which is much less varied than that for flint (Callahan 1987; Lindgren 2004). This under-valuation of quartz has also contributed to an under-valuation of other cultural expressions. Users of a second-rate raw material could hardly have any intricate or complex social structure or forms of expression. A view that has steadily gained ground is that certain forms of artefacts were expressions of a social distinction rather than a practical function (Larsson 2003). A sharp edge is always a sharp edge, regardless of where it appears. The fact that there are clearly shaped tools is rather an expression of an affiliation to a geographically defined group or a marker of the continuity of a tradition. The fact that sites with quartz in the majority of cases were located in environments which did not preserve organic material has further accentuated the alienation *vis-à-vis* the southern Swedish sites and find complexes.

Analysis of a small number of sites in northern Götaland and southern Svealand revealed a boundary between settlements dominated by flint and those dominated by quartz (Welinder 1973a). The dividing line ran down Vättern from north-west to south-east.

The boundary between flint- and quartz-using societies has been perceived, if not explicitly then at least implicitly, as something of a civilization boundary. In flint environments, trained archaeologists have rarely considered the quartz-using societies of southern Sweden. It has gradually become clear, however, that sites in northern Sweden, corresponding to the southern Swedish quartz sites, actually had features that were well worthy of attention. These included houses with sunken floors (Loeffler 2005) and graves (Halén 1994).

The Mesolithic of the Swedish east coast first attracted attention in the 1970s (Welinder 1973b, 1977; Åkerlund 1996a). Welinder's works were based on a number of specially selected sites. Otherwise the finds have come from rescue excavations, which means that the majority are discovered in what are now densely settled areas. It mostly requires special find conditions and antiquarian staff with special competence to detect Mesolithic sites among the remains that are excavated. When one site attracts attention, it usually generates several new ones of the same kind.

It is not uncommon for scholars to claim that the lack of remains of Mesolithic settlement sites is due to the fact that there were none. We can now state with good reason that no large area of land was ignored by humans after the physical conditions for settlement were provided by deglaciation. The supposed lack of settlements is a result of a lack of field surveys and possibly also a lack of the knowledge needed to recognize these remains.

Despite the extensive information at our disposal concerning remains from the Neolithic (Janzon 1984; Browall 1986), our knowledge of Mesolithic settlement in Östergötland was still extremely limited well into the 1990s (M. Larsson 2003; Browall 1999, 2003; Kaliff, this volume).

Fig. 1. A general view of the Motala site after the second year's fieldwork. The site is largely covered by the infrastructure of a modern society. The parts that were excavated sloped gently northwards down to Motala Ström.
Photo: National Heritage Board.

A place of special attraction for Mesolithic settlement

The excavation of the site in Motala was occasioned by the fact that there were remains of medieval settlement in the surroundings. The fact that the area also had a significant Stone Age settlement was not noticed until the preliminary excavation. Before this there had not been any excavations in the area, so it is perfectly understandable that the character of the site was not initially perceived as suitable for Mesolithic settlement.

Several excavations of Late Mesolithic sites in southernmost Scandinavia have yielded considerable knowledge about optimal settlement locations (Fischer 1975). A look at the location of the Motala site shows that there were extremely good conditions here for a large-scale Mesolithic settlement. The outflow of Lake Vättern beside the site, in the form of Motala Ström – the river which discharges a few kilometres later into Lake Boren and ultimately into the Baltic Sea – existed about 9,000 years ago. The outflow is located in a sheltered bay of Vättern with yet another similar bay in the immediate vicinity, which facilitated water transport around the outflow. The fact that the distance from the former Baltic coast was only about 30 km at the end of the Mesolithic also helped to make the area attractive for settlement. All in all, there are very few places in the Vättern area which could have been so favourable to settle in. In fact, there ought to be several sites of both Mesolithic and later age in the vicinity. The location of the site, sheltered by a headland, gave it relatively good protection against later erosion. Natural decomposition processes such as powerful currents in combination with the intensive development of the shores on both sides of Motala Ström, and the dredging of the navigation channel for the entrance to the parallel Motala Canal, may however have had the consequence that very few remains are still *in situ*.

As regards the geographical position of the site, a couple of aspects should be considered. When one discusses the location of the site, the designation "inland settlement site" is in this case somewhat debatable. There is no doubt that the site was beside Lake Vättern and that the coast of the Baltic Sea was at least thirty kilometres to the east. In this case, however, one can question the terms "inland" and "coastal" settlement. In the Mesolithic the coastal zone of the Baltic Sea was, as today, somewhat ambiguous. Just off the actual shoreline comes an inner archipelago where the open waters between the coast and the islands were usually very limited (Åkerlund 1996a). Beyond this was the outer archipelago. Waves and currents occurring in the Baltic Sea rarely affected the actual coast directly, with the result that there were sheltered conditions and particularly favourable circumstances for animal life – including humans – in the coastal zone. If the settlers needed to get out to utilize the resources of the open sea, they mostly had to travel considerable distances by water. The situation at the "inland settlement site" in Motala was completely different. Lake Vättern, which today has an area of 1,900 km^2, was slightly larger during the Mesolithic and can almost be termed an inland sea. Vättern is relatively deep, with a mean value of 40 m, has steep shores and no real archipelago. Beside the Motala site the water is about 30 km at its widest. The open water mirror gives free scope for winds, and the lake is notorious for its high waves. This means that the settlement site was located on a shore which was more like the environment on an open coast than the settlement sites found in former waterside locations on the Baltic coast. Moreover, the water in Vättern in the initial phase of the Mesolithic was the same as the freshwater in the Ancylus Lake stage of the Baltic. The shoreline zone at the site was compressed into a couple of small bays, in contrast to the archipelago in the coastal belt of the Baltic. This must have influenced resource utilization as well as the physical and mental relation to water. The use of the fish stock in Vättern required special fishing methods, and water transports required the same sturdy boats as the open sea of the Baltic. The quick fluctuations in the weather, especially in the winter half of the year, for which Vättern is still notorious, must have made the settlers particularly attentive to the fickleness of nature.

Another aspect which makes the site special in a broader geographical perspective is its stability. As the underwater excavation showed, the water level beside the site seems to have been the same for much of the Late Mesolithic as it is today. From an inland perspective this is not unproblematic but it is in a Scandinavian coastal perspective. In southernmost Scandinavia, recurrent transgressions during the Mesolithic reduced the areas of land by about a third. Suitable site locations were transformed into skerries and then covered by water (Larsson 1995). Along the east and west coasts of Sweden the isostatic and eustatic changes meant a constantly changing relationship between land and water, resulting in new landforms. Yet another significant change was the increasing salt content, from the freshwater of the Ancylus Lake to the first admixture of salt in the Mastogloia stage and the growing salinity in the Littorina stage.

The oligotrophic lakes of southern Scandinavia, with their accelerating filling of organic material towards the Late Mesolithic, also led to palpable reductions in the water mirror. In the present region Lake Tåkern is an example of this change (Browall 2003). Vättern was likewise subject to changes as a result of heavier uplift in the north than the south, flooding areas at the south of the lake and exposing areas in the north. Through these changes, there arose at *c.* 7000 cal. BC a new outlet in the form of Motala Ström. After this there seems to have been an unaltered relationship between land and water for many generations – an area where the world in one important respect stood completely still. For the Mesolithic people who came into contact with large water basins, this must have been an unusual state of affairs, which surely influenced their perception of the region.

The fact that the relationship between land and water did not change in the surroundings of Motala ought to have resulted in sites with a very long settlement time. As the radiometric values show, however, the settlement was relatively short-lived (Carlsson, this volume). Yet there is one dating which suggests an early use of the site. It seems to be earlier than the coming of the outflow in the form of Motala Ström, and thus at a time when the place was not as attractive. The fact that all the datings of activities after *c.* 5000 cal. BC are based on the bone points found out in the water suggests that the place was abandoned as a camp site (Bergstrand, this volume). The water beside the former settlement was still used for leistering fish, however. This is yet another indication of the existence of nearby sites whose occupants were familiar with the area and its conditions.

Social structures, central places, and cultural designations

One of the articles in this volume, by Magnus Rolöf, discusses the social structures during the Mesolithic which have been presented in different contexts (Rolöf, this volume). There is usually a teleological outlook on the form of social structures during the Mesolithic, implying a development with increasingly large and complex units. From ethnographically based analyses of hunter-gatherer societies, on the other hand, we know that they can display a great variety of social structures in both diachronic and synchronic perspectives (Knutsson 1995; Ingold 1999). This means that we should be critical of excessively static models for social structures and patterns of movement. Instead we should reckon with variations in the size of social units and in the extent of movements during the Mesolithic. Depending on different conditions, both physical and social, the social unit may have taken different forms, both on the site under consideration here and in the area used by a social system.

In the temporal perspective of a few centuries during which the site was probably used, the settlement may have taken several different forms. In certain periods it may have been a short-lived, perhaps seasonal, camp, while in others the settlement could have been more permanent.

The combination of ecological environments that existed at the outflow of Motala Ström was exceptional, and the resource utilization provided a base for a greater population density than other parts of eastern Sweden. This must have meant that the concentration of settlers, and probably also settlements, was much greater here than in other parts of eastern Sweden. This could have meant that special social structures occurred at the outflow of Motala Ström compared to other parts of the region. It is also possible to use the term central place – as for other parts of prehistory – in the sense of social constellations, structures, and activities that are exceptional in a larger region (Larsson 2003). A bigger and denser social unit requires clearer rules for the participants' interaction, which can be reflected in expressions of a symbolic nature and in traces of rituals – in the former case in the form of decorated objects, in the latter in the form of votive deposits and graves. A central place also functions as the hub of centripetal and centrifugal network patterns. Centripetal refers to both the accumulation of raw material, especially of an exotic nature, and the function as a focal point for the inhabitants of the region, a place where they met on certain occasions. As a centrifugal effect, objects which required time-consuming labour or high technical skills were produced at the central place and then distributed from it.

As regards the Motala site, the composition of the flint material testifies to an extensive network of contacts. The house and the fishing platform constructed just off the shore indicate that the place was used for permanent operations, as is also suggested by the occurrence of finds which are unusually copious for the region. The leister points reflect the production of relatively stereotyped forms, which in itself is an indication of advanced manufacturing know-how. Finds of human bones on the site may likewise mark the occurrence of rituals. The fact that no graves were found may be a reflection of their absence. On the other hand, large parts of the slope above the settlement site could not be excavated. From what we know of the spatial relations found on large settlement sites in south Scandinavia, the slightly higher parts of the slope, which are now under the railway embankment, ought to have been a suitable area for graves (Larsson 2004).

As regards features and the composition and quantity of finds, there are significant similarities to conditions in southern Scandinavia, as well as northern Europe. In the history of archaeology, socially advanced forms of expression have been easily associated with a material culture including a number of well-defined, morphologically distinguishable tool forms classified in a familiar culture. The fact that a site is related to a well-known culture designation has made the continued discussion easier (Kozlowski 1975, 2003). But the conditions in areas which lack clear culture designations or culturally distinguished units are much less certain. In such areas it has been difficult for some scholars to accept anything but basic social structures. No culture designations – no culture. This is especially noticeable in areas like eastern Sweden where archaeological excavations started relatively late. For understandable reasons, younger generations of archaeologists have been reluctant to employ culture designations which too easily petrify general and not infrequently erroneous notions about a particular phenomenon. Unfortunately, this attitude also makes it difficult to satisfy our need to systematize in order to create channels for learning. A mental blockage can be the result, when areas that lack remains with a specific culture designation are difficult to memorize.

Views of cultural identity

The aim of this article is not to examine the finds in detail. One artefact will nevertheless be highlighted since it serves as a foundation for reflections on cultural identity. It is a bone point classified as Type C (Bergstrand, this volume). It has been shown to have striking similarities to the objects that are called harpoons in southern Scandinavia. Because of the environment in which they are found they have usually been taken to be tools used for seal hunting (Larsson 1999). It is therefore interesting to find a fragment which can be linked to a setting specifically intended for leister fishing. It is probable that similar harpoons had several different applications, since harpoons of Early Mesolithic age have been found in freshwater lakes where both leister fining and hunting for aquatic mammals may have occurred (Larsson 1996).

Fig. 2. Broken leister or harpoon point found in the water at the fishing place in Motala.
The find corresponds to Type C, F11698, table 1, Bergstrand, this volume. Photo: National Heritage Board.

Apart from the form, which is the sole example of a regular harpoon in the material from Motala, it is also the only identified tool showing ornamentation in the form of small, regular incisions, on the sharp outside of both the preserved front barbs and on both edges of the broad inner part of the intermediate barb base.

In the presentation of the points the author notes parallels with finds from a couple of sites in southernmost Sweden (Bergstrand, this volume). It is interesting that this form of harpoon has a distinctly eastern distribution in the south Scandinavian Ertebølle culture (Vang Petersen 1984). This type of harpoon also occurs in both the Boreal and the Atlantic periods (Larsson 1999), the latter corresponding to the period of the main settlement at Motala.

Decorating harpoons was probably a way to stress a distinct identity (Weniger 1995). Decoration comparable to that on the Motala harpoon occurs on a small number of Late Mesolithic harpoons (Larsson 1999). Decoration on the barbs is found on three of four harpoon finds from southern Skåne, whereas this decoration is totally lacking in present-day Denmark, despite a considerable quantity of harpoons (Andersen 1972, 1976, 1997).

Both the form of the harpoon and the decoration of the barbs indicate a link with an easterly tradition in the south Scandinavian Late Mesolithic. Another phenomenon which distinguishes southernmost Sweden from Denmark, but which has its counterpart in the Motala site, is that fine-toothed bone points still occur in the Late Mesolithic (Bergstrand, this volume). Yet another phenomenon which seems to distinguish southernmost Sweden from Denmark is evidence of burials in seated position. This position is also found on the west coast of Sweden and on Gotland (Larsson 1989, 2004). Otherwise there are such obvious differences between the sites in the area that it is scarcely realistic to classify them in a uniform culture – a form of more internal cultural identity

The geographical distance between Motala and southernmost Skåne is about 400 km. By way of comparison, this distance is shorter than the area covered by the Ertebølle culture (Vang Petersen 1984). The extent of the Kongemose culture is believed to have been slightly smaller (Sørensen 1996). In the analysis of the Motala site, parallels have been drawn with areas such as the west coast of Sweden, with Kinnekulle flint at a distance of roughly 200 km to the west, and with the Stockholm region, roughly the same distance to the north-east, where slate-like tools like those in Motala occur (Carlsson 2004b). There has only been marginal consideration of the form taken by these contacts and the significance they had for cultural identity.

The clear link between morphologically distinguishable tool forms of lithic material and cultural identity that is found in the south Scandinavian Kongemose and Ertebølle cultures did not exist in the same obvious way in the area around eastern Vättern, and scarcely in eastern Sweden as a whole. This is marked by the fact that the Motala site contains only a few of the arrowhead forms characteristic of southern Scandinavia. In view of the large number of microblades, special forms of combination points may have

Fig. 3. Part of a human skull found at the Motala site. The osteological analysis showed that the bone comes from the occiput of a man who must have been aged 20–40 at death. Photo: National Heritage Board.

existed, made of wood, bone, and antler. It must be regarded as surprising that no flint-edged bone and daggers or fragments of these were found in an environment with unusually good preservation conditions for these organic materials. From the other side of Vättern there is a find of a flint-edged bone point, and the form is well known on the west coast. This type of tool also occurs further north in the form of arrowheads and daggers (Larsson 2005). In the main area for flint-edged tools, southernmost Scandinavia, there are a few regular forms. Towards the north it seems that several different forms occur at the same time, which might suggest that cultural identity was marked through these artefacts.

In view of the variation in arrowheads of flint that occur in southernmost Scandinavia (Vang Petersen 1984: fig. 5), one gets the impression that almost any point of any hard material is adequate for penetrating animal bodies (Fischer *et al.* 1984). The varied osteological material is also evidence that hunting could be successfully pursued without any special arrowhead forms. The different types of arrowheads that are so characteristic of the Mesolithic both in southernmost Sweden and on the west coast have to do with other than purely functional factors. In eastern Sweden no need was felt to shape any identity markers in the form of arrowheads or points for light javelins. Here this need was marked in a different way. On large settlement sites in eastern Sweden, for example, the one in Motala, there is a considerable number of rock axes (Lindgren 2004). Here we have an important functional form which may in addition have functioned as a symbolic marker. The finds of leister points are an indication of the proportion of the presumably large toolkit that must have been made of organic material. An important part of the symbolic language could have been expressed in this material.

Settlement area and duration of settlement

An earlier article in this publication discusses different cultural relations to the environment and the utilization of place (Carlsson, this volume). As examples the author used the observed differences between settlements from the Kongemose and the Ertebølle cultures at the Tågerup site in southern Sweden (Karsten & Knarrström 2003). Here there are considered to be explicit differences in the perception of flint working (whether it was specialized or practised by the majority of the settlers), in hunting (whether it was selective with little impact or maximized the use of resources), in the size of settlement sites (small or large), and in the execution of art (stringent or careless). The conclusion is that people in the time of the Kongemose culture lived in harmony both with nature and with surrounding groups, while people in the Ertebølle period were exposed to stress caused by intensive resource utilization and conflicts with other settlements.

When transferred to the results of the excavation in Motala, this perception can be interpreted as indicating that the remains reflect the period when resource utilization was intensified not just in southernmost Sweden but also in the area around Vättern.

It is obvious that there are clear differences between the remains in the two south Scandinavian Late Mesolithic cultures. Yet distinct changes in lithic crafts can also be found both earlier and later. In a broader geographical perspective, certain stages of the Ertebølle culture display more specialized craft than others. With only one site to go by, some of the other interpreted differences between the two cultures can be uncertain and even misleading. In the temporal perspective of several centuries that we have here, a large amount of finds can easily give a distorted picture of the use of the site. The differences observed between the two cultures could equally well be interpreted as traces of different utilization of place and resources depending on seasonal conditions. During the early Kongemose culture a location beside a river slightly inland from the coast was used for repeated seasonal stays, but at a later point in time when the area was in direct contact with the coast, utilization was maximized.

An aspect that is difficult to handle as regards the lack of classifiable arrowheads is that, despite some questioning (Karsten & Knarrström 2003), they are excellent chronological markers. A settlement site like the one in Motala, in such a favourable location, ought to have been used for a long time. Since the number of arrowhead forms is reduced to a microlith and a few transverse arrowheads, all we have to rely on are the radiometric datings to establish the time of settlement. There is some difference in time, for example, between the two houses discovered by the excavation. However, it is not so large as to prevent us from assuming that there was continuous settlement for a few centuries. It is only when we work with these lengths of time that the large quantity of finds and traces of activity stand out in a different light. During a period of, say, three hundred years, an average of three bipolar quartz cores should have been worked each year, and quartz waste would not even amount to one kilo. This does not suggest a large number of settlers. It is more likely that there were gaps in the occupation, as indicated by the radiometric datings. We should also bear in mind that the dig did not cover the entire site. The excavation area was limited to the west by the railway embankment. Several significant features such as the two identified houses are located close to this limit.

In the southernmost part of the site it was possible to investigate a slightly longer and higher part of the slope. Within this section, located furthest from the water and thus a peripheral part of the site, the excavation uncovered a microlith and the oldest radiometric dating of the earliest remains of settlement. This might suggest that the older parts of the site were slightly higher up the slope. This could explain why there seems to be a period without settlement from the formation of Motala Ström around 7000 cal. BC until the establishment of more long-term settlement on the site around 5500 BC. Despite a seemingly unchanged relationship between land and water, small changes caused by climatic factors may have meant that the older habitation area was located on a spot further up the slope which is today under the railway embankment.

Survey findings

The surveys conducted in the vicinity of the Motala site, and in a larger region of eastern Sweden, yield interesting insights. In the immediate vicinity there are sites suggesting relatively short-lived settlements and sites with a higher degree of utilization, with finds on a scale indicating settlement comparable to that on the Motala site (Molin, this volume; Wikell, this volume; Wikell & Ericsson, this volume).

It is also clear that the interest in field surveys in the region has only arisen in recent years, as knowledge of Stone Age settlement has been stimulated by the excavation of the Motala site.

How physical conditions can affect survey findings is more evident from a survey in a different part of eastern Sweden, conducted after a forest fire which removed all the undergrowth. A density of settlement sites that is extreme for the region was discovered here, with 70 find spots per square kilometre, an increase of 1,600% on previous surveys of the area, clearly showing that surveys give only an indication of the occurrence and density of sites, and definitely not a total view of Stone Age settlement. The nationwide inventory of Sweden is unique by international standards (Pettersson & Wikell 2004). It is nevertheless evident from the focused surveys presented in this volume that the results have considerable problems as regards representativeness. The experience of a special survey of an area in southernmost Sweden shows that only about 3% of the existing settlement sites were detected by the nationwide inventory (Larsson 2001). This is of particular importance since the antiquarian authorities often use the results of the nationwide surveys as a direct reflection of the actual situation as regards Stone Age settlement.

Another aspect which can be rather problematic is the fact that settlement sites detected on the surface are usually more or less destroyed since soil preparation may have removed many finds from their original location and seriously damaged features. Because of the heavy cultivation, chiefly starting in the nineteenth century, extensive areas have been subjected to soil preparation. Today these areas have in many cases been taken over by forests, but the damage has been done. This means that a significant proportion of the finds are in the topsoil that is removed before the excavation starts. The perception of the content and quantity of finds on the site, based on an excavation after topsoil stripping, will differ considerably from the information obtained by an inspection of the soil before stripping. A site which is relatively limited when excavated can be the last remaining vestiges of what was originally much larger. A significant share of the finds has been ploughed up into the topsoil where it is noticed by field survey. But when this layer is bulldozed away before the excavation begins, a significant source of knowledge disappears.

Home, sweet home
The spatial story of Mesolithic settlement organization in Östergötland

Tom Carlsson

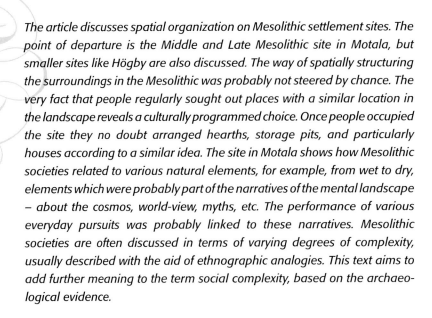

The article discusses spatial organization on Mesolithic settlement sites. The point of departure is the Middle and Late Mesolithic site in Motala, but smaller sites like Högby are also discussed. The way of spatially structuring the surroundings in the Mesolithic was probably not steered by chance. The very fact that people regularly sought out places with a similar location in the landscape reveals a culturally programmed choice. Once people occupied the site they no doubt arranged hearths, storage pits, and particularly houses according to a similar idea. The site in Motala shows how Mesolithic societies related to various natural elements, for example, from wet to dry, elements which were probably part of the narratives of the mental landscape – about the cosmos, world-view, myths, etc. The performance of various everyday pursuits was probably linked to these narratives. Mesolithic societies are often discussed in terms of varying degrees of complexity, usually described with the aid of ethnographic analogies. This text aims to add further meaning to the term social complexity, based on the archaeological evidence.

But what did it look like?

All archaeologists ask the question: what did it look like? Whether it is a routine antiquarian assignment intended to make room for a road or a new house, or a pure research investigation of a previously known dwelling site, we ask the same question: *what did the place look like* when the people we are interested in lived there? Where did the water go? Were there houses? Where did they cook their food? When did they performs crafts? What environment did the people create around their homes? We more or less consciously create a picture of the place, an idea of how space was organized.

Different places naturally offer differing potential to create pictures of the past. Preservation conditions, cultivation, modern-day damage, and so on erase a great deal of the original picture. A few pieces of worked stone found on an islet in the archipelago or in a newly ploughed field are in all likelihood just fragments of a much richer whole. Our picture of what many places looked like is probably vastly oversimplified, lacking in nuances and perhaps hopelessly wrong as well! The often obvious lack of analysable traces which could have helped us to answer the question of *what it looked like* unfortunately has the consequence that much of the picture is clear to us even before we have started our excavation. Our "advance view", our pre-understanding, of Mesolithic settlement sites and the society that created them is in large measure complete and waiting to be confirmed. We look for recurrent features, for patterns, for comparable finds and places. We check the empirical testability of the material. Perhaps we also find ethnographic analogies. Comparison is the implicit foundation for archaeological research, and of course we cannot do without it, particularly if we want to have our interpretations approved and accepted in the academic world in which we act. In the creation of the composite whole, however, we know at the same time that the variations were probably much greater than what we describe, than what is palpable.

This text seeks to understand Mesolithic settlement sites: surviving traces of how people arranged their homes: *what did it look like* and *why did it look like tha*t? No attempt is made in the article to define or even demarcate the term "settlement site". Settlement site – a home, a farm, an area (a space) – is probably far too broad a term to allow itself to be defined. Narrow definitions perhaps give security, but they impede our potential to make interpretations of the prehistoric picture rather than helping us to describe variations created by the people who perceived the site as their own. Nor can a settlement site be demarcated physically; in several dimensions it was also a perceived reality, filled with symbols, names, and narratives (Burström 1995:163). The surroundings can also be viewed as a narrative: space was organized according to a network of activity components: hearths, pits, wells, occupation layers, craft, and so on were assembled in a picture woven to create "a spatial story" of events and activities (Thomas 1993:81). Everyday chores were planned and carried out on the basis of this mental image of *how* space was constructed. Every archaeological investigation thus leaves fragments of this total world-picture, this context of meaning, imbedded in the seemingly unstructured remains.

A house in the country

Since the 1990s several Mesolithic sites have been excavated in Östergötland, offering varied levels of analysis for the settlement site. At all the places treated in detail in the text, houses have been found. From what may be a modern-day perspective, the house must surely have been crucial for the people on the site. The houses may be seen as the hub from which many of the other activities were spatially organized.

Up to the 1990s our knowledge of Östergötland's Mesolithic consisted almost exclusively of stray finds. In 1911 the archaeologist Birger Nerman, with the aid of finds of pecked axes, singled out the western part of the province as a central area for the earliest population. The shores of Lake Tåkern are also still highly interesting today, containing many important find spots (Browall 1980, 2003). Large-scale investments in the infrastructure starting in the 1990s boosted our knowledge of Mesolithic settlement sites in the province. Extensive stripping of topsoil by machine diggers exposed large areas where small and large settlement sites have been discovered.

Högby

In 1992 the construction of a road led to the discovery of Mesolithic remains at Högby (M. Larsson 1996). The settlement site was located on the slope of a sandy ridge close to a now completely vanished wetland. Several radiocarbon datings showed that the site was used during a long part of the Mesolithic. An early period occurred *c*. 8400 BP, a second phase around 7900–7300 BP, and a third 7000–6300 BP. The finds may be said to be representative: a mixture of different lithic raw materials but with a clear predominance of quartz, about 79%. The difficulty of defining quartz tools means that the analysis is based on the spatial distribution of the total find material and on the flint tools (Carlsson *et al*. 1999:52ff.).

For the purposes of this article the spatial analysis is most important, although the finds of objects such as microblades of Cambrian flint (from Kinnekulle in Västergötland) are very interesting for the question of contacts over large geographical areas. The features and the finds at Högby were concentrated within two small areas. In both these clusters of pits and post-holes, two semicircular houses could be discerned. The structures were supported by posts and they represent a living area of roughly three square metres. The openings were to the west, probably facing the wetland, affording a view of the activities performed on the shore and the properties that the wetland represented in people's cosmology. In one case a hearth was excavated and interpreted as having belonged to the house. A short distance away some more finds were made, but no houses could be detected among the post-holes in the area. Radiocarbon analyses show two separate settlement phases, an early phase 8970–8330 BP and a later phase 7600–6000 BP (ibid.:54ff.).

Mörby

In connection with excavations of Early Iron Age remains at Mörby in 1996, the stripping of topsoil uncovered Mesolithic settlement remains over a large area. The Mörby settlement site was on the sandy shore of a vanished wetland. The area was now arable land. Several streams flowed through the dwelling area in the Mesolithic. The settlement remains consist largely of radiocarbon-dated features, a very small quantity of finds varying widely in character, and possibly also a large (undated) quartzite block used as a source of raw material. Seventeen ^{14}C analyses date the settlement site to the time between 9200 and 8095 BP; this thus represents the earliest known settlement hitherto in Östergötland (Kaliff *et al*. 1997; Carlsson *et al*. 1999).

The excavated area is interpreted as having two dwelling sites and a workshop area. Two Mesolithic houses were found. Both were semicircular structures open to the south-west, towards the former wetland. The house remains consisted of post-holes and shallow trenches, with a living space of approximately 5–6 m² each. House I was dated to 9200 BP and House II to 8275 BP, the Early Mesolithic. The houses and the immediate surroundings were almost totally lacking in finds. It is possible that cultivation by modern methods, such as deep ploughing, has disturbed the soil and moved any finds away from the vicinity of the house (ibid.:57ff.). Hearths, pits, and a small amount of finds, including microblades, were discovered within a small concentrated area about fifty metres from the houses. It is worth mentioning that this area had not been disturbed by modern-day cultivation. Despite this, there were no traces of any more buildings; this area has been interpreted as an activity area for cooking and other tasks. Just beside it was the large quartzite block which was used for repeated working, as was evident from the sides and the large quantity of waste. Two hammerstones were found but no finds that allowed any more exact dating of the raw material extraction (ibid.:59).

Lilla Åby, Slaka Parish

The third example is a parallel to the Högby and Mörby settlement sites. On a sandy ridge, just a short distance from the shore of the ancient Ancylus Lake, a cemetery and settlement site remains from the Iron Age were excavated in 1988. Eleven features were subsequently radiocarbon-dated to the Early Mesolithic. The excavation methods were wholly geared to the Iron Age remains, and it is therefore possible that the considerable amount of quartz and flint gathered is not representative of the site. It is interesting that a barbed point of flint was found. This belongs to the earliest phase of settlement and is usually assigned to the western Swedish Sandarna culture (Appelgren 1995) (fig. 4 page 19, this volume).

The interpretation of the Mesolithic phase was not made until after the end of the excavation was over and the ¹⁴C datings showed quite a different result from what was expected. In the excavation report there is no attempt to interpret the Mesolithic phase. By reading the plans drawn during the excavation one can see a cluster of post-holes and pits from the Mesolithic. In this concentration of post-holes one can detect a semi-oval structure, about 5 x 5 m in size, with the opening to the south. The dating of the post-holes and pits is between 9000 and 7900 BP (Carlsson *et al.* 1999:61).

Storlyckan

In 1997 remains of a relatively well-preserved Early Mesolithic house were found at Storlyckan. The house was at the edge of a steep slope running down towards a watercourse. Unlike the three examples above, the Mesolithic remains were known when the excavation started. The site had not been cultivated by modern agricultural machinery as it was a pasture. The working methods were geared right from the start to discovering as many finds as possible. Finds and features were concentrated in two small nearby areas, and in one of these there was a post-hole belonging to a small house (Molin & Larsson 1999). The vast majority of the finds were encountered in the area of the house. The material consists of roughly 43% quartz, 47% flint, and the remaining 10% of the local rock, rhyolith, which is a completely different picture of lithic raw material than that from other settlement sites where quartz tends to predominate. It is possible that the amount of finds/raw material gives a skewed picture. If the finds are instead calculated by weight, then quartz dominates with 80%, while flint accounts for 15% and rhyolith for 5%, which is a more "normal" distribution of the raw materials for Östergötland (M. Larsson 2003:30).

All that remained of the house were traces of three post-holes, but an area cleared of stone shows that the structure was about 15 m² in area. Most of the stones along the walls may also have been part of the structure of the house. There was also a hearth pit in the house. No interpretation has been made of the direction that the opening faced. About ten metres from the house an activity area was excavated with a large hearth, filled with fire-cracked stone. A very small amount of finds including microblades was found around the hearth. Two ^{14}C datings showed that people lived on the site around 7905–7865 BP (7000–6500 BC cal.) (ibid.:30f.).

Motala

In Motala, on the banks of Motala Ström, there is a completely different settlement site from the ones described above. The picture of small scale displayed by the Early Mesolithic settlement sites in Östergötland is contradicted here at Motala by enormous quantities of finds and features. During the three years (2000–2003) while the excavation lasted, thick occupation layers were dug out containing some 180,000 finds. The investigation of occupation layers with well-preserved organic finds – bone, pollen, and macrofossils – took place both on land and under water. It is worth stressing that the entire site could not be excavated, but only the part that was in the way of a new railway bridge. There is a great deal to suggest that the site covered a much larger area.

The location of the settlement site at Strandvägen in Motala is unique in that the physical conditions, from a microperspective, have remained similar for at least 9,000 years! The water in Motala Ström still flows by at the same level. During the Atlantic period the Littorina Sea probably incorporated Lake Roxen as a broad bay while Lake Boren was a shallow lake. There was salt sea about 30 kilometres away. Motala Ström was almost certainly important for communications. Via the lakes was the simplest way to travel in all directions. A simplified reconstruction of the local environment during the Atlantic period describes it as a meeting place of several different ecological areas. In the south was what is today a plain, an extensive area of small lakes, swamps, and dried eskers sticking up. In the north large forests spread in rocky terrain (Carlsson *et al.* 2003).

Fig. 1. Aerial photograph. Lake Vättern and Motala Ström. Photo: Jan Norrman.

The Mesolithic phase is dated 5900–4000 BC. A large number of features, hearths, post-holes, and presumed storage pits testify to intensive use of the site around 5500–5000. According to the radiocarbon dates the site might have been used in different ways later on in the Mesolithic. The youngest ^{14}C dates are all from artefacts found underwater: leisters, worked bone, and a red deer antler. This means that the organization or the use of the settlement might have changed. But we still do not know what the site looks like outside the limits of the excavation area; houses, hearths, stone knapping areas, and so on could have been in different areas at the settlement during the latest phase of the Mesolithic. Another explanation could be that at this time the site was visited just for varied but very special reasons – exclusively for fishing and/or for ritual activities. There is only one Neolithic ^{14}C dating (3950 BC), but a small amount of finds including polished flint fragments show that the site was probably also visited in later periods.

The site was well chosen in its micro-environment: in the lee of the westerly winds on a gentle slope down towards the water that is a calm part of Motala Ström. The whole area was covered by a Mesolithic occupation layer 20–50 cm thick. This layer was thickest closest to the water and then gradually got thinner up the slope. The layer was excavated and water-sieved, but not before the layer was wholly removed were the Mesolithic features discovered. Post-holes, waste pits, hearths, and so on were placed along the length of a dry zone. There were very few features near the water, and no Mesolithic activities, such as hearths, were found away from this zone.

A Mesolithic long-house

On a slight terrace in the transitional zone where the occupation layer ceased, a concentration of post-holes was excavated and interpreted as belonging to the remains of a house. The internal structure consisted of the remains of three post-holes from the roof-bearing central posts of a two-aisled house running north–south. In the west there were several post-holes interpreted as having supported the wall of the house. There were no traces at all of the eastern wall, but this area had been disturbed by a number of pits containing brick and other modern material. Judging by the line of the wall and the fragmentarily preserved gables, the house was probably almost elliptical in shape. The southern gable (?) was wider and much more rounded than the northern one and was also placed further from the central posts. The gable in the south was interpreted as running close to the central post. In the house the excavation also uncovered a hearth with fire-cracked stone and leached soot and charcoal. The documented post-holes (and their presumed counterparts in the eastern line of the wall) form a structure about 10 x 4 m with a rounded south gable and a slightly more pointed gable to the north.

The house ran north–south. No opening/door was observed, but one interpretation suggests that it was in the east wall. This would then give the hearth a functional position just inside the door and it would mean that the opening/door faced in the direction where many activities were performed, on the river bank. The western wall of the house gave protection against the constant westerly winds from Lake Vättern. Another possibility is that the opening was in the south.

When the entire occupation layer in the area had been excavated, it was also noticed that the house had stood on a levelled surface that had been partly dug out. The ground was probably prepared by the people who built the house, or else the house was placed on a site that was naturally flatter than the surroundings. The post-holes varied in diameter between 0.3 and 0.4 m. They were usually lined with small stones and were strikingly like each other in form and appearance. The filling contained layers of soot, charcoal, and occasional pieces of worked quartz. In one post-hole in the line of the wall there was a hammerstone. Inside what was interpreted as the walls of the house there were comparatively few finds. Objects were however found immediately outside the wall

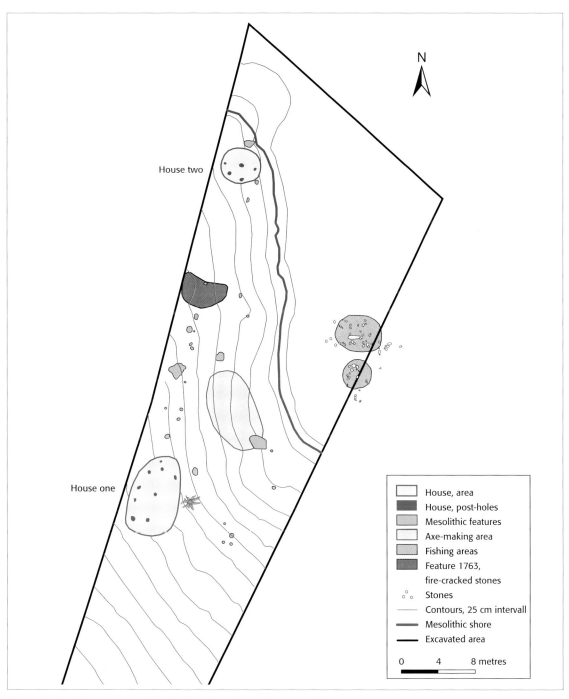

Fig. 2. The long-house, a Mesolithic dwelling house? Graphics: Lars Östlin.

of the house, chiefly small flakes and debris. The interpretation is that the house mainly functioned as a dwelling and that stone working mostly took place outdoors or in other buildings (see below). Some handling of tools (resharpening? manufacture?) nevertheless resulted in the deposition of waste, chiefly along the walls. The house was in all probability cleaned, which has naturally affected our potential to reconstruct the activities performed indoors.

Charcoal from the three roof-bearing posts and the hearth was selected for ^{14}C analyses:

- 5630–5470 BC (calibrated, 2 sigma), 6580 ± 55 BP. Oak.
- 5490–5310 BC (calibrated, 2 sigma), 6440 ± 55 BP. Oak.
- 5480–5250 BC (calibrated, 2 sigma), 6370 ± 55 BP. Hazelnut shell.

All three roof-bearing post-holes yielded datings within a narrow range. The variation of a few hundred years seems like a reasonable interval, but it is also conceivable that the oak that was used as building material or firewood had a high initial value, in other words, that it was relatively old when felled. The hazelnut shell, on the other hand, can scarcely have had any initial value. The charcoal in the hearth could not be dated, unfortunately, since it dissolved while being prepared for the AMS datings. The question whether the hearth belonged to the house thus remains unanswered.

Cooking

Outside the house, close to the river bank, there were several small hearths and cooking pits. This area yielded the largest concentration of fish, vertebrae, bones, and also scales. Scrapers of flint and quartz, bone needles and other tools were found in the same area. One interpretation is that this area was intended for everyday cooking. Just outside the house the excavation also uncovered more anonymous pits, perhaps used for storing food. These too have been dated in the same range as the house.

- 5380–5200 BC (calibrated, 2 sigma), 6315 ± 50 BP.
- 5370–5190 BC (calibrated, 2 sigma), 6580 ± 55 BP.

These datings are slightly later than the mean value obtained for the house, but they agree closely with that of the hazelnut shell.

Axe production

A short distance from the house, traces of axe manufacture were found within a small area; among other things there were 30–40 whole and fragmented axes. In form and appearance the axes resemble the eastern Swedish axes with their polished surfaces and great variation in form. The datings probably also agree with these, around 6000–4500 BC (Lindgren 2004:48). At least four workpieces for a greenstone axe was found, along with flakes of greenstone and heavy hammerstones of red porphyry within the same area. The finds of several large grindstones suggest that axe edges were polished and sharpened on the site. Petrographic thin-section analyses on the grindstones showed that they consisted of Visingsö sandstone. One type occurs within limited areas around Vättern and very sporadically in other places. The nearest occurrence to Motala is Lemunda, approximately 10 km to the north of Motala. The grindstones that were analysed, however, are almost identical to sandstone from the southern end of Vättern.

Judging by the number of workpieces and the amount of debitage, it was not industrial manufacture of axes that took place. We should instead envisage self-sufficient axe production.

A workshop on the point

Yet another Mesolithic building (House II) was found, this time at the very tip of the original point. This house was probably round or semicircular and, unlike the longhouse, it also contained large quantities of finds. In terms of the number of finds per square metre, this area has the densest quantity of finds. They were concentrated almost entirely within the walls. What remained of the house were four post-holes making up

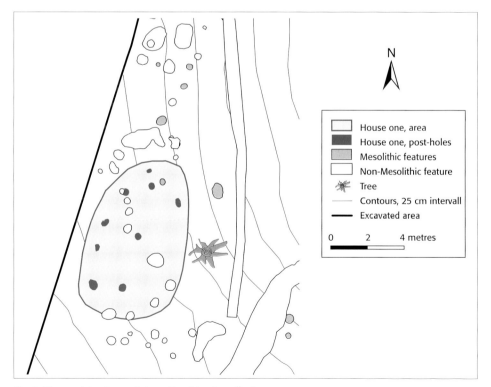

Fig. 3. The semicircular workshop. Graphics: Lars Östlin.

a semicircle (about 5 m in diameter) with the opening to the north-east. In the middle of the house there was yet another post-hole. The wall posts did not show any sign of leaning in towards the central post, so it is likely that a number of rods extended from the central post to rest against the wall posts. Inside the house the excavators also noted a thin layer of clay which was probably a floor.

Hammerstones, axes, axe flakes, heavy hammerstones, grindstones, and debitage from tool manufacture using different kinds of stone suggest intense activity. In the water just outside the house there were also large amounts of waste from stone working. This is probably the result of cleaning out the house. The large number of finds and the limited space have led to the interpretation of House II as a workshop for stone working and not a dwelling.

The specimens for dating House II come from charred hazelnuts found in the four post-holes. The ^{14}C analysis yielded the range 5470–4700 BC.

- 5470–5200 BC (calibrated, 2 sigma), 6305 ± 55 BP. Hazelnut shell.
- 5300–4960 BC (calibrated, 2 sigma), 6185 ± 55 BP. Hazelnut shell.
- 5070–4770 BC (calibrated, 2 sigma), 6040 ± 55 BP. Hazelnut shell.
- 5210–4790 BC (calibrated, 2 sigma), 6070 ± 55 BP. Hazelnut shell.

An important question is whether the two houses were used at the same time or at least belong to the same settlement structure. According to the ^{14}C datings, the workshop is slightly later than the larger long-house. Judging by the dates from hazelnut shells only, however, the two houses might have formed one settlement unit. The two ^{14}C dates from oak probably result from the collecting of old branches for fires, or else the posts for the roof might very well have been made of oak. The interpretation of the two houses is that the dwelling house and the workshop were, at least partly, used at the same time. Most probably there were even more houses or different structures in use, but this could not be confirmed by the excavation.

Food for the day and for the next

Between the two houses a layer of fire-cracked stone measuring roughly 2.5 x 3.5 m was documented. Just beside it were several small hearths. The finds consisted of a large amount of worked stone and organic material. There was also a concentration of craft tools, for example, slate knives, hammerstones, anvil stones, grindstones, scrapers, and an axe. The organic material is copious and varied: bones from terrestrial animals and fish bones, hazelnut shells, and polished bone/antler. Charcoal from the layer of fire-cracked stone was dated to:

- 5370–5050 BC (2 sigma, 6265 ± 60 BP).

A hearth just beside it was dated to:

- 5470–5200 BC (2 sigma 6325 ± 60 BP)

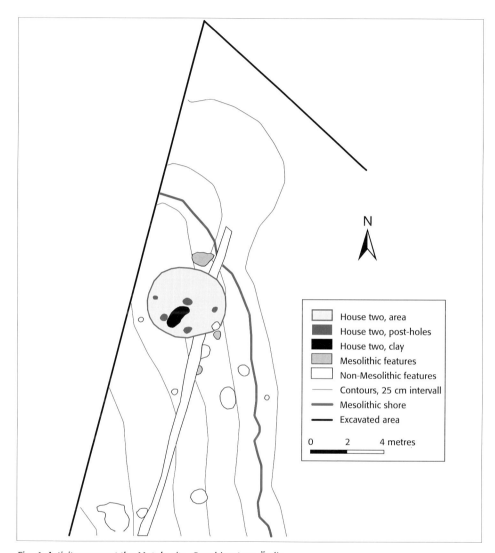

Fig. 4. Activity areas at the Motala site. Graphics: Lars Östlin.

Fishing in Motala Ström is partly seasonal, with an abundance of salmon in certain periods. Drying and/or smoking of fish and perhaps also of meat from other animals in certain periods was probably practised. Conservation and storage of foodstuffs for future use was probably part of the Mesolithic economic cycle. The fire-cracked stone may be remains of the hearths used in the conservation process. To this interpretation we can add that slate knives were found. A proposed use of these in the Södertörn archipelago was for flaying seal (Wikell 2003). It is possible that the same type of knives for big fish and perhaps also for terrestrial animals at inland sites like Motala.

Fishing places

A few metres out from the bank the marine archaeologists found two stone foundations built of large stones (0.3–0.6 m). Around this foundation was a concentration of leister points. Some leisters were found *in situ*, driven down obliquely under stones. They probably broke off against the stone when the leister missed the fish. Fishing was evidently practised in the water just off the actual settlement site, as has also been documented on Danish Ertebølle sites (Enghoff 1995; Pedersen 1995 *et al.*; see also Bergstrand, this volume).

Wet and dry – functional rituals

The Mesolithic settlement site at Motala was a well-organized place for a long time. Around 5500–5000 BC a number of houses were built, differing in appearance; several of them probably existed simultaneously. The settlement site had activity areas which were well demarcated spatially: cooking, lithic craft, axe production were carried out at specific places.

The excavated area is a cross-section through the site from the highest point along the bank and out into the water. The cross-section cuts from the dry land down towards the water, and the Mesolithic settlement site organization follows this gradual natural division. Different activities were performed in *relation* to the bank and the water. The distribution of finds reinforces this picture. Furthest from the water were the dwelling houses, hearths for cooking, and hearths which probably represent a place for drying or smoking of food in certain seasons. The next zone, between the dry land and the water, was used for crafts such as manufacturing, polishing and sharpening of axes. Lithic craft, the manufacture of various tools, was also pursued here. In the water, people threw residue from tool manufacture; they also fished there.

Yet another division can be discerned *along* the entire dry zone near the river bank. In very few cases there are traces of various activities: axe production was pursued in one area, hearths were lit in another, a third was used for cooking food or knapping flint. This may of course reflect a highly functional division of the site. No one wants to sleep in a damp house; fishing can only be done in the water; rubbish was thrown in the water to get rid of the smell; and so on.

Perhaps there are other ways to explain where activities took place and where things were left. The shore of the river, where the waves constantly splashed the stones, should perhaps not be regarded merely as a functional area for rubbish. The classification of finds suggests that the relation between objects and places has many profound meanings. Part of the top of a human skull was found at the water's edge. Of course this could be the remains of a damaged grave, the content of which was scattered among other refuse, but in view of the number of similar finds of human parietal bones in wetlands near Ertebølle settlement sites, coincidence is not an acceptable explanation for the finds of skull bones in such similar circumstances (Karsten 2001). Another interpretation is that the individual after death was buried in some way – above or under ground – and the body decomposed. The body may also have been disarticulated to hasten the decomposition process. When the time was ripe, part of the skull was knocked off. This part was "buried/deposited/offered" in what we today call the refuse layer of the settlement site. The skull fragment and perhaps above all its actual deposition was probably part of a religious ritual. Finds in the same area included a bone point with double barbs, leister points, and a decorated antler artefact.

A total of roughly 28 kg of animal bones was found, but in only two cases was carved decoration noted on these. An artefact about 20 cm long (fig. 5), made of red deer antler, was found between the long-house and the water, just a few metres from the human bone. The decoration consists of two rows of triangles filled with scratched lines. The function of the object is unknown. Yet another small decorated antler fragment, some 6 cm long, was found in one of the wall-bearing post-holes of the round house. The decoration in this case was very simple, consisting merely of two parallel lines which narrowed at one end to a point. The original appearance and function of the object cannot be guessed today, but it was probably a fragment of a larger objects. The original decoration may possibly have consisted of one or more rhombi. Both objects are undated, but the decoration agrees well with that of south Scandinavia in the earliest phase of the Ertebølle culture (Andersson & Carlsson 2005).

The same wet shoreline zone also held concentrations of handle cores. The number is disproportionately large in comparison with finds of microblades from the same zone. The fact that handle cores are found in wet environments at several places in Scandinavia has attracted attention. These too have therefore been interpreted in terms of spatial ritual organization on settlement sites (Knutsson et al. 2003; Karsten 2001).

Further out from the bank the marine archaeologists found on the bottom a red deer antler, a pressure flaker, and a pecked axe. The water and the part of the site nearest the water probably had a special meaning in the people's perceptual world. The objects could be explained as waste, but since similar finds occur in comparable settings in southern Scandinavia they can more probably be interpreted as ritual offerings (Karsten 2001).

But what did it look like? To obtain a picture of vegetation in the immediate environment of the settlement site, macrofossils were collected from sediment in the water for analyses. Our "preconceived" picture that the settlement site was a bright, open place where the big trees had been chopped down to create a space in the depths of the surrounding Atlantic deciduous forests proved wrong. Pollen and macrofossils showed, on the contrary, that people had very little impact on the big trees. It was probably only the undergrowth that was cleared to make way for houses and other activities in the leafy shade of the trees (Regnell 2003). This picture of a settlement site under the tree canopy is not unique for Motala. The Ertebølle site at Bökeberg in Skåne was established in the same way without the trees being cleared (Karsten 2001). Bonsall *et al.* (1987:201) have presented the same result from a Late Mesolithic settlement site in north-west England. The settlement sites and cultivation plots of the Linear Band culture (LBK) were likewise incorporated under the trees (Whittle 1996:149).

A functionalist conclusion is that the leafy environment at the Motala settlement site enabled fishing with leisters from stones just a few metres from the shore. Another interpretation could be that the trees growing on the site were part of the people's world-picture. It is not uncommon for trees to be a part of myths. The tree of life, spirits in trees, and trees as animate beings are found in many ethnographical descriptions. The relationship of Mesolithic people to trees in other than a functionalist perspective is described by Jenny Moore (2003:142ff.). Instead of chopping down trees to open up a glade, people carefully selected which trees to let stand, because they contained living narratives which could not be destroyed.

Living space and "the Mesolithic house syndrome"

Remains of houses on Mesolithic settlement sites are a controversial topic in Stone Age archaeology. In cases where building remains have been interpreted as belonging to the Mesolithic, the interpretations have usually encountered massive criticism from scholars. The source criticism has concerned, among other things, the basis for the dating and the validity and representativeness of the ^{14}C analyses; even the excavation methods have been questioned (Johansson 1989; Browall 1999). In Denmark there has been a fixed view since the 1970s of what the houses of the Maglemose culture looked like and how they were structured (Petersen 1972; Andersen *et al.* 1982). This has had the consequence that remains of settlement or houses from this time which differ in any way from the accepted picture, with differences in find distribution, have been dismissed. The narrow criteria and the definitions have impeded the discussions instead of taking them forward (Schilling 2001). The tough source criticism has been criticized by Lars Larsson as something he calls "the Mesolithic house syndrome" (Larsson 1995:101). He wonders how a similar scrutiny of house remains from other periods would have affected discussions of these. The few house remains may nevertheless seem strange in view of the number of Mesolithic sites that have actually been excavated. A significant reason was of course for a long time the limited areas excavated, but our traditional outlook when excavating Stone Age sites probably also affected the number of houses found. Stone Age sites are mainly identified through finds of artefacts, and for traditional reasons the excavations have then concentrated on the areas richest in finds. The settlement sites described in Östergötland with house remains show variations in ways of spatially structuring the settlement site. Depending on the purpose, social strategies, cosmological ideas, and so on, activities were performed in different and often separate selected places. The two houses from the Motala settlement site probably reflect completely different activities;

lithic crafts at least were performed in a concentrated area near the small round house. If any craft work was done in the bigger house, it has not left any traces.

The best survey at present of Mesolithic building remains is by Cecilia Cronberg (2003), and despite the fact that Ola Lass Jensen (2001:122) singles out houses with sunken floor levels as the typical Ertebølle house, and despite attempts by Erik Brinch Petersen (1972) and others to define the Maglemose house, the lasting impression in Cronberg's survey is still the wealth of variation, in the shapes of houses, in their size, and in the distribution of finds. The state of our knowledge of Mesolithic houses is much better today than it was fifteen years ago, although the opposition to interpreting post-holes as belonging to houses is not as solid as it used to be, the work of gaining accept-ance for every new house is a struggle waged on the academic barricades.

A summary of settlement sites with houses in Östergötland gives a picture of well-organized small-scale settlement: small houses, a small amount of finds, and a clear divi-sion of activities in the habitation area. Another common denominator is the proximity to wetlands and water. The small amount of finds may be due in large measure to the excavation methods; at Mörby and Lilla Åby especially they were geared to other types of ancient remains. The Mesolithic remains were all discovered at a late stage of the digs, when finds had possibly already been bulldozed away. Yet at Storlyckan and Högby too, the number of finds is small compared with south Scandinavian settlement sites from the same time. Working stone was obviously not the most important reason why people spent time on these sites.

The discrepancy in the ^{14}C datings from the nearby houses in Högby and Mörby makes it uncertain whether the houses were used at the same time. It is more likely that the scattered datings show that people returned more or less regularly to the same plac-es. The division of space simultaneously reflects how activities on the settlement site were performed within specific areas during these visits: habitation, cooking, waste manage-ment were rarely mixed spatially; instead there were places intended for each purpose. This spatial organization may very well reflect a microcosm, the physical expression of a Mesolithic world-view (Grøn 1995; Grøn & Kuznetsov 2003; Carlsson *et al.* 1999).

Comparisons with Danish Maglemose houses, for example, Ulkestrup, show both similarities and differences with respect to those in Östergötland. The Danish houses are small, 5–10 m^2, are close to the water, and large quantities of finds have been discovered inside the houses or immediately outside them. The similarities are mainly in the size of the houses and the localization near water, but unlike in Denmark the Maglemose houses in Östergötland have very few finds. There is no room here to discuss seasonal use, but after his analysis of Maglemose houses Olle Grøn suggested that the orientation of the door can help us to interpret what time of year the settlement sites were used. The openings of houses on summer sites mostly faced the water, while those of winter houses usually looked east or in some direction that gave shelter from the wind (Grøn 1995). If the parallels with the door openings are comparable and applicable over such large geographical distances, Högby and Mörby could be interpreted as summer dwelling sites. Storlyckan and Lilla Åby, unfortunately, do not offer this type of interpretation about seasonal occupation based on door openings.

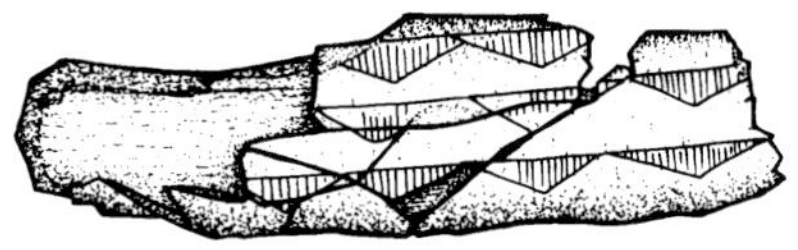

Fig. 5. A decorated artefact from the Motala site. Drawing: Anna Molin, National Heritage Board.

Man before fish?

The question is, finally, what picture of the Mesolithic do the interpretations of the settlement sites in Östergötland (re)produce? Much of the text above has been about describing the settlement sites and not so much has discussed what this means for an understanding of the society that created the remains. Far too much Mesolithic research has concerned "What we have found – not what we have found out" (Knutsson 1995). A similar criticism was made by Marek Zvelebil after the conference "Man and Sea", where he said that, after decades of accumulated knowledge about the big sites and highly developed fishing of the Ertebølle period: "the time has come to put man before fish" (Zvelebil 1995:422).

Very briefly, changes during the period in southern Scandinavia are usually described as a smooth, slow development from small groups and settlement sites in the Maglemose period to increasingly large settlement sites during the Ertebølle culture (L. Larsson 1990). Large settlement sites, permanent fisheries, shell middens, and so on in southern Scandinavia mean that the Late Mesolithic societies are now thought to have attained a greater level of social complexity than previously believed. Most scholars today also agree about the existence of permanently occupied settlement sites (Karsten 2001:84ff.). There is a risk of interpreting the changes in evolutionist terms. The results of the large-scale excavations at Tågerup in Skåne show, if anything, the reverse development. The controlled lifestyle of Kongemose society, in visible harmony with the ecological surroundings, with advanced flint craft, elaborate art, and so on, was succeeded by a settlement site from the Ertebølle culture whose people hunted and fished indiscriminately and made flint objects which were solely functional. Injuries to skeletons from the Ertebølle period further suggest increased violence between rival groups (Karsten & Knarrström 2003). Complexity perhaps cannot be equated with development.

Of course, one can not directly transmit different Mesolithic societies from southern Scandinavia to Motala, Östergötland. Ertebölle culture in Denmark and Scania is not Ertebölle culture in Motala or elsewhere. But in many ways in coping life there are great similarities over vast areas in northern Europe at the time for the late Mesolithic(Zvelebil 1995). The broad spectra economy, together with special purpose sites and large settlements, that are characteristics fore the time, I believe does not reflect economical or social stress at all but rather changed relations to the environment and a changing cosmology in society. But by which way are increased risks of being killed not a matter of stress? All together the material culture from the Motala site shows a society not in stress but "takers of opportunities".

More aspects of Mesolithic societies than the purely economic ones can be analysed through the ways of structuring the surroundings. For the three Early Mesolithic sites, Högby, Mörby, and Lilla Åby, it has previously been suggested that the spatial organization at least partly reflects a cosmological idea, that activities were assigned to places within the habitation space that had a deeper meaning than can be explained merely in functional terms (Carlsson *et al.* 1999). The surroundings consisted of places where events (real or mythical) were enacted. Together the places constituted narratives which included people's everyday activities. The fact that this organization is not exactly the same at settlement sites in different times and places does not mean that the people had different perceptions of reality; instead it reflects variations on a theme.

The physical expressions at Motala show striking differences from the small-scale character of the Early Mesolithic settlement sites. In the relationship between people and fish, Motala is possibly yet another example of how society at this time emphasized fishing. The evidence of extensive leister fishing in a river that was extremely rich in fish in certain seasons, and the traces of drying/smoking food for the future reflect a society which practised economic cooperation, at least periodically. But the choice of settlement site could just as well have been determined by the good communications. To continue the parallels with southern Scandinavia and Tågerup, the natural harmony and balance seemed almost ideologized during the Kongemose period, but the later Ertebølle culture, in contrast, manifested space. The physically deposited traces of culture that we see at Motala are remarkably similar to those of the Ertebølle sites at Tågerup, Bökeberg in Skåne, and several other settlement sites in Denmark, for instance through their thick occupation layers, stone-lined hearths, building remains, fishing places, and so on (Karsten 2001). Activities around the dwelling houses were organized according to the distance from and relationship to factors such as water. The space was filled with symbols, names, and narratives. The increasing permanence of settlement may have required a change in the content of the narratives. Instead of, as before, toning down their presence, the people physically manifested their place during the Ertebølle period. The significance of this should not necessarily be interpreted as territorial markers. It can equally well be interpreted as expressions of a greater need for physical accentuation of the cosmological narratives.

The excavation of large areas gives us opportunities to interpret what Mesolithic settlement sites looked like and perhaps we can also can discuss why they looked the way they did.

Leister fishing
in Motala Ström during the Atlantic period
A typological study based on the finds from the Motala site, Östergötland

Thomas Bergstrand

The article deals with leister fishing in Motala Ström, based on finds and results from an excavation of a Middle and Late Mesolithic settlement site in Motala, Östergötland. Since the site was located beside the river, parts of the adjacent water area were also investigated, revealing refuse layers and a fishing place constructed of stone, around which there was a large number of broken leister points. An analysis of these allowed two types to be distinguished, A and B, both of which have counterparts in south Scandinavian finds from both the Boreal and the Atlantic periods. Among the finds there is also a small quantity of what can be compared to harpoon points and a large number of coarsely shaped bone points which are also believed to have been used as leisters. Radiocarbon datings of finds deposited in the water indicate two phases of activity, corresponding to the settlement phases on land. The Type A points represent a phase around 5600–5300 BC (cal.) followed by the slightly later Type B points. The other bone points and antler finds correspond to a phase 1,000 years later. The conclusion, on design criteria, is that the manufacture of leister points was a specialized craft, with the form of the tools changing over time, to disappear completely in the later activity phase and be replaced by simpler bone points. The design and type of decoration of one of the harpoon points is almost identical to finds in southern Skåne, indicating long-range inter-regional contacts.

Introduction

This article deals with finds of leister points and a fishing place discovered by an underwater archaeological investigation in Motala Ström, Östergötland, in the summer of 2003. The investigated area was part of a larger shoreline settlement, dated to the Middle and Late Mesolithic, which goes under the name Strandvägen 1, here referred to as the Motala site. The text also includes a discussion of pointed pieces of bone found in the same contexts, along with a smaller number of finds belonging to a refuse layer. Since this material is of such a scale, quality, and chronological distribution, it inevitably leads us to consider the state of our knowledge about the Mesolithic in Östergötland, which has for a long time been problematic. In the shadow of the flint-based Mesolithic culture groups of south and west Sweden, it was long thought that much of Östergötland, lacking identifiable settlement sites, consisted of virtually uninhabited badlands. Lake Vättern was used as a dividing point and an explanatory model separating a united south Scandinavian region on the one hand and small, sporadic coastal sites in Östergötland on the other hand (see Carlsson, this volume).

The major transformation of the infrastructure in western Östergötland in recent years, however, has had the consequence that a fairer picture of the region's Mesolithic period has emerged. With the archaeologist's focus on the quartz as the raw material on which the culture was based, it has been possible to identify more and more sites, and our potential to interpret the Mesolithic landscape has improved. With the results of the Motala investigation, Vättern need no longer be regarded as the physical dividing line in the landscape; it was on the contrary a communicative bridge for interregional exchange with both the west and the south.

The results from the Motala investigation can also be said to be an incentive for an almost classical discussion concerning the view of the change of the south Scandinavian culture groups in the Middle and Late Mesolithic. On the basis of the thousand-year interval between the two best-documented settlement phases at the Motala site, which is also significant for the finds treated in this article, it is possible to discuss analogies with the overarching discrepancies in material culture which are used to distinguish the Ertebølle/Lihult culture from earlier tool-using cultures. Mainly on the basis of the Tågerup excavations in western Skåne, Karsten and Knarrström use the formula *quantity and quality* to illustrate the difference between the generous technique of the Ertebølle culture and the economical flint technology of the Kongemose culture: "The artefacts in the latter period [Ertebølle] are certainly made in a functional and rational way, but all concern for visually attractive forms has vanished" (Karsten & Knarrström 2003: 228ff.).

A similar judgement has been passed concerning western Sweden. One verdict issued by Fredsjö (1953) is that the Lihult culture can be regarded as a degenerate Sandarna culture, or as Karsten and Knarrström laconically put it (2003:230): "It did not matter how the tools were shaped as long as they worked".

As this article will show, there are clear changes in the studied find material, changes that rest on a secure typological and dating foundation. In that sense the study ultimately deals with what is perhaps the most fundamental question in archaeology: why change? To what extent this find material should be used as evidence for a major local-regional change in society is, however, uncertain, particularly in view of the poor state of research on Östergötland.

The Motala site

The underwater archaeological investigation in Motala Ström was part of a larger excavation of a Mesolithic settlement site where the two most intensive periods are dated to 5500–5000 BC and 4200–4000 BC (cal.). The site is officially designated Strandvägen 1 (RAÄ 173, Motala parish). Since other articles in this publication deal in detail with the overall investigation and the results of the excavation on land, only what is of direct relevance for the interpretation of the fishing place and related finds need be mentioned here by way of introduction.

The settlement site was right on the south bank of Motala Ström, the river that drains Sweden's second largest lake, Vättern, into the Baltic Sea. The roughly 3 km long and narrow river is judged on geological grounds to have had basically the same course and shoreline level since the Mesolithic. It was not until the regulation of the river in the 1920s that the water level was altered. The change, however, is deemed to have had a marginal effect on the level of the shoreline at the site since it is at the upper end of Motala Ström. The modest rise in the water level, approximately 0.5 metres, was later confirmed by stratigraphical observations in connection with the investigation (Bergstrand 2004).

The area of water that was investigated was a calm backwater outside the actual stream of Motala Ström. Although the shore zone in modern times has been somewhat reshaped by the filling of the shallowest sections, there is an explicit orientation of the settlement site and its activity areas towards this backwater. The investigation of the settlement site within a combined area of land and water, with almost permanent shoreline conditions, resulted in a better all-round view than is otherwise normal. The set of questions guiding the investigation was defined by the project as such, but there were also more concrete problems demanding a solution. Briefly, these questions concerned the stratigraphy and age of the sediments, the level of the shoreline during the settlement phase, the occurrence of different types of deposition such as waste, storage, and offerings, the occurrence and spatial distribution of finds and structures, and the character of the natural and cultural environment.

The investigation comprised a total of about 20 m^3 of find-bearing layers spread over an area of 67 m^2. This volume consisted of three distinct stratigraphical layers which were protected under more than 80 cm of later gyttja (fig. 1). Counting from the bottom, they consisted of calcareous gyttja, coarse-detritus gyttja, and gyttja silt (A1628, A1627, A1626). It was primarily the latter two layers that contained finds, consisting of waste, leister points from fishing activity, and structures in the form of deliberately placed stones. The layer of gyttja silt was on average 0.19 m thick and should be viewed as the stratigraphical settlement horizon in which the majority of the finds were deposited, while the underlying layer of coarse detritus, with an average thickness of 0.08 m, can be considered the stratigraphical "bottom".

Fig. 1. Section marking the three find-bearing layers. Photo: Bohuslän Museum/National Heritage Board.

Depending on the type of find, one can see a pattern in what was deposited and how. The finds that were of waste character, that is, thrown away, washed away, or dropped, were mostly found in the uppermost layer of gyttja silt. The majority (twelve items) of the broken-off leister points were likewise found in this layer, while eight were found in the underlying coarse-detritus layer, and only one in the layer of calcareous gyttja. The fact that most of them were found in vertical position clearly shows that the points were deposited when the tool was broken off and that the leister was pushed deep into the bottom, depending on how much force was used.

A fishing place

Within the central investigation area we found a large structure consisting of stones placed in the layer of gyttja silt (A1626) According to Quaternary geological expertise, this cannot be a natural occurrence in this part of the stratigraphy; the stones must have been put there by humans (Mats Regnell, pers. com.). The stones varied in size between roughly 0.15 and 0.3 m in diameter. Although the stones were not documented in detail, the impression was that the stone structure was strikingly level in shape. The stones were probably selected according to their shape and size and placed in concentrations in the shallow water. Through the plan documentation one can distinguish a number of concentrations within this trench and in the trench to the south of it. The roughly 1.5 m long and 0.3 m wide area at the centre of the bigger trench is a dense stone packing of fist-sized washed stones (fig. 2).

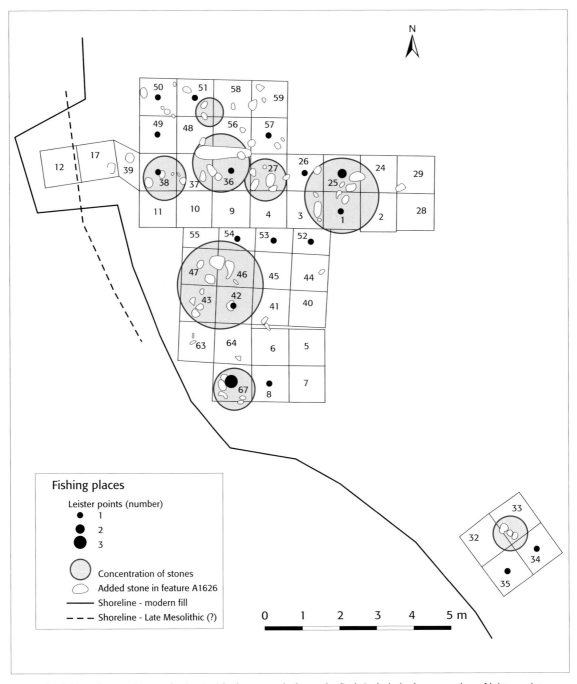

Fig. 2. The fishing place at the Motala site. Beside the stone platforms the finds included a large number of leister points (black dots). The Mesolithic shoreline is estimated on the basis of the stratigraphy (dashed line). Graphics: Lars Östlin.

The concentrations of stone marked with circles on the plan are an attempt to see a pattern, and thus a function for the features (fig. 2). Also overlaid on the plan is the distribution of leister points and the presumed Mesolithic shoreline. If the relation between the concentrations of stones and leister points can be assumed to be sufficiently clear, the stone concentrations can be interpreted as platforms for leister fishing. Of 23 finds, all except one were broken points which in several cases were retrieved *in situ* in vertical position. The finds are explicit evidence that leister fishing was pursued in these shallow waters right beside the settlement site, and the platforms of stone can very well be envisaged as having facilitated the fishing. Without the stones, people would have sunk in the soft bottom sediment and frightened the fish away.

Description of the leister points

A total of 21 finds from the underwater excavation are classified as leister points, and only one of these is intact. In addition there are one or two other points which look so different that they should probably be called harpoon points. The major part of the finds thus consist of broken leister points. The fact that they are broken off agrees perfectly with the interpretation of the site as a fishing place. When an archaeologist finds a broken point standing vertically in sediment, it is interpreted as a result of the fisherman missing his prey and also having the bad luck to break his implement. At comparable find spots in Denmark the rear ends of the broken tools have moreover been discovered on the settlement site beside the water where the broken points were left. The fisherman simply had to leave the water and replace the broken point with a new one (Johansson 2000:110). At Motala two or three rear ends of points were found in the water. The finds from land are harder to classify since the preservation is so much worse, but the material nevertheless gives us an opportunity, if not to refit individual finds, at least to link the process and the use of the settlement site.

The 16 most prominent leister points are relatively similar in form. Despite this, an attempt has been made at a typology of the finds, to distinguish if possible any morphological or functional features that changed over time. The result was that two types were discerned, called Type A and Type B. The two remaining points with a discrepant, harpoon-like form are called Type C and Type D (table 1).

Type A

The number of points of Type A is nine (nos. 8868, 12409, 12417, 12421, 12422, 12651, 13001, 13030, 13490, fig. 3). The type is a single-row, fine-toothed point, straight or only slightly curving (concave). The teeth are regular in shape, of almost uniform size and at regular intervals. The notch for the teeth is an acute angle and almost at right angles to the longitudinal axis of the workpiece. The thickness of the points varies between 6 and 9 mm, and the width is between 11 and 20 mm. The cross-section is pointed-oval or

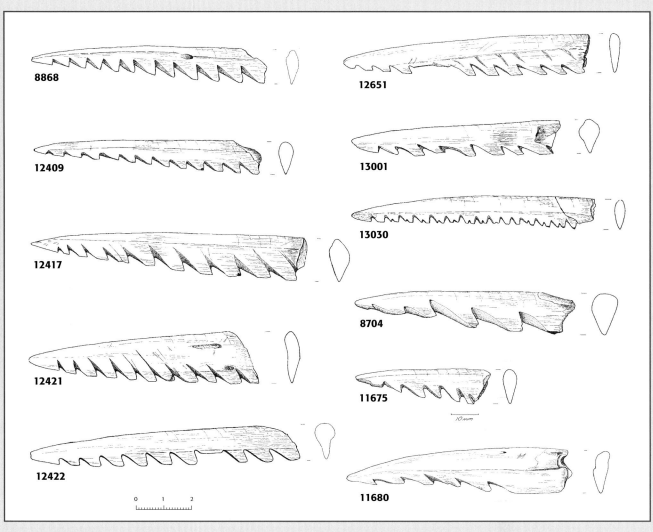

Find no.	Species	Bone	Material	Class	Teeth	Length	Width	Thickness	Type
8868	Red deer	Tibia	Bone	Leister point, part of	11	98	14	6	A
12409	Red deer?	Diaphysis	Bone	Leister point, part of	12	90	12	7	A
12417	Red deer?	Radius or tibia	Bone	Leister point, part of	10	108	18	9	A
12421	Red deer?	Radius or tibia	Bone	Leister point, part of	10	87	20	6	A
12422	Red deer?	Metatarsal?	Bone	Leister point, part of	10	102	15	9	A
12651	Red deer	Radius	Bone	Leister point, part of	11	93	15	5	A
13001	Red deer	Metatarsal?	Bone	Leister point, part of	7	78	13	9	A
13030	Red deer?	Diaphysis	Bone	Leister point, part of	15	91	11	5	A
13490	Red deer?	Diaphysis	Bone	Leister point, part of	6	45	13	6	A
8704	Red deer or elk	Unidentified	Bone	Leister point, part of	5	85	15	10	B
11675	Red deer?	Unidentified	Bone	Leister point, part of	6	47	12	6	B
11680	Red deer?	Radius or tibia	Bone	Leister point, part of	4	103	20	8	B

Table 1. All 21 leister points and the two possible harpoon points (nos. 11698, 13447b), classified as Types A, B, C, and D. Dimensions in millimetres. Drawing: Anette Olsson.

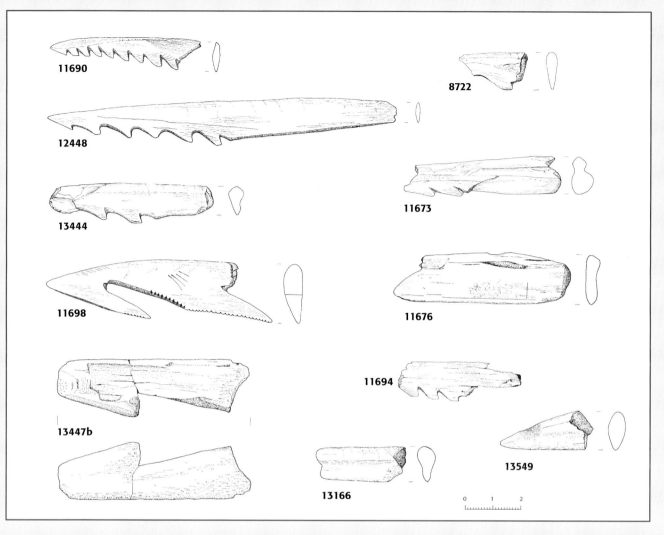

Find no.	Species	Bone	Material	Class	Teeth	Length	Widh	Thickness	Type
11690	Roe deer?	Diaphysis	Bone	Leister point, part of	8	62	13	3	B
12448	Red deer	Radius	Bone	Leister point, intact	5	157	10	3	B
13444	Red deer?	Diaphysis	Bone	Leister point, part of	2	66	14	8	B
11698	Red deer or elk	Antler	Antler	Leister or harpoon point, part of	2	98	21	8	C
13447b	Red deer?	Antler?	Antler?	Leister or harpoon point, part of	1	70	20	4	D
8722	Unidentified	Unidentified	Bone	Leister point, part of	0	21	15	4	—
11673	Red deer	Metatarsal	Bone	Leister point, part of	2	79	18	10	—
11676	Red deer?	Diaphysis	Bone	Leister point, part of	0	64	19	6	—
11694	Mammal	Diaphysis	Bone	Leister point, part of	3	50	15	4	—
13166	Red deer	Diaphysis	Bone	Leister point, part of?	1	35	15	8	—
13549	Unidentified	Antler?	Bone	Leister point, part of	0	42	18	8	—
	Median					79	15	6	

drop-shaped, depending on the workpiece and/or the degree of polishing. The distance between the teeth varies from 3 to 10 mm, but never more than 3 mm for the same point (counting from rear edge to rear edge). As a rule the height of the teeth is 3–5 mm or 6–9 mm. All are made of bone, the majority of which have been identified as red deer. The bones used were from the radius or tibia, the metatarsal, or diaphyses in general.

The design of the points in Type A is so uniform that they could have been made by one and the same person. The uniformity and the proportions in the way the teeth were cut out are striking. The sharpness of the teeth is particularly noticeable, showing that the artefacts must have been virtually new when they were lost. Only one find differs in the design of the teeth. No. 13030 can be described as double-toothed; ten of its fifteen teeth have small cuts which make it even more fine-toothed.

Type B

Type B is represented by four points, one rear end and one intact point (nos. 11675, 11680, 11690, 8704, 13444, 12448, fig. 4). A common feature of the type is that they are a little more concave and slightly asymmetrical. The teeth have a softer, almost wavy design which is not as regular and uniform as in Type A. The thickness of the points varies between 3 and 10 mm while the width ranges from 10 to 20 mm. The teeth are as a rule a little larger/wider. The distance between them is generally 12–13 mm up to 14–17 mm, and even 22 mm. The cross-section is similar to that of Type A. The raw material has in most cases been identified as red deer, and possibly also roe deer (no. 11690) and red deer or elk in one case (no. 8704). The bones used were radius/tibia or diaphyses in general.

Find number 12448 is the only intact point in the material. It is 157 mm long, 10 mm wide at the base, and 3 mm thick. The rear end is finely ground, which indicates how it was intended to be mounted to the shaft. The point has only five teeth, which underlines the difference *vis-à-vis* the Type A points with twice the number of teeth.

Type C

Type C consists of a single point which is more like a harpoon in form (no. 11698, fig. 5). The broken point is made from antler of red deer or elk and is 98 mm long and 21 mm wide. The point has two full flukes on the edges of which there are small, shallow notches. Whether these notches were intended as a functional or decorative element is uncertain. Four short, shallow lines are scratched on one side; if they are intentional they should be regarded as decoration. Comparable finds from Bredasten and Skateholm in Skåne, as well as in Denmark, are richly decorated (Andersen 1997:57ff.).

The size of the point and the design of the flukes are without counterpart in the rest of the finds from both land and water. In view of the find spot it is likely that they were used for leistering, but it cannot be ruled out that they were used for hunting larger prey, on land or in water. On the settlement site there are finds of seal bones, suggesting larger-scale and probably seasonal hunting in the Littorina Sea only 35 km to the east (Carlsson 2004a:24).

Type D

Type D, like Type C, is represented by a single find which, despite its fragmentary state, is more like a harpoon than the leister types above (no. 13447b, fig. 5). The object is a point 70 mm long, broken into two parts, and probably of red deer antler. Although the point is rather eroded, the manufacturing technique is obvious. Like Danish Ertebølle harpoons, the workpiece was cut from the antler and thus acquired an outside and an inside (Andersen 1972:79). In view of the eroded condition of the find, it is uncertain whether it was lost in connection with leister fishing. It is perhaps more likely that it comes from a refuse layer.

Unclassified

The remaining six points are smaller fragments and rear ends, which makes it difficult to fit them into a typology (nos. 8722, 11673, 11676, 11694, 13166, 13549, fig. 6). As a complement to all the points, it can be said of the finds of the three rear ends that they measure 35, 40, and 50 mm from the end as far as the first tooth. If we extrapolate these values for the Type A and B points, they were probably originally about 140–150 mm long, which can be compared with the intact point that measures 157 mm (no. 12448). The assumption is uncertain, however, since the finds from land have teeth almost all the way out to the rear end (nos. 12339, 10619).

Among the unclassified finds there is also a point consisting of the outer tip (no. 13549). The break occurred at the outermost notch for the tooth. It differs totally in size from the other finds, 42 mm long, so it is likely yet another type. It should possibly be compared with no. 11698 (the harpoon point), which is also made of antler and of larger format.

Finds on land

From the excavation of the settlement site on land there are a total 18 finds of leister points (fig. 7). Owing to the terrestrial environment they are less well preserved, generally consisting of small, eroded fragments. The majority are points (10 in number), but there are also three rear ends and five middle pieces or other fragments. We could perhaps have expected a greater quantity of rear ends from this context, in view of the large number of broken points in the water, but this is not the case.

One of the rear pieces can be compared with a Type B point, but the distance between the last tooth and the rear edge is about 60 mm. The other two finds are more like Type A and have teeth almost all the way down to the rear edge. Of the points it is no. 9471 that

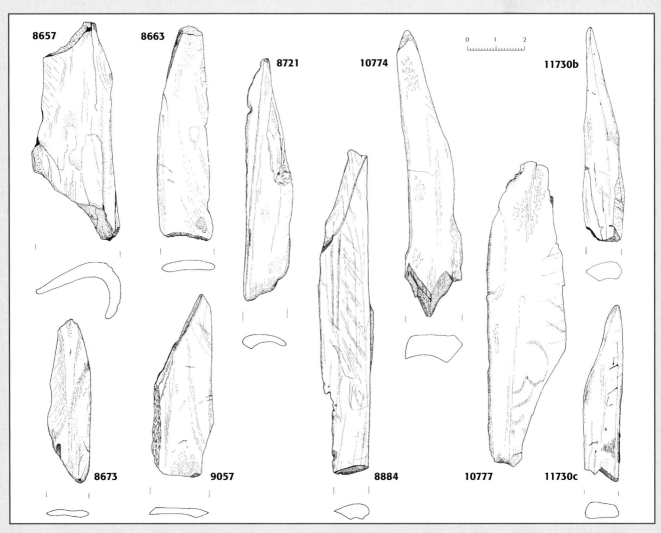

Find no.	Species	Bone	Material	Class	Length	Width	Thickness
8657	Large mammal (red deer/elk?)	Tibia?	Bone	Leister point, preform?	78	30	5
8663	Red deer	Femur	Bone	Leister point, preform?	75	19	4
8673	Red deer?	Femur	Bone	Leister point, preform?	58	15	7
8721	Red deer	Metatarsal	Bone	Leister point, preform?	87	17	8
8884	Red deer	Metatarsal	Bone	Leister point, preform?	115	20	10
9057	Large mammal	Unidentified	Bone	Leister point, preform?	65	22	5
10774	Elk?	Femur or tibia	Bone	Leister point, preform?	102	20	8
10777	Red deer?	Femur and tibia?	Bone	Leister point, preform?	109	28	6
11721	Red deer?	Diaphysis	Bone	Leister point, preform?	33	15	7
11730b	Red deer or elk	Diaphysis	Bone	Leister point, preform?	75	20	7
11730c	Red deer or elk	Diaphysis	Bone	Leister point, preform?	62	12	8

Table 2. The 21 finds of bone of the type "pointed bone piece" or "leister point, preform?". The finds are heterogeneous in design but are all pointed. Unlike the others, find no. 13082 is wholly in proportion with Types A–B but lacks teeth. Dimensions in millimetres. Drawing: Anette Olsson.

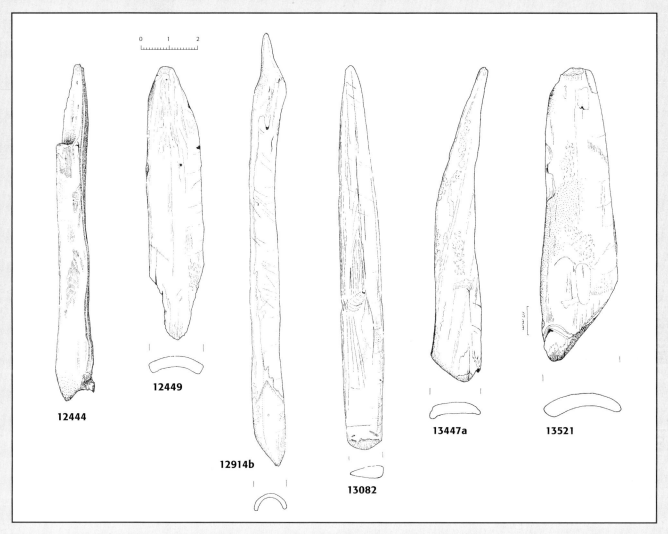

12444

12449

12914b

13082

13447a

13521

Find no.	Species	Bone	Material	Class	Length	Width	Thickness
11895	Red deer?	Metatarsal?	Bone	Leister point, preform?	110	19	10
11922	Red deer or wild boar	Diaphysis	Bone	Leister point, preform?	76	25	5
12444	Red deer	Metatarsal	Bone	Leister point, preform?	119	18	10
12449	Red deer	Femur	Bone	Leister point, preform?	122	24	6
12451	Not analysed	Not analysed	Bone	Leister point, preform?	138	16	7
12914a	Red deer?	Tibia?	Bone	Leister point, preform?	42	17	5
12914b	Roe deer	Splinters (foramen nutricum)	Bone	Leister point, preform?	155	10	4
13082	Red deer	Diaphysis	Bone	Leister point, preform?	135	13	4
13447a	Red deer?	Diaphysis	Bone	Leister point, preform?	113	17	6
13521	Red deer	Femur	Bone	Leister point, preform?	105	28	8
				Median	102	19	7

distinguishes itself as yet another type. Unlike the others it has two rows, that is, with teeth on both edges, which are remarkably small and shallow. The material is compact thin bone, probably a diaphysis. Judging by the scale, it should be regarded as a leister point.

Bone points or leister points?

Apart from 23 clearly identifiable leister and harpoon points there is also a collection of 21 pointed bone pieces (table 2). The finds are heterogeneous in design, the majority being very crudely cut (fig. 8). In view of the find spot in the layer of gyttja silt (A1626) and the fact that they are all pointed, it is likely that they should either be regarded as semi-manufactured leister points or that they were used just as they were. Some of them were even found standing vertically in the sediment, like several of the leister points proper.

With the exception of find number 13082, the shared feature of the finds is that one end is cut or broken off crossways while the other is pointed. The length varies between 58 mm and 138 mm. As table 2 shows, the greater part are made of femur, metatarsal, or generally diaphysis of red deer. Some could be of elk bone. Compared with the leister points in table 1, there are more finds made of femur from red deer. It should be borne in mind that the pointed bone bits are not worked as much, making it easier to identify the species.

Find number 13082 differs from the other finds in this class. Found standing vertically, it can best be described as an intact leister point, conforming exactly to Types A–B, but without teeth. The point, which is made of a red deer diaphysis, is 135 mm long, 13 mm wide, and 4 mm thick. On the sides one can see distinct traces of the processing but no hint of any notching for teeth. How should this design be explained in relation to the other types? Was it intended to become a fine-toothed leister point but used before it was finished, or did someone think that a polished bone point was an adequate fishing tool? As an isolated find with this design it should perhaps be regarded as having been half-finished when it was lost.

Datings

Of the ten finds that are ^{14}C-dated, half are of the class *Leister point, part of*. As table 3 and fig. 9 show, the Type A points fall within a narrow chronological interval, 5640–5310 BC (2σ, 6590–6470 ± 55/65 BP), while the B point is suggested to be marginally later, 5390–5050 BC (2σ, 6290 ± 70 BP) and the D point slightly earlier 5740–5530 BC (2σ, 6745 ± 55 BP). The datings of the two finds of the class *Leister point, preform* are noticeably later (nos. 8884 and 8721). The former is dated 4620–4350 BC (2σ, 5660 ± 50 BP) and the latter 5070–4770 (2σ, 6040 ± 60 BP). Unlike the Type A points, these seem rather to belong to a phase of activity almost a thousand years later, which also included the three other finds of antler (nos. 8867, 9531, and 11890). A comparison with the ^{14}C datings of the features on land reveals interesting parallels. Of the two settlement phases, the earlier corresponds to the period 5500–5000 BC (2σ), that is, the time of the Type A and B points, while the later phase reflects the period 4200–4000 BC (2σ), which may be considered to lie within the margin for the younger finds (Carlsson, this volume).

With reservations for the fact that only one B point has been dated, this could mean that the type is later than the A type. What does it mean if the types are chronologically distributed? Is the design a distinctive cultural feature that reflects a specialized craft whereby individuals made numerous tools according to a set template, or is the design functionally conditioned for specific prey? It seems reasonable to conclude that the two settlement phases on land correlate to the two distinct groups of finds. In the earlier group there also seems to be a chronological change which calls for an explanation, along with the question why the leister points were replaced by coarse bone points in the later phase. Since the changes are so definitive, the answers should include far more than functional aspects and instead comprise questions of material culture and identity.

Lab no.	Find no.	Layer	Class	Material	^{14}C years BP (uncal.)	^{14}C years BP (cal., 2σ)	Type
Ua-22961	8867	1626	Pressure flaker	Antler	5660 ± 65 BP	4680–4350	–
Ua-22967	11890	1626	Artefact	Antler	5710 ± 50 BP	4690–4450	–
Ua-22964	9531	1626	Artefact	Antler	5770 ± 55 BP	4730–4490	–
Ua-22963	8884	1626	Leister point, preform	Bone	5660 ± 50 BP	4620–4350	–
Ua-22960	8721	1626	Leister point, preform	Bone	6040 ± 60 BP	5070–4770	–
Ua-22965	11675	1627	Leister point, part of	Bone	6290 ± 70 BP	5390–5050	B
Ua-22968	12421	1627	Leister point, part of	Bone	6470 ± 55 BP	5530–5310	A
Ua-22962	8868	1627	Leister point, part of	Bone	6570 ± 65 BP	5630–5460	A
Ua-22969	12422	1628	Leister point, part of	Bone	6590 ± 60 BP	5640–5470	A
Ua-22966	11698	1627	Leister or harpoon point, part of	Antler	6745 ± 55 BP	5740–5530	C

Table 3.
^{14}C-dated finds of bone and antler sorted according to class (BP uncal. and BC cal., 2σ).

Fig. 3.
Diagram showing the ^{14}C datings of the finds.

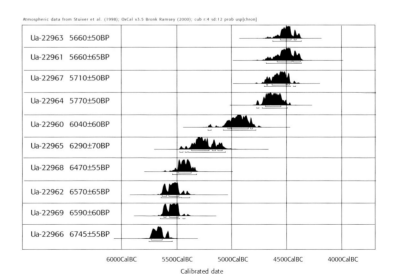

Comparative finds

Finds of leister and harpoon points are unusual. In Scandinavia they started to appear as stray finds in the second half of the nineteenth century, often in connection with peat cutting in bogs and regulation of lake levels (Montelius 1917:I:1:7; Brøndsted 1938). It was not until some way into the twentieth century that leister points were found by excavations of Mesolithic inland settlement sites (Althin 1954; K. Andersen 1983; Larsson 1978b, 1982, etc.). The development of underwater archaeology in Denmark in the second half of the twentieth century has also had the result that preserved artefacts of bone and antler are found during inspections and excavations of submarine sites. That it is mainly harpoons that are found can be said to corroborate the current distinction between the use of leisters and harpoons: the latter were chiefly intended for hunting marine mammals while the more fine-toothed leisters were used for fishing in lakes and rivers. There is also a third type of tool that is common on Danish coastal sites, a composite tool with which the fish can be caught between curving toothed branches. The type that is mainly assumed to have been used for eel fishing is also represented on inland sites in Skåne (Larsson 1983:61f.; Andersen 1995:57ff.).

The nomenclature for leisters varies somewhat in different publications. Older descriptions use the terms leister, bone point, and harpoon without making any major functional distinctions, while Andersen thinks that tools with a simple point should be designated as fishing spears, whereas tools with composite points are by definition leisters (Andersen 1983:163f.). In addition, the term *single-pointed leister* has been used in the presentation of the Tågerup excavations in Skåne. The find in question lacks a separate point of bone or antler, consisting of a pointed hazel rod over three metres long, which is assumed to have been used to spear fish (Mårtensson 2001:292). In the work with the finds from the Motala site, the designation *leister point* has been used without any specific technical sense, mainly because the term is slightly more generally employed, unlike, for example, *fish-spear point* or equivalent. In addition there are different descriptions of what constitutes large- or fine-toothed and barbed bone points. For the finds from the Motala site the designation "tooth" has been used throughout, even though their design has been significant for the present typology.

Sometimes, however, the archaeological classification of how the different tools can be assumed to have been used may seem rather stereotyped. Like the occasional harpoon points from the Motala site, it is probable that the different tools were used to the extent that they served their purpose, even if there was a specific intention in the manufacture. For example, S. H. Andersen sets up two criteria for the design of a harpoon: the rear end should be made so that it can easily be separated from the shaft and so that a line can be applied between point and shaft. The fact that harpoons are predominantly found on coastal Ertebølle sites is seen as indirect evidence that they were used for marine hunting (Andersen 1972:74). There is, however, a small number of finds from lakeside contexts, which qualify the picture of their function (Andersen 1971:114; Andersen 1983:172f.; Rex Svensson 1988:154ff.). Larsson (1978b) problematizes the functional identification of different types of bone points from the Ageröd excavations in Skåne. The two types of leister points that occur – fine-toothed and barbed – are both considered to have been used for leister fishing, while the latter type could very well have been used for hunting game too. This assumption is reinforced by finds from Åmose in Denmark, where a point of Mullerup type was found together with a red deer skeleton (Andersen 1983:173).

The earliest antiquarian presentations of leister points in south Scandinavia are in *Minnen från vår forntid* (Montelius 1917) and *Danmarks Oldtid* 1: *Stenalderen* (Brønd- sted 1938). On typological grounds the Swedish material is placed in the Mesolithic, albeit with the reservation that virtually all are stray finds. Of the few that are docu- mented, the geographical distribution is wide: Öland, Blekinge, Skåne, Östergötland, and Södermanland (Montelius 1917:I:1). Compared with the finds from the Motala site it is only find no. 42 from the Hörninge bog on Öland that has typological features similar to Type A (cf. also Åberg 1923). Find no. 50 is likewise not a typological parallel but it is interesting in that it was found beside Lake Tåkern, only about twenty kilometres from Motala Ström.

The find from Hörninge bog on Öland is not the only one. The 1968 excavation of a settlement site at Alby in eastern Öland uncovered 4–5 fragments of fine-toothed leister points. The largest object is a rear end with seven teeth preserved, of a design similar to Type A from the Motala site. The find, which is of bone, with no exact identification, also has scratched decoration consisting of points and zigzags on one side (Königsson, Lepiksaar & Königsson 1971:35). The settlement site is not exactly dated other than to the range 8000–5000 BP, that is, the entire Atlantic period. The article also presents further leister points, collected as stray finds within a radius of a few kilometres from Alby. The find registered as SHM 6799, Stenåsa parish, shows similarities to the two-row find from the Motala site (no. 9471) and to SHM 6219, Stenåsa parish; in its entire design it is almost identical to the Type A points (ibid.:38f.). There are no datings for these finds.

From Spjälkö in Blekinge there is a stray find of a leister point with great similarities to Type A. The point, which is broken, is 108 mm long, 10 mm wide at the base, and has 24 teeth. The point is made from cannon-bone of elk. The find itself is not dated but there is a dating for the stratigraphical layer in which it was found: the sediment is dated by pollen analysis and radiocarbon to the range 6480 ± 75 (–200) to 6670 ± 75 (–200) BP, that is, the Middle Atlantic period (Liljegren 1982:56). Liljegren, together with Welinder, maintains in his discussion that the tool as a type was used for a long time, connected to the environment rather than to any specific culture group (ibid.; see also Liljegren & Welinder 1976).

Further leister points from Blekinge were presented by Sigurd Erixon in his article on the Stone Age in Blekinge (Erixon 1913:131ff.). All of the so-called bone points are stray finds from bogs: Istaby, Mjällby, Lörby, and Väby. They are described as "long, narrow, smooth, small-toothed tools" of bone. Since these finds come from different places, it is perhaps natural that the design differs, while on the other hand, with occasional exceptions, they stand out as one-row, fine-toothed, polished leister points. Erixon does not adduce any typological grounds for dating but considers it probable that they belong to "the time around or slightly after the Littorina Sea maximum", that is, *c*. 8200 BP, or the Early Atlantic period.

In Skåne there are finds retrieved by recent years' excavations. The Ageröd I:HC site on Lake Ringsjön is a late Maglemose settlement site which was localized beside the former shoreline. The finds of eight leister points are classified by Larsson into three types: fine-toothed, barbed, and a combination of the two (Larsson 1978b:41). The Type A and B points from the Motala site can best be compared with the barbed type from Ageröd. Otherwise it can be said that there is a discrepancy in the definition of what should be called fine-toothed. The finds from Ageröd came from all four stratigraphical layers with no clear typological distinction. From comparisons with Danish, Swedish, and north German finds Larsson concludes that that the fine-toothed leister, as a type, lasted over a much longer time during the Mesolithic in southern Sweden than in Denmark (ibid.:43).

The Ageröd find also contains 66 bone points which, according to Larsson's interpretation, were used as prickers for leather and/or as arrow/spearheads. The latter is indicated by resin on one find, which can be interpreted as showing that the point was shafted (Larsson 1978b:38f). In Althin's publication of this site from 1954 there are several polished points, without teeth, designated as "bone points", which are virtually identical to find no. 13082 from the Motala site (Althin 1954:307–309). Bone points probably had a great many functions during the Mesolithic, but in the light of the results from the Motala site one should consider the possibility that coarsely made bone points could also have been used as leisters.

The excavations at Segebro and the nearby Bulltoftagården in Skåne unearthed two leister points of the fine-toothed type. Based on find contexts, the object from Segebro is dated to the Late Boreal and the find from Bulltoftagården slightly earlier, to the early Maglemose culture (Larsson 1982:78). The Segebro find also includes, albeit from a later settlement phase in the Early Atlantic period, a large number of bone points of the same heterogeneous character as the finds from the Motala site. In the discussion of functional identification Larsson says that the longer examples may have been used as spearheads and leister points (ibid.:64f.). S. H. Andersen has an analogous interpretation for similar finds from the Danish Ertebølle site of Tybrind Vig on Fyn. These bone points, according to Andersen, could have been used either as single points for leisters/fishing spears or as "middle points" in a composite eel leister (Andersen 1995:59).

Other interesting finds from southern Skåne come from the sites of Skateholm and Bredasten. The latter is a coastal settlement dated to the early Ertebølle culture, 4500–4000 BC (dating on typological grounds), which contains, besides a fragment of a small fine-toothed point, a point of bone which is virtually identical to find no. 11698 from the Motala site, that is, the large harpoon-like point of antler (fig. 5). The fragment is only 7.5 cm long but seems to have been shaped in the same way, with long decorated teeth/flukes (Larsson 1986:35f). The similarities between the finds must be considered amazing in view of the fact that the datings differ by about a thousand years, which in itself can be used to cast doubt on the datings of the Bredasten site. A very similar find, among several others, comes from one of the graves at Skateholm I. It has the same stout design but differs slightly in decoration from the examples above (Larsson 1984:10ff.).

In Denmark, especially Sjælland, there have been many finds of leister points which have been associated with the Maglemose culture. The find spots are numerous: Mullerup, Sværdborg, Lundby Holmegaard, and others, but by far the richest must be Åmose in western Sjælland (Mathiassen 1948). Peat cutting in the 1940s and 1950s and archaeological excavations have resulted in hundreds of finds which because of their context are ascribed to the Maglemose culture. The finds come from what Andersen describes as "fishing places", large in area and mostly localized at the different currents of the former lake. The points were only exceptionally found in concentrations; the majority are single finds in areas where the water depth at the time is estimated to have been 0.5 to 1 m. Although a small number of find contexts indicate composite tools with several points – what Andersen terms leisters – the predominant type is referred to as fishing spears. Finds show that the single point was applied to a shaft of hazel with the aid of bast (Andersen 1983:155ff.).

The points, which are dated on contextual grounds to the Maglemose period, are divided by Andersen into three types: A: bone points of ribs with barbs; B: bone point of tubular bones with barbs; and C: flat and round bone points without barbs. In Denmark the first two types go under the name Mullerup type and are characterized by being made of ribs, 11–25 cm long and with 1–3 barbs (Andersen 1983:158ff.). The C type is only worked in exceptional cases, and like the finds from Motala and Segebro, and possibly also from Ageröd, it shows that they were used for leister fishing. The discrepancies in design between the Danish Mullerup type and Type A and B from the Motala site are striking, but at the same time they can be described as being subordinate to the purely functional aspects since they were demonstrably suitable for leister fishing in shallow water with fast currents.

From Åmose there is also what Andersen describes as large-toothed and fine-toothed bone points. They are fewer in number than the others, and on the basis of comparable finds in northern Germany and stratigraphical observations in the growth of the bog, the large-toothed examples can be assigned to the Bromme culture (Younger Dryas) and the fine-toothed ones to the Preboreal (Andersen 1983:166ff.). Neither these types nor the later Mullerup type can be connected with the Ertebølle sites at Åmose, which supports Larsson's thesis that the finer-toothed points lasted for a longer time during the Mesolithic in southern Sweden than in Denmark (Andersen 1983:158; Larsson 1978b:43). Karsten and Knarrström (2003:55) also agree with this, having found only one "barbed" bone point on the Tågerup site in western Skåne. The point has been ^{14}C-dated to the middle of the Kongemose culture and is presumed in this context to be "an example of an earlier technology that survived for functional reasons".

What did they fish for?

The investigation of the Motala site yielded only a small amount of fish bones. The species are confined to eel, perch, pike, and carp. The modest volume of fish bones should be explained by the poor preservation conditions on land and/or deposition patterns that the excavation did not detect. There is no sign at all of the Vättern salmon trout, caught in large volumes in historical times. By comparison we may mention the Danish site of Åmose, where similar fishing resulted in large quantities of bones, chiefly from pike and wels, species which live in biotopes that are suitable for leister fishing (Andersen 1983:156f.).

The amounts of bones found at Danish Mesolithic coastal sites are as a rule large but it is hardly fair to compare them with an inland site (Enghoff 1995). Since certain sites have leisters similar to those from Motala, however, it may be of interest to attempt some comparisons. Bredasten is particularly interesting in view of the similarities in the find material. Both the fine-toothed leister and the barbed harpoon-like point are represented on the two sites, which traditionally reflect two different hunting biotopes: sheltered inland waters and coastal waters. The osteological evidence from Bredasten includes seal, pike, and perch, which highlights the good potential for subsistence in a lagoon environment on the boundary between land and sea (Jonsson 1986:50f.).

Finally, one may ask whether other fishing implements were not found at the Motala site. As in historical times, Motala Ström was suitable for fixed structures to catch both migratory and more stationary species. It is therefore not impossible that uninvestigated areas at the settlement site could contain traces of fixed fishing devices. As regards modern-day leister fishing, there is an ordinance from 1866 banning the practice on the grounds that it was far too efficient, besides which it was considered cruel (Arvidsson 1923:20f.).

Conclusion

The problems in the analysis of this material and comparisons with a selection of south Scandinavian finds have been twofold: the difficulty of distinguishing a local typology and chronology and the heterogeneous comparative material which in many cases lacks absolute datings. The typological features that distinguish Type A from B can and should be discussed further, while Types C and D are indisputable. An important, but fragile, factor in this context is the datings, which suggest that the proposed typological classification also has a chronological parallel: Type A is followed by B. The preforms, which have their counterpart in the material from Åmose and elsewhere, represent a later phase which lies closer to the dated antler finds. Apart from the fact that the datings are grouped around two phases with almost a thousand years in between, this also indicates a discontinuity in the manufacture of leister points from the early phase. Why did people use coarsely cut bone points and not the elaborately made ones? Did they concentrate on other fish species that were easier to catch, did the leister fishing become less important for their livelihood, or did they start using other types of tools such as hooks, nets, and fixed devices which were more efficient? The large number of coarse bone points shows clearly that leister fishing also occurred during the later phase, but that the stock of implements had changed. In contrast to what Liljegren and Welinder (1976) state, that the leister was connected to the environment and not to the culture, the present findings allow us to say that the form of the implements changed, not because of functional aspects but probably because of a perception of the tool as part of the material culture. The rigid uniformity that characterizes the Type A and B points loses all its significance and is replaced by a tool that was not necessarily less functional but much less conspicuous. A hint at a parallel can be discerned in the Tågerup site, where a leister point of bone was found, dated to the Kongemose phase, whereas the Ertebølle phase shows only two pointed hazel rods which are interpreted as leisters (Karsten & Knarrström 2003:183). This therefore seems to confirm Karsten and Knarrström's (2003:230) view of the ideal for the Ertebølle stock of tools: "It did not matter how the tools were shaped, as long as they worked."

As a counterpart to the distinctive typological features and the datings we have the stratigraphy, which only reflects the chronological stages to a limited extent. The Quaternary geological assessment of the stratigraphy describes the water as a calm limnic environment with moderate sedimentation corresponding to that of a lake. The sedimentation must have been very modest since the same layer with an average thickness of 0.19 m contains finds from two phases of activity at an interval of about a thousand years. The picture is further complicated by that fact that many leisters were pushed down into the underlying layer, which in no way corresponds to the contemporary deposition horizon. For the Motala site, however, there are stone platforms which may be said to tie together the activity in the stratigraphy if not in time. From this we can learn that leisters found in "lost" contexts can rarely be dated using the frame dating of the stratigraphical context but only on the basis of good typological grounds or preferably ^{14}C dating.

The comparative material used in this article comes from both Preboreal and Atlantic times. Although the majority of the finds can be ascribed to the inland sites of the Maglemose culture, there are several finds from Atlantic coastal sites which show that the leister, or the fish spear, was still frequently used. The finds from Ageröd I:HC are an interesting parallel to the Motala site in that the material includes three different types and that they occur without any stratigraphical consistency. Larsson (1978b:42f.) runs into dating problems here, namely, that the typology and presumed age of the finds does not correlate with where in the stratigraphy they were deposited. Judging by the chronology of the datings of the Motala finds, the design of these tools was rigid during their period of use, probably representing a specialized craft. The argument is reinforced by the Danish Mullerup type, which, although several hundred examples have been found, is always made of ribs and designed with one to three barbs.

The uniformity also applies to the Type C point in comparison with the finds from Bredasten and Skateholm. The finds show definite typological similarities and can, according to S. H. Andersen's typological schema for Danish Ertebølle harpoons, be called type B (Andersen 1997:57ff.). What makes the comparison even more interesting, in view of the distance between the sites and the difference in their age, is the virtually identical decoration. There are, however, more links between Skåne and Motala Ström since Kristianstad flint was also found at the Motala site.

The future will no doubt see the discovery of places similar to the Motala site in the water system that links Vättern with the Baltic Sea. With the Motala site as a backdrop, in coming excavations it will be possible to ask many questions that have hitherto remained unanswered. Besides problematizing the tool typologies and their datings proposed in the article, it would be interesting to see whether there are fishing places with a comparable construction. Another question is whether only leister fishing was practised or if there are traces of fixed fishing devices and/or fishing with nets and hooks, as the find of a fragmentary fish-hook suggests. More finds of leisters and harpoons will also mean greater opportunities for inter-site and regional comparisons as regards similarities in design and decorative elements, the existence of which is suggested by the Motala finds.

To conclude, we return to the question of what generates change. Behind the switch from leister points of exquisite craftsmanship to coarse bone points there must be a significant structural change; although this can be detected at the level of detail, it can only be explained by studies of a far more overarching design. If the change is also found in other groups of finds on the settlement site between the two activity phases, there is good reason to add Östergötland to the south Scandinavian culture groups' break-point between quality and quantity in material culture during the Middle and Late Mesolithic.

From the hunter's point of view
Animal bones from the Motala site

Joakim Åberg

Several excavations in Östergötland in recent years have yielded a growing corpus of source material for the oldest phases of settlement in the province. The osteological material from these excavations, however, has been very limited as regards the number of bones found and the number of identified species. The osteological evidence from the recently concluded excavation of the settlement site beside Motala Ström is much more extensive, with a relatively large amount of bones from both terrestrial and marine species, which gives new opportunities for discussions of economy, selection, and patterns of settlement. Together with the very large lithic material, the spatial division of the site, house remains, and so on, this material suggests a much more complex society than has previously been demonstrable in this area.

Introduction

Several excavations in Östergötland in recent years have yielded a growing corpus of source material for the oldest phases of settlement in the province. Sites like those at Högby, Mörby, and Storlyckan have stimulated discussions on topics such as localization and settlement patterns, find compositions, and resource utilization (Molin 2000). As regards the osteological material, however, only a very limited number of bones and species have been found (M. Larsson 1996; Kaliff *et al*. 1997; Larsson & Molin 1999). The lack of preserved organic material is a recurrent phenomenon on Mesolithic sites in much of Sweden, with the exception of Skåne and Bohuslän (Knutsson *et al*. 1999). This absence of source material has made it difficult to attempt comparisons of the economy of different sites. The osteological evidence from the recently concluded excavation of the settlement site by Motala Ström is much more extensive, allowing new opportunities to discuss economy, selection, and patterns of settlement. Together with a very large amount of lithic material, the spatial division of the site, house remains, and so on, this material conveys a picture of a much more complex society than has previously been demonstrable in this area (see also e.g. Carlsson and Rolöf, this volume).

A preliminary analysis of the osteological material from the Motala site in Motala has revealed a relatively large quantity of bones from both terrestrial and marine species, and above all the number identified species is large. The geographical location and size of the site, with remains of houses, well-situated osteological and lithic material, and the spatial division of the site, open the way for many interpretations of the place. The osteological material provides us with new opportunities to understand and discuss the relationship between man and landscape.

Bones from settlement sites in Östergötland

The osteological material from previous excavations in Östergötland is at best inadequate. Poor preservation conditions for organic material, partly because of the location of sites on sandy soils, have had the result that bones have been retrieved at only a few of these sites, namely, Högby, Mörby, and Storlyckan. At the Högby site the excavation found bones of red deer and beaver. The osteological analysis comprised only burnt material, mostly obtained by sieving material dug from squares. The bones were badly fragmented, which made identification difficult. Of 278 fragments, the species and bone type could be determined in only 26 cases, with beaver as the dominant element (Vretemark 1996). It is clear that beaver was an important prey, which agrees with observations from Mesolithic sites around Lake Hornborgasjön in Västergötland, where the species also dominates (Ericsson 1985). The material is too small, however, for a discussion of settlement patterns and seasonal utilization. The material from the settlement site at Mörby, despite the water sieving, consists of only a few burnt and unburnt bones. One of these could be identified as hare (Sigvallius 1997). At Storlyckan a very small amount of exclusively burnt bones was collected during the excavation of a hut. The bones were mainly found by sieving the material dug from squares. All bone fragments were badly worn, as a result of which only two fragments could be identified, both of them from wild boar (Molin & Larsson 1999).

The number of identified species from these sites is thus very small. This in itself is hardly surprising, since there are very few bones and most of them are burnt. Comparisons between collections of burnt and unburnt bones have shown clearly that the former represent a much greater variety of species than the unburnt material, and an over-representation of certain body parts and species (Bäckström 1996). The latter applies also to unburnt material, but a larger assemblage of osteological material like that from the Motala site, consisting mainly of unburnt bones, allows much greater opportunity for analyses of livelihood and economy.

The animals at the Motala site

The bones have been analysed by the osteologist Berit Sigvallius, National Heritage Board (Sigvallius 2001, 2004). Since Mesolithic research by tradition often proceeds from discussions of the animals on settlement sites, one of the most explicit goals of the project was to obtain such a large and varied amount of osteological material as possible. The whole Mesolithic occupation layer was water-sieved. About 25 kg of burnt and unburnt bones was found during the fieldwork between 2000 and 2003. The individual bones were badly fragmented, unfortunately, which means that for many bones it has not been possible to determine the species or even assign them to larger families of species. The identified material consists above all of teeth, although bone fragments from other parts of animal bodies occur.

Below is a presentation of the animal species found, along with a brief description of the behaviour and occurrence of different species. It should be pointed out, however, that studies of the latter can involve problems of interpretation since they usually come from later times and often in partly different environments from those surrounding the settlement site in the Atlantic period (Magnell 1995).

Red deer (Cervus elaphus)

Judging by the proportions of identified bones from red deer, this animal was the most frequently hunted quarry throughout the Atlantic period. Large amounts of osteological material from red deer on sites in Skåne and Denmark also indicate that the species was numerous throughout the period. In the osteological material from the Motala site, 59 fragments of red deer have been identified with certainty. They are mostly teeth, but bone fragments from the skull and front/rear extremities also occur. As many as 659 fragments are not identifiable more exactly than as deer of some kind, which probably means that the statistics for the species are uncertain. Red deer are considered to be relatively flexible in the choice of biotope, but they prefer forested land with glades and fens (Dahl 1989:33). The Atlantic deciduous forest has also been described as a varied forest with open elements here and there, which could be a result of deliberate shaping of the surroundings of settlement sites. This has been observed, for instance, in a pollen-analytical study of Dags Mosse, near Lake Tåkern (Göransson 1989:378, 391f.) and at the Late Mesolithic site of Bökeberg III (in Skåne), where variations in the occurrence of charcoal in macrosamples and pollen curves indicate the deliberate opening of the landscape to favour red deer (Regnell *et al.* 1995:82).

Wild boar (Sus scrofa)

The osteological material suggests that wild boar was also an important prey in this area, as at most other Late Mesolithic sites (Magnell 1995:154). A high frequency of wild boar can however be explained in part by the fact that the skeleton of the species consists of many more bones and teeth than, for example, deer (Jonsson 1986). It is nevertheless clear that wild boar played a significant role in the economy on this site, as demonstrated by the 663 fragments. The material is almost exclusively unburnt. Bones from all parts of the body are represented, although the material mainly consists of teeth.

Elk *(Alces alces)*

Elk does not seem to have been hunted to any great extent. Only 14 fragments have been found in the osteological material. As with red deer, however, the statistics are uncertain in the general category of big deer. Because of its size, this species may have been of great economic significance in any case. A full-grown elk has a large slaughtering weight compared with other species, and the yield per killed animal is thus very high. The fact that the Motala site was in a varied biotope with both forests and wetlands also indicates that the conditions existed for the species to flourish.

Roe deer *(Capreolus capreolus)*

Roe deer are common on Mesolithic sites, although the species was not as important for the economy as red deer and wild boar (cf. Magnell 1995:153). The Atlantic deciduous forest with its rich herb and shrub vegetation ought to have been optimal from the nutritional point of view (Lepiksaar 1982:110). Since the species is sensitive to severe winters, it must have been favoured by the milder climate at this time (Berglund 1982). The reason roe deer were not a more common prey may be that the population was kept down by predators like wolf, lynx, and bear, and that competition from red deer and wild boar may have had a negative effect on the stock of roe deer (Jochim 1976:101). In addition, the more predictable habits and size of red deer may have made the species an easier and more desirable quarry than roe deer. In the material studied here there are only two certain toe bones from roe deer, but 254 fragments are with great probability from roe deer. As in the group of big deer, however, roe deer and sheep/goats are gathered in one group because of the great similarities in the appearance of the bones. The stratigraphical find circumstances nevertheless indicate that most of these bones do actually come from roe deer.

Brown bear *(Ursus arctos)*

There is a great deal to suggest that bear was not hunted to any great extent in this area, even though the species gave fur and considerable amounts of meat. Only two teeth were retrieved. The distribution of bear today is associated with coniferous forest and mountains (Bjärvall & Ullström 1985:135). When denser deciduous forests spread during the Atlantic, the bear was probably pushed further north to more open forests with pine and hazel. The very low reproductivity means that the species is sensitive to high hunting pressure.

Seal *(Phocidae)*

In the material from the Motala site there are only two fragments from seal in the form of a tooth and a toe bone. It is nevertheless worth highlighting these fragments because the nearest seal hunting place is about 35 km to the east, on the Littorina Sea. Bones from seal are common on Mesolithic sites in southern Scandinavia. They are hard and therefore are well preserved. Remains of grey seal (*Halichoerus gryphus*) are otherwise often found on sites located right on the coast. Other species retrieved on sites in Skåne and Denmark are common seal (*Phoca vitulina*), harp seal (*Phoca groenlandica*), and ringed seal (*Phoca hispida*). Two of these species occur in coastal areas of eastern central Sweden: grey seal and ringed seal. Harp seal has also lived in this area, but the species no longer occurs in the Baltic Sea. Modern populations are found in outer archipelagos or around beaches and tidal ridges (Bjärvall & Ullström 1985). The exact species of the seal tooth and the seal bone from the Motala site has not been identified.

Beaver (Castor fiber)

Beaver bones have been found on many Mesolithic sites, although generally speaking they have often accounted for a rather small proportion of the retrieved osteological material. The species requires a biotope with watercourses which do not freeze solid in the winter, and plenty of available deciduous trees (Mathiasson & Dalhov 1987). On sites located beside rivers, such as Hög and Ringsjöholm, beaver is therefore relatively well represented (Iregren & Lepiksaar 1993; Jansson *et al*. 1998). In view of the location of the site, the material from the Motala site may seem small. A total of 16 fragments have been identified, most of them teeth.

Otter (Lutra lutra)

Otter occurs at a large number of Mesolithic sites, and was presumably hunted for its fur. Yet the occurrence of butchering marks on bones from Late Mesolithic sites shows that the species was at times also used as food (Noe-Nygaard 1995). The species is associated with coasts and watercourses. Bones from otter are rarely found in large quantities on settlement sites, however. At the Motala site only three fragments of this animal were discovered.

Dog (Canis familiaris/Canidae)

Dog bones occur commonly at Mesolithic find spots. Dogs no doubt had several important functions for humans, particularly as watchdogs and to assist in hunting. The special relationship to dogs is shown by the well-known graves at Skateholm in Skåne, where dogs figure both together with people and in graves on their own (L. Larsson 1988). Sometimes, however, dogs were also used for their meat and fur. Examples of this come from Bökeberg III in Skåne and Danish sites where dogs bones were split to extract the marrow (Aaris-Sørensen 1988:163; Eriksson & Magnell 2001b:64). A total of 12 fragments of teeth, jaw bones, toe bones, and metatarsal from dog have been identified in the osteological material from the Motala site. They are probably from several individuals since they were found both scattered over the site and in features. A further five fragments cannot be identified more exactly than as either dog or fox.

Fox (Vulpes vulpes)

Five fragments have been identified as fox or dog. The fox was common on Mesolithic sites both on the coast and inland. The species is highly adaptable and can live in most environments (Bjärvall & Ullström 1985). The area around this site may very well have been home to a rather large stock of foxes.

Hare (Lepus timidus)

The hare has been found on only a few Mesolithic sites. This has sometimes been interpreted as showing that the species was uncommon during the Atlantic period (Jonsson 1988:83). There are three tooth fragments of hare in the material from the Motala site, indicating that the species was hunted, albeit on a small scale.

Pine marten (Martes martes)

Pine marten was probably common during the Atlantic, as demonstrated by its occurrence on several excavated sites from the Late Mesolithic. The species, which lives on small birds and rodents, is chiefly hunted for its fur. This is underlined by the fact that concentrations of marten bones from the same individual are relatively often found on sites, indicating that the meat was not used; instead people disposed of the skinned bodies (Møhl 1978:60). In the material from the Motala site, however, there is only one fragment (an ulna) from pine marten. It is possible that the species was not hunted to any great extent.

Squirrel (Sciurus vulgaris)

This species occurs, albeit rarely, on Mesolithic sites. One explanation for this is that the bones are rarely preserved. The evidence usually consists of teeth, but at the Motala site there were also two fragments of humerus. Yet another explanation why squirrel is relatively uncommon in the osteological material could be that it mostly prefers a biotope with coniferous forest (Eriksson & Magnell 2001:185). The environment during the Atlantic, however, was not in any way unsuitable for the species (Mathiasson & Dalhov 1987:178).

Hedgehog (Erinaceus europaeus)

Bones from hedgehog have been discovered on large coastal sites, which might suggest that the species was more common around settlements where the population was larger and human presence more palpable (Magnell 1995:166). In the material from the Motala site there are 94 fragments of hedgehog bones. The majority came from the same animal and were found in a context which might be much later than the Mesolithic settlement site.

Mouse or vole (Muridae)

In the osteological material there are 14 fragments which cannot be identified more specifically than as mouse or vole. Vole bones occur on most Mesolithic sites. This has often been interpreted as a secondary admixture. It cannot be ruled out, however, that the animal was trapped, although its economic significance was not particularly large. The northern water vole (*Arvicola terrestris*), which is the most common species of vole on Late Mesolithic sites, normally occurs along shores and in wetlands (Bjärvall & Ullström 1985). It was presumably common in the surroundings of the settlement site, and although it was probably not of any great significance as food, it could very well have been trapped for its fur. Examples of flaying marks on vole bones are found on Late Mesolithic sites in Denmark (Noe-Nygaard 1995).

Birds

Only four fragments of birds have been found in the osteological material. One of these has been identified as coming from domestic hen (*Gallus gallus*) and is thus obviously of later date. In addition, there is an intact humerus from a sparrow, finch, or lark, probably also recent.

Fish

Bones from fish are probably under-represented in the material from Motala, as on many other Mesolithic sites. Fish bones are preserved more poorly than bones from mammals, partly because they are comparatively small and thin. Certain species are preserved better than others, however. Bones from pike and perch, for example, are more resistant than bones from oily fish like salmon, trout, and eel, which form fatty acids during decomposition, thus hastening the process. The presence of dogs on a settlement site reduces the chances of bones being preserved, and it is also possible that birds could have removed some of the material. A total of 1,269 fragments of fish bones were found. Of these, 107 have been identified, with 37 from pike (*Esox lucius*) and 69 from perch or pike-perch (Percidae). Apart from these two species, a fragment of carp has been identified. The material from pike consists chiefly of vertebrae, while the remaining material is fragments from the upper jaw and teeth. The bone fragments from perch/pike-perch are mainly fin rays and vertebrae, along with skull fragments. Only a few fragments are affected by fire.

Some critical aspects

As hinted at above, the find material includes bones which cannot be identified or are recent intermixtures. Osteological assessment is often an interpretation. The similarities in many bones are sometimes even greater between different species than between individuals of the same species (Sigvallius 2004). Source criticism is important with this material. The archaeological interpretation has often been done in isolated cases and assessed according to stratigraphy and signs of recent impact on the environment where the bones were found. Some material has an obvious recent character, for example, the bones of cattle and horse, and therefore can be ascribed to the use of the place in later periods.

One of the purposes for the collection of the bones and for this text is to discuss strategies. Interpretations of economic strategies are of course dependent on what we find on a settlement site, but it is equally obvious that a great many critical aspects must be taken into consideration. The problem of representativeness constantly arises; often only a few per cent of the remains of different animal species once deposited on the site can be identified. Apart from the degree of preservation and the preservation conditions, selective behaviour during hunting could also have had the effect that only a portion of the animals that existed in the fauna at this time are represented in the material. The absence of certain species need not mean that they did not exist or were rare in the area. Tabooed or low-priority species will also be missing in the material. Certain species, such as birds or fish, were also available at different times during the year. People's interest in and use of different species can also vary with the season (Cegielka *et al.* 1995:7).

Problems of representativeness are also caused by how the bones were treated after the animal's death. Marrow fracturing and gnawing by predators are just two examples of how the decomposition of the bones and the distribution of species and elements can be affected. The bones from most Mesolithic sites in southern Scandinavia are fragmented. The general interpretation is that the bones were fractured by humans to extract marrow, since the typical marks left by this have been noted on most Mesolithic sites (Noe-Ny-gaard 1977; Lövgren 1998; Eriksson & Magnell 2001a:168). Gnawing marks from dogs have been observed on several occasions. It is mostly bones with very spongy tissue, such as vertebrae and bones from young animals and from fish and birds that are destroyed. Dogs fed with fish remains may be responsible, for example, for much of the loss of fish bones (cf. Eriksson & Magnell 2001a:170). There are several examples showing that dogs ate a great deal of fish, for instance from Mesolithic sites in Denmark, where high contents of ^{13}C have been measured in dog bones (Noe-Nygaard 1988:88ff.). Experiments have also shown that dogs consuming fish can break down up to 80 per cent of the osteological material (Jones 1986). Dogs can make scatter analyses of bones difficult or even impossible if they have been fed butchering waste and food remains (Kent 1981). Big birds like crows and gulls can also conceivably lie behind the loss of bones from, for example, fish and small animal species (cf. Lepiksaar 1982:118).

Another controversial question is whether the Mesolithic hunters really took the whole prey home. If for some reason they chose to consume the prey where it was killed or to leave parts of the animal at the spot, this affects the composition of the identified material (Eriksson & Magnell 2001a:166). It has sometimes been argued that body parts from large prey, such as red deer and elk, were left behind, for example, for logistic reasons. It is likely, however, that all parts of the animal body were equally valuable, either as food or as raw material for making tools. Transporting a large animal need not involve any great problems, especially if there was access to water routes (Eriksson & Magnell 2001a:203).

In osteological analyses it is thus of the utmost importance to try to form an opinion as to how representative the material really is. Possible sources of error may seem overwhelming, and for understandable reasons interpretations are extremely rarely made on the basis of representative material. With sufficient consideration for taphonomic aspects and processes, however, the bones from Mesolithic sites can serve as a foundation for theories about, say, seasonal use and discussions of sedentary habitation. An excessively critical attitude to the osteological material, for example, in a seasonal analysis, could mean that certain seasons are excluded even before the analysis is performed, and that evidence is thus found for only brief periods. It should be at least as important to subject the results of an analysis to critical scrutiny, and to try to find a plausible explanation for the *reasons* for a specific use (Eriksson & Magnell 2001a:214).

Human selection

There can be no doubt that the composition of the fauna in the forests and the waters around the Motala site largely dictated which animal species were hunted and trapped by humans at this time. The question is, however, whether it is possible to trace any selection process in the osteological material. The fact that bones from certain species are better preserved than others can result in a misleading over-representation of these species in the material. In other words, it may look as if one species was hunted more frequently than happened in practice (Magnell 1995:169). In the same way, the absence or infrequency of particular species need not mean that they were missing or rare in the area, as the discussion above shows. This could be an indication that a selection took place. It is possible that the few bones of elk, for example, at the Motala site actually do reflect the fauna around the site at this time. It could also be the case that this species was given low priority for some reason, thus reflecting the hunters' conscious choices. The same could also apply to bear. Knowledge of the low reproductivity of the species and its sensitivity to hunting could very well have been part of the Mesolithic awareness. Nor is it unlikely that the distribution of species in the material from a settlement site was affected by factors of which it can be very hard to find traces, such as religious ideas or taboos prohibiting the hunting of certain animals, at least at certain times (Magnell 1995:148).

Bones of elk are uncommon on Late Mesolithic settlement sites (chiefly coastal sites). Generally speaking, they seem to be fewer the later the sites are. Bones from this species rarely account for more than one per cent of the identified bones, with a few exceptions such as Bökeberg III and Ageröd V, where the proportion rises to 8 and 10 per cent respectively of all the bones identified as coming from artiodactyls (Magnell 1995:151). The frequency of elk in osteological material seems to be higher at inland sites. It is possible that elk was favoured by large areas of wetland, as seems to be the case, for instance in Skåne (Eriksson & Magnell 2001a:177). Ecological variations in the landscape around the Motala site at this time (see Strucke 2003) would probably have provided biotopes for elk. One explanation why elk was not a more common quarry could be that these animals seldom form flocks or dense populations as red deer do. Moreover, the movements of red deer in the landscape were easier to predict, partly because they form trails and move over smaller areas. Altogether, this must have meant that red deer was an easier prey and people therefore preferred to hunt it rather than elk (cf. Magnell 1995:152).

Further examples which could suggest that a selection was made can be detected in the evidence from fish. The fact that a large amount of leisters of bone and antler and fragments of bone hooks have been found on the Motala site, and that tools in the form of fish traps and nets are absent, may indicate that more selective fishing was practised. Fishing with leisters is considered an effective method for pike, especially since this species moves to shallow waters to spawn, and is then inattentive and easy to get close to. Pike is also easy to catch with a hook, especially directly after spawning. Features which have been interpreted as platforms for leister fishing have also been found in the water near the site. The fact that only pike and perch have been identified could be viewed as a result of selective fishing. At any rate it is clear that bones from only two species, such as pike and perch, do not reflect a normal fish population.

Hunting or fishing?

As regards the economy of the Motala site, fishing was not used to the full as an economic resource, or else the surviving material does not reflect the whole reality. The lack of fixed fishing devices and the few fish bones suggest the former while the number of leister points and permanent fishing places suggests the opposite. The leister points nevertheless indicate that fish was an important part of the diet, at least seasonally (see Bergstrand, this volume).

Judging by the identified bones, hunting for deer and wild boar was highly valued, while species which are chiefly grouped in the category of fur-bearing animals (e.g. bear, beaver, fox, and pine marten) account for only a small share. Red deer is usually considered easier to hunt than wild boar because of its more predictable habits. A red deer also yielded a large amount of meat and raw material such as antler and skin, along with several nutritious by-products such as marrow, blood, brain, heart, liver. This, together with the fact that the low fat content of the meat made it suitable for drying (L. Larsson 1983:133) undoubtedly meant that the species was well worth hunting. The low reproductivity of red deer, however, meant that hunting had to be done selectively if it was to be possible to cull a large number and simultaneously maintain a vigorous population (Eriksson & Magnell 2001a:198). A species like wild boar can withstand a much greater hunting pressure, since the reproductivity of this species is high (Göransson 1987:31).

At inland sites like Bökeberg III and Ageröd V, hunting was mainly focused on red deer (Lepiksaar 1983; Cegielka *et al*. 1995), and there are also examples of settlement sites where people mainly hunted wild boar, such as Bredasten and Ringkloster (Jonsson 1986b; Rowley-Conwy 1998) or specialized in hunting birds and fur-bearing animals, such as Aggersund (Møhl 1978). In the material from the Motala site there are no signs of any specialization of this kind. Instead we see the broad-spectrum economy that is typical of a base site of sedentary character (Karsten & Knarrström 2003). If the seal bones can be interpreted as showing that people made their way to the coast to hunt seal, this hints at the use of resources within a large geographical area. The harpoons/ leisters could also have been used for hunting seal.

Economy versus settlement pattern

The discussion of the Late Mesolithic settlement pattern has mainly concerned whether people moved between different natural settings on a seasonal basis. Sites on the coast have been taken to represent base settlements where a large group of people stayed for most of the year. In the summer, smaller groups moved inland to more specialized sites beside lakes to utilize resources which were seasonally and geographically limited. Sometimes there has even been talk of a coastal and an inland population (e.g. Larsson L. 1980; Larsson M. 1996:39; Kaliff 1999:26). This seasonality has often been taken virtually for granted in analyses of Mesolithic settlement sites, although there have been hints or explicit statements from several scholars in recent years that certain "populations" were stationary much earlier than used to be assumed (e.g. Carlsson *et al*. 1999:65; Knutsson *et al*. 1999:93; Karsten & Knarrström 2003:212).

The reasons stated for settlement based on annual movements have often been grounded in ecological factors, such as the unavailability of resources in the vicinity of the settlement site during all the seasons of the year (Rowley-Conwy 1987:76), and the fact that sites have only a limited and unrepresentative assemblage of finds (Carlsson *et al*. 1999:65). Conversely, the favourable placing of a settlement in an environment beside several varied biotopes has been viewed as one of the primary reasons for a "liberation" from the mobile life (cf. Jennbert 1984; Kaliff 1999:26; Nordquist 2001:73). A permanent or long period of use is also thought to be corroborated by a larger, well-used habitation area with a large accumulation of waste, along with a considerable quantity of tools and remains of tool manufacture (Nilsson 1995:184; Karsten & Knarrström 2003:120). Graves beside the settlement site are likewise usually seen as a sign of permanence (e.g. Karsten & Knarrström 2003:212; Jennbert 1984). The picture of sedentariness is further confirmed by the varied osteological material, which represents a wide range of species from both local and partly non-local biotopes. A broad spectrum and variety of species is also considered to be a characteristic of base settlements or year-round sites (e.g. Rowley-Convey 1987; Eriksson & Magnell 2001b:76; Karsten 1999). An osteological analysis should, perhaps must, be a part of the quest for the totality. It should not attempt to decide what Mesolithic people ate on the basis of some taken-for-granted food-intake determinism.

Actions in quartz
Some reflections on shiny white stones in eastern central Sweden

Roger Wikell

Quartz can be difficult to see. But it is like everything else – something to learn; how to read quartz. The shiny white stones have been neglected because they do not look like the flint that archaeologists expected to find. But the intentions of the toolmaker are written in the stones. The stones in the landscape enable us to see the Mesolithic cultural landscape.

Introduction

In Motala the find lists are dominated by quartz, as is also the case at other Mesolithic settlement sites in Östergötland and eastern central Sweden. Quartz is the very backbone of the material culture we encounter on Mesolithic sites in the region. Quartz occurs at virtually all these places. The amount of quartz per site can vary from a few scattered bits to several tens of thousands. Because of its abundance, it is chiefly quartz that first signals Mesolithic sites during surveys. Knowledge of the material is therefore important when fieldwalking and conducting preliminary archaeological investigations. More and more settlement sites can then be discovered and excavated. The ever-present quartz distinguishes eastern central Sweden chiefly from southern and western Sweden, where flint predominates. The use of quartz was not just a matter of "making do with what we've got"; the material was important for the identity of the groups using it.

With increased knowledge in recent decades, quartz has achieved greater acceptance among archaeologists and the interested general public. But this has not always been the case. It used to be axes that were studied primarily, but since the 1930s the white stones have attracted increasing attention. One of the first to notice quartz flakes as man-made, and moreover of significance as tools of some kind, was Torsten Engström. Together with the geologist Harald Thomasson, Engström pursued Stone Age studies in Kolmården in north-east Östergötland. He declared with foresight: "If quartz does not seem suitable for the retouch treatment of flint technology, this was not necessary, since razor-sharp edges could be obtained by knapping. A piece of quartz from which splinters were struck seems to suggest that this may have occurred on the site. The large number of sherds on the settlement sites may mean merely that dull tools were discarded, since the supply of raw material was copious" (Engström 1935:36). The two scholars also say: "The structure of quartz is quite different from that of flint, and one therefore cannot expect a similar technique" (Engström & Thomasson 1932:37). As late as the 1980s there were archaeologists, although not with the Stone Age as their speciality, who were sceptical about quartz and its Mesolithic context (Nordström & Ferenius 1984:10). According to them, the quartz could possibly belong to nearby Neolithic settlement sites; quartz flakes had been observed early on at several places like these (Hansson 1897:7; Almgren 1906b:102; see also Ahlbeck 1995).

This attitude is not unique or hard to understand. Quartz has seemed difficult and abstract, and has often been met with scepticism by those who are unfamiliar with the material. It has not been made any better by the fact that the archaeologists who have previously tackled the material have been looking among the quartz for artefact forms known from the flint industry, such as scrapers, burins, and microliths. It is the outward forms, not the manufacture or technique, that have been the foundation for the finds that were sought after or identified. This has proven to be incorrect, for as far as we can understand, people did not make formal tools in the true sense from quartz, although there are in fact retouched pieces. Most objects have been interpreted as scrapers. Compared with other regions in Sweden, however, the proportion of intentionally formed tools is very small. This causes frustration for an archaeologist in eastern central Sweden who is interested in the Mesolithic. How can one handle mass material which is so anonymous, which so tantalizingly eludes all attempts at traditional functional divisions, typology, and dating? Nor are there obvious points of contact with the research tradition in southern Scandinavia or on the west coast of Sweden, with their chronologically distinct culture groups: Maglemose, Kongemose, and Ertebølle in the south, and Hensbacka/Fosna, Sandarna, and Lihult/Nöstvet in the west. All these are based on a plentiful supply of flint.

"The flint syndrome" – the tendency to translate quartz pieces, or the forms one thinks one sees in the material, into formal objects of flint – has impeded research (Knutsson 1998). A well-known example of this is Ville Luho in his works on the Askola and Suomosjärvi cultures in Finland (Luho 1956, 1967). (For a critique of Luho's assumptions see Siiriäinen 1977; Knutsson 1998.) Stig Welinder, in his influential works from the 1970s, likewise saw different tools in the quartz, for instance through his publication of the now famous Late Mesolithic site of Sjövreten on the Södertörn peninsula south of Stockholm (Welinder 1973). Yet another example from Södertörn is the presumed Late Mesolithic material from Flemingsberg, where Evert Baudou claimed to see arrowheads and the like (Baudou 1962). The objects that Welinder identified from a toolbox made in Flintland were, for example, "core scrapers, angle burins, flake scrapers and blade fragments" (Welinder 1973:28).

It is not unusual that archaeologists who see quartz for the first time in the field see objects they recognize from their undergraduate courses in archaeology. This categorization is evidently common among archaeologists. We want to see a toolbox with contents that we recognize. When we do not, we become uncertain about what is knapped or not. At the beginning of one's career in quartz one often includes *all* white stones, since one is uncertain whether they are worked or not. Other white stones and minerals such as feldspar are often placed in the find bags. Archaeologists evidently do not want to miss anything. The registration work then yields a considerable pile of natural gravel. This is mentioned as an illustration of what a process it is to learn to see quartz (cf. Ahlbeck 1995). It is understandable that quartz can be difficult and abstract for a beginner; this could be called a "quartz syndrome". The mass material is felt to be beyond understanding. It does not seem to say anything about the society and the people who once used it. "Slivers which do not even look like an arrowhead – what do they tell us?" the unaccustomed beginner seems to wonder.

Christina Lindgren has shown how difficult it can be to see retouched quartz. The dazzling white surface of quartz seems to camouflage the retouches. With a simple experiment she demonstrated in her article "Shapes of Quartz and Shapes of Minds" how tricky it is for inexperienced archaeologists to "read" quartz. She had a small group of colleagues register retouched and unretouched pieces. The result was rather depressing. Only 59 per cent of the material was correctly registered (Lindgren 1998). The example shows how important it is to be familiar with the material. You have to see a lot of quartz to be able to read it. It is a good idea to perform experiments of one's own. I am optimistic, despite Lindgren's study, and I believe that it is possible to see, if not all, then many of the retouches. What is required, besides experience, is cleaned pieces and good lighting. Otherwise it is easy to be afflicted by the "quartz syndrome" and believe that there is nothing to see or learn. But there is hope; several scholars have tackled quartz in particular and the Mesolithic in eastern central Sweden in general. Several dissertations and articles have appeared in the last twenty years. It is in this light that we should view the Motala excavation.

Errett Callahan's work from 1987 and Kjel Knutsson's dissertation from 1988 have paved the way. They are primarily about reduction strategies and use-wear analysis. Nor should we forget Noel Broadbent's dissertation from 1979, where quartz quarrying, quartz reduction (especially the bipolar technique), coastal settlement, and seal hunting are discussed in detail, a track on which Stig Welinder had already started in the same decade (Welinder 1977). Broadbent studied a coastal Late Mesolithic settlement site complex at Lundfors in northern Sweden (Broadbent 1979). The sites are very similar to those in eastern central Sweden from the same time.

It was Callahan and Knutsson who tackled quartz in earnest. Callahan studied lithic material from four places in eastern central Sweden. His first impression was: "Here and there a recognizable tool type emerges – a scraper, a microblade, a greenstone axe – but most seems as if it were produced in a gravel factory" (Callahan 1987:18). The disheartening impression of the finds was partly due to the fact that "the excavators had indeed picked up much non-artifact material and fire-cracked rock" (Callahan 1987:18). The material collected by the archaeologists with little experience of stone underlines the importance of lithic knowledge. Callahan, with many years' experience of stone-smithing and experimental archaeology, had the right knowledge. A pattern gradually crystallized in what had once looked like a pile of gravel. Callahan drew up a reduction schema, from platform (freehand), via anvil and bipolar technique, with variants (Callahan 1987:60, fig. 97). Callahan's model seems to hold water, since platform cores are fairly uncommon compared with the amount of platform flakes and flake fragments, which is quite large. The explanation, according to Callahan, is that the cores and flakes were reused by the application of the other methods. The anvil method is rather uncommon, either because it is difficult to distinguish from bipolar technique in its final stage, and from platform in its initial stage. On the other hand, bipolar cores, the last phase in this envisaged reduction chain, are very common. There are both flakes and cores in large quantities. The reduction process looks like a method that uses material economically, a rational way to get a great many flakes out of hard and brittle material. Callahan concludes that the bipolar technique was common: "Bipolar method of lithic reduction seems to lie at the heart of Middle Sweden technology" (Callahan 1987:12). Figs. 1 and 2.

There are different kinds of bipolar cores in the material from eastern central Sweden, everything from the classical, often "cushion-shaped" ones worked from the top down to those reduced from the outside in. Different variants among the cores suggest that there was an active strategy in the bipolar craft. Bipolar-knapped quartz is not necessarily random knocking on stone. Some typical cores can be seen in figs. 1 and 2. Some of the cores knapped from the outside in are worked all the way around and can then be bewilderingly like conical blade cores. The spalling surfaces can also have a similar size. It may be tempting to view these as conical microblade cores, but the question is whether this can be done without problems. What was the intention of the stonesmith? Are they chronologically relevant for other regions? In any case, there is a great deal in the archaeological material which reveals strategies, choices, and actions in quartz.

The size of the bipolar cores of quartz that we have found allows us to suspect that the flakes were not worth bothering about when the core was less than about 2–3 cm high. The width varies somewhat, but is seldom greater than the height. Flakes from bipolar cores on an anvil are often narrow and straight, but they sometimes occur with a curved line. It is nevertheless characteristic that the flakes are fairly thin and narrow. It is possible to strike thin flakes by platform technique, but with the technique described here it can be done more regularly. Several archaeologists have wondered whether the thin flakes can be viewed as microblades.

Of the cores in the material which are worked from the top down, a fairly representative sample can be seen in figs. 1 and 2. It may be noted that they are of almost the same size, which shows where the stonesmith felt that the core had been used up. Since we are justified in assuming that it is not one and the same person who knapped all the thousand and more bipolar cores in Motala, we can see here a "normative" picture of how far people were prepared to go in the reduction. Since we may assume that it was not the core itself that was the primary thing but the flakes, we have here a measure of the smallest desirable size of these. It is possible to strike flakes from small cores. Among the finds there are cores which my colleagues and I, in a travesty of Callahan, called in the field "note small size" – bipolar cores (Callahan 1987:24, fig. 14). These need not necessarily have been knapped by children or fine-limbed people. With a fresh cleft branch one can simply hold the core fast and continue working the stone without risk until really small proportions are reached.

The reduction schema presented by Callahan was significant for continued research. The fundamental work continued by Kjel Knutsson and others, partly together with Callahan, has given archaeologists new tools with which to achieve order among all the quartz. Based on theories from solid mechanics about the strength of fragile materials, principles have been drawn up for how quartz breaks up when worked. The seemingly chaotic disintegration, with large quantities of broken pieces and debris, proves to be regular. Mesolithic people knew this and took advantage of it. Based on controlled experimental knapping series, it was possible to build up a picture of how quartz breaks. The different pieces that were formed could now be explained. Fracture pictures of what could be expected became a tool for understanding the variation in the material and what one could expect to find in it. A sorting schema could thus be created (Knutsson & Lindgren, in Lindgren 2004). A foundation was laid for giving a culture-historical meaning to the hitherto anonymous quartz (Callahan et al. 1992). There was a need before this, as we have seen, but it became urgent in connection with the large-scale excavations for the high-speed railway line from Stockholm south to Södertörn. The excavations, which were the first modern ones of their kind, comprised large areas of Mesolithic settlement sites. The large quantity of excavated quartz soon became unmanageable (Callahan et al. 1992). Before this, Mesolithic settlement sites had often been investigated by means of test squares, keyholes which are far too small to glimpse the prehistory of which archaeologists try to gain some idea.

Based on Knutsson and Lindgren's sorting schema, a range of simplified variants have been used. In the registration of the material from Södertörn, we have often applied the categories of core, core fragment, flake, flake fragment, debris, and debitage. Pieces have also been identified as to method: platform, anvil, and bipolar. This basic division has been used for parts of the material from Motala, and a simpler variant with cores, knapped pieces, debris, and debitage. This is a good way to proceed with the material. There is obviously more than just the simple reduction classification. It is not only the disintegration of the quartz that is written in the pieces. I am thinking of the pieces where the stonesmith did more than just reduce a quartz core – striking flakes, quite simply. Strategies and choices are readable. Actions in quartz are recorded in the many shiny stones. The intention is often more than simply smashing the stones to obtain sharp edges. These small stories take us close to the toolmaker.

To return to the bipolar cores that are worked from the top down: We can ask whether the cores themselves were the primary thing. Were they used as tools? They have sometimes been viewed as wedges. With their often slightly cushion-like shape they acquire a relatively strong form. Is it scrapers or planes that we see in the material? Platform cores have often proved to be this (Knutsson 1998). We should remember certain examples of handle cores and keel scrapers (Olofsson 1995). Luho viewed the bipolar cores as tools, and even in more recent times the idea has been put forward about Late Mesolithic material from eastern central Sweden (Granath Zillén 2001). The idea is not entirely wild, since the bipolar crushing edges have a certain, albeit distant, similarity to a finely retouched edge on an ordinary scraper. The retouch is primarily made to strengthen the scraper so that the extremely thin part does not split immediately under strain. In addition, people would have wanted to reduce the material's cutting properties when scraping skins. Future use-wear analyses may possibly confirm or falsify this hypothesis. If it should be proved correct, we would suddenly have access to an easily identifiable object which can be connected to different activities. We would then have yet another variable to analyse.

If we look at the distribution of bipolar cores in Motala, it is clear that they were found over virtually the whole excavated area, but with a distinct preponderance along the banks of the river Motala Ström, like the distribution of other categories of quartz. Other finds – axes, hammerstones, grindstones, etc. – likewise show this concentration along the banks. There is a clear rise in the number of cores between the presumed hut and the water (Carlsson, this volume). Bipolar flakes are also more numerous at this place. We have here, presumably, a place that was used repeatedly or intensively for knapping. But how should we understand the other cores? Did people knap cores in more than one place and then discard them when they were considered used up? Or were they carried away from the find-rich knapping place and then dumped? This procedure has been observed at Skumparberget in Närke. In that case it was not just cores that were carried away, but larger usable flakes. Kjel Knutson sees parallels to the procedure described by Lewis Binford among the Inuit: a "toss zone" surrounding the knapping place (Knutsson & Melchert 1995; Binford 1978).

When we look at the first step in the presumed reduction strategy – the platform – we find a picture similar to that for the bipolar cores. It is mainly platform cores that are found within the same area. This is a strong indication that the platform and bipolar technique can be regarded as a continuous series of elements in stone-smithing, as Callahan suggested. It was probably the same person who used both techniques. We can imagine

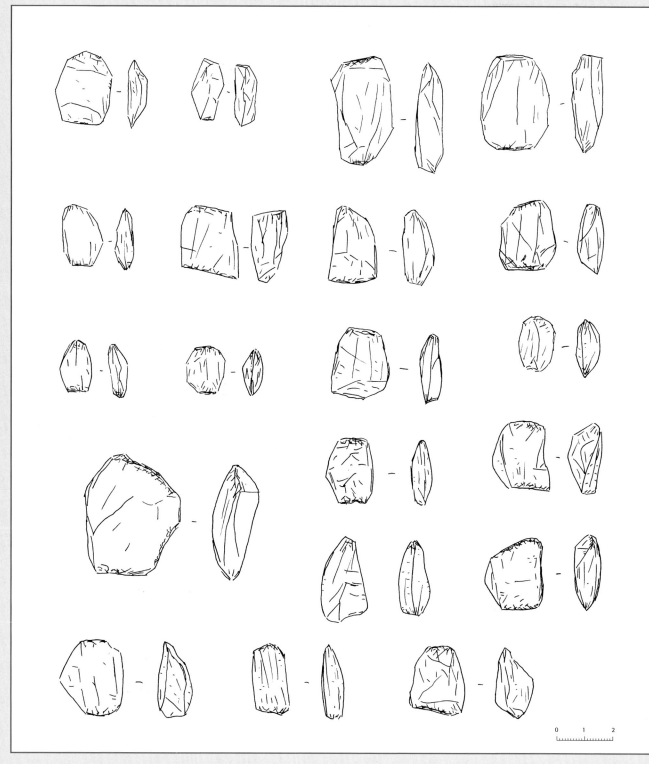

Fig. 1. Bipolar cores from Motala. Drawing: Roger Wikell.

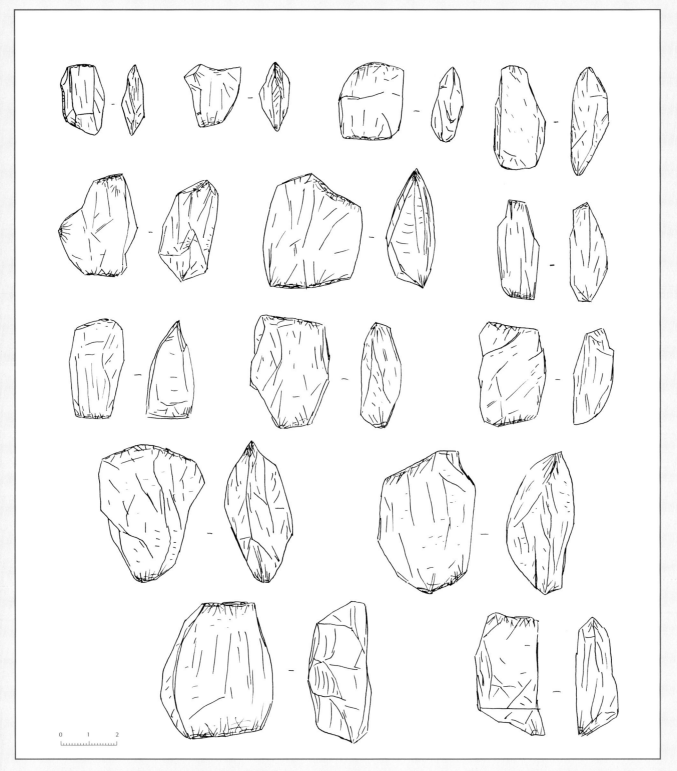

Fig. 2. Bipolar cores from Södertörn. Drawing: Roger Wikell.

that it is the place that is constant, while different people went there. Christina Lindgren has tried to problematize the knapping places in terms of action theory. The different reduction methods can then be read as parts of a social strategy whereby a person could take up both a spatial and a social place within the settlement site through the body movements required by the technique. The strategies can be given different performative characteristics which, according to Lindgren (2004), can be viewed as a way of communicating. If people wanted to express different things with the knapping techniques, they evidently did so within the same parts of the settlement site, which is perhaps not so diametrically opposed to the hypothesis. There may not have been any social opposition between the reduction methods, since one and same person can perform both methods in the same knapping action.

The settlement site in Motala closely resembles the settlement sites in Södertörn. It is chiefly the quantity of quartz and the distribution/presence of the reduction strategies that we discussed above. The types of axes, grindstones, and stone knives are also very similar (Lindgren 1997; Wikell 2003; Carlsson 2004b). The datings agree too. They are roughly grouped between 6500 and 5500 BP. Yet there are some essential differences to which the scholars in the region have drawn attention. They chiefly concern the presence of microblades and especially their manufacture. Handle cores are found regularly in the western part of eastern central Sweden, but are mostly absent in the eastern part. During the Mesolithic, it seems as if handle cores and the manufacture of microblades were associated with the mainland in the west, or with islands close to the mainland. The archipelago area, on the other hand, has no manufacture of handle cores (Lindgren 2004). The presence of microblades in the archipelago is explained by finished tools, which included microblades, finding their way out to the distant islands. There was no proper manufacture, however. Now handle cores of fine-grained material have actually been found (Sven-Gunnar Broström pers. com.) and rejuvenation flakes have also been discovered on excavated sites in Södertörn, at Eklundshov (Lindgren 2004) and Myrstugeberget (Granath Zillén 2001). These exceptions, as we view them today, only confirm the rule that there was no large-scale production of microblades in the archipelago area. Handle cores are conspicuously absent in both excavated and surveyed material.

The complex of handle cores is chiefly dated to the Late Mesolithic in eastern central Sweden, but there are places which can be assumed on good grounds to be older (Knutsson *et al.* 1999). The site at Storlyckan, Östergötland, where microblades were found in a feature interpreted as a hut, has been radiocarbon-dated, indicating that the site was used around 7905 and 7865 BP, or 7000–6550 cal. BC, 1 sigma (Larsson 2003:30). Welinder viewed the handle cores as part of what he called the flint group, akin to the Late Mesolithic Lihult/Nöstvet culture on the west coast (Welinder 1977). The many excavations of the last few decades have not been able to confirm this strict division; it now seems more as if the flint group is found on the mainland and the quartz group in the archipelago, as mentioned above. The Motala settlement site definitely belongs to the mainland group, not just geographically because it was on the mainland as it was then, but also in terms of technology, with several different kinds of material among the handle cores. In Motala there is both white quartzite and Cambrian flint among the cores (Carlsson *et al.* 2003; Holm 2004). Lindgren and Åkerlund would interpret the presence and absence of handle cores in eastern central Sweden as culturally conditioned. Different groups chose either to learn and adopt handle cores or not to. Alex Gill has criticized the view that this necessarily reflects identity markers of two groups. He sees a more prosaic/functional explanation why people felt a need to adopt the handle core tradition. Gill (2003) suggests that hunting on land required microblades for both functional and ritual reasons. In the archipelago, different tools were used for fishing and seal hunting.

The discussion about the microblades is significant, and it is obvious that the handle core tradition was important in Mesolithic society in eastern central Sweden. But that does not mean that we can forget the quartz. The backbone of the lithic strategy in the region is the frequent use of quartz, and the palpable presence of bipolar technique is, in Callahan's words, "at the heart of Middle Sweden technology" (Callahan 1987:12). In Motala 1,000 bipolar cores have been registered, not counting all the core fragments which conceal a higher number. The total number of quartz pieces retrieved at Motala is over 120,000. The weight of the quartz collected, brought there, and left behind is about 230 kg. The area of the site and the amount of finds means that Motala can be classed as a large settlement site for the region (Åkerlund *et al.* 2003; Lindgren 2004). Another large settlement site which has been excavated and published is the Jordbro Industrial Estate in Södertörn. Over 80,000 bits of quartz were found there, and the number of bipolar cores is just over 1,000 (Lindgren & Lindholm 1998; Lindgren 2004). The weight of the excavated quartz from Jordbro Industrial Estate is about 242 kg.

The impression gained from the registration work at Motala is that the pieces are smaller than they tend to be in Södertörn. They seem to have been used to the full and knapped down to the smallest possible size. In Södertörn, on the other hand, one is struck by how often large pieces are found. The average weight of the quartz from Jordbro Industrial Estate and from Motala can exemplify this impression. The bits of quartz from Jordbro weigh on average 3.0 grams. In Motala the corresponding weight is just 1.6 grams. Does this indicate a shortage of material? (Or a difference between archipelago and mainland?) Small pieces of knapped material, meaning far-reaching exploitation, can sometimes be explained that way. It may be correct, since the same procedure can be seen for flint, both in southern Scandinavia and that from Kinnekulle, in the material from Motala. In this procedure, then, quartz and flint are similar.

The quartz in Motala seems in large measure to come from quartz nodules. The proportion of pieces with till-worn surfaces is large compared with Södertörn. Once again, Motala and Jordbro Industrial Estate can illustrate this. Pieces with a till surface are much more common in Motala and from the settlement site in Södertörn. This may reflect the surrounding landscape. Around Motala there are large areas with gently undulating moraine slopes. Exposed rock is decidedly rare. The Atlantic mixed oak forest grew dense on the clayey till plains. Quartz is thus rather hard to get at (cf. Knarrström 2000). Natural sources of quartz in a landscape like this are where the ground is damaged. We can ignore windfallen trees and the like since they are far too temporary. There are no large blocks which could contain veins of quartz. The most important place in this landscape is the shore, in this case of rivers and lakes. Living and open shores are important, the kind that do not become overgrown with peat and other vegetation. Such shores are mainly found along Vättern and Motala Ström. Here quartz nodules in till can be continuously washed out by waves and spring floods.

Compared with Södertörn, however, the extent of available shore in Motala is small. In Södertörn and in the Mesolithic archipelago landscape there were washed till shores and rock slabs. In the fissure valleys of Södertörn, exposed rock is common, presumably with the most important source of raw material: quartz veins. In addition to this favourable situation, the ongoing uplift constantly exposed new land; new shores and cliffs with quartz veins. Motala and Vättern lack this growth in the lithic economy. There the shore, in principle, stands still, so the supply may have been very scanty, unless the till itself is rich in quartz nodules.

When viewed in this light, the heavy exploitation of quartz in Motala is like the use of flint. Flint is also an inaccessible raw material, one which moreover comes from places far outside the home district. Quartz, on the other hand, could be found at home. And people preferred to knap it on the beach. Did they want to imitate the archipelago situation? The relentless or efficient use of the quartz, the final stage of which is done by bipolar technique, has sometimes, as we saw above, been considered crude. But it is easy to learn. The reduction techniques as a whole are easy to learn. Suitable stones to use as hammerstones are found in abundance on the beaches, although we see that Mesolithic people chose their hammerstones with care. In Motala we found over 800 hammerstones, which is an indication of the extent of quartz-smithing. Moreover, the quartz on Mesolithic settlement sites is often "beautiful" compared with the quartz that was worked in later periods. A personal impression is that one can tell by looking at quartz whether it is knapped in a Mesolithic manner, even though one is justified in saying that quartz reduction can be summed up as: "you make do with what you've got, you get what you knap". Yet there is on the whole a trend in Mesolithic knapped quartz. The aim was to obtain flakes and not, as one might believe, cores, as discussed earlier in the text. The number of retouched pieces is small. The previously cited Torsten Engström likewise notes that the quartz from the Middle Neolithic settlement sites in Kolmården is "clumsier" in its execution than the quartz on the preceramic settlement sites at higher altitudes (Engström & Thomasson 1932:37).

The predominant technique among the cores is bipolar. This reduction method has been regarded as temporary. But now when the temporary seems to be permanent, how are we to understand that? What is the relation between bipolar cores, from which one can make thin, small flakes, and microblades? Jenny Holm, who has discussed the relationship between quartz and microblades from Närke, in the region north of Motala, has formulated this problem pithily: "Quartz, Microblades and the Meaning of Life" (Holm 2003a).

The quartz and the microblades are related to each other. The quartz, and its craft, can be described as, if not crude, then at least unsophisticated compared to handle cores. But the amount of quartz in the eastern central Swedish Mesolithic shows that this material was important. It was part of the meaning of life. Quartz was the backbone of lithic culture for a long time in eastern central Sweden. Mesolithic people were fond of the bipolar method. Quartz was a natural part of their lives; this may seem like a banal statement, but in view of how difficult it has been for archaeologists to accept quartz, it is not obvious that quartz is important. The meaning no doubt went beyond the functional properties of the flakes. It is not just the cutting and scraping edges that were the purpose of using quartz.

It is only when the Mesolithic changes that quartz loses its significance and becomes clumsier. The properties of quartz, diametrically opposed to those of flint, and its bright white colour distinguish the lithic material in the area from that of surrounding areas. The simple technique with its economical use of material served its purpose. The quartz, which originated in the landscape where the people had their homes, was an integral part of their identity. The fairly rich, or at least widespread supply of quartz gave freedom in a mobile life. Quartz für alle!

The flint from the settlement site in Motala
A study of raw material, technology, and function

Nicklas Eriksson

This article presents the results of analyses of some of the flint found at the Late Mesolithic site in Motala. Through analyses of the raw material, technology, and function of the flint, an attempt is made to demonstrate how the material from the site can serve as a basis for discussions about the contact network of Mesolithic people at Motala and how they arranged their immediate environment in various ways.

Introduction

The Mesolithic site in Motala is in the borderland between two lithic traditions. Quartz and ultramylonite dominate to the east, while to the west of Motala flint is the most frequent raw material on settlement sites. The different raw materials and certain technological attributes show that the different influences met here in a cultural mixture, although the quartz tradition is dominant. It should be mentioned that flint does not occur naturally in Östergötland but must be brought here in some way.

The reduction methods in the flint areas were predominantly platform techniques of varied character, and many places had developed the specialized manufacture of blades and microblades (Karsten & Knarrström 2001:319; Knarrström 2000a:54ff.; Knarrström 2001:52ff.). Blades were mainly knapped using a soft, indirect technique with an antler punch, and an almost standardized form could be achieved in this way. Microblades were chiefly made from conical microblade cores and handle cores with a punch or pressure flaker. The bipolar technique was more common in the quartz areas. East and north of Vättern it is quartz, ultramylonite, and other types of rock that dominate the lithic material on settlement sites. This raw material behaves differently from flint when knapped, and implements were shaped more in accordance with the nature of the material (Knutsson 1998), which limited the potential to plan the appearance of the tools. The microblade tradition is nevertheless the common denominator for Middle and Late Mesolithic societies.

The parts of the site that were chosen for investigation were a relatively central area around a two-aisled long-house and an area which in the Mesolithic was the outermost tip of the site where another, slightly smaller building had stood. The distribution of finds from the two-aisled house indicates that it was cleaned out, since the major part of the finds were outside the walls of the house and down towards the former shoreline to the east. The interpretation is therefore that the house functioned as a dwelling and that stone working was done outside or in other buildings (Carlsson 2004a). The area outside the house running down to the water was therefore selected for analysis, since the material from here represents activities taking place in or outside the long-house.

The finds in and beside the smaller building are copious, and unlike the case of the long-house, the hut does not seem to have been cleaned to the same extent. Many finds of hammerstones, axes, axe flakes, heavy hammerstones, grindstones, and debitage from tool manufacture indicate varied and intensive activities inside the building (ibid.). The dating of the two houses by radiocarbon analysis of charred plants shows that they were used simultaneously, at least during part of the time when the site was occupied. The area between the long-house and the shore has also been dated through samples from hearths, cooking pits, and waste pits, showing that it was occupied within the same interval as the house (ibid.). In this article the area with the long-house will be called area 1 and the area with the smaller house will be called area 2 (se Carlsson, this volume, fig. 2).

How our knowledge is obtained: aim, material, and method

Since the Motala site was in this "border zone", and since the two houses had different functions, this gives us an excellent opportunity to study raw material, technology, and function in order to obtain knowledge of how the people on the site arranged their immediate environment, and also the network of contacts in which they were involved. To achieve this, the following questions have been formulated:

- What raw materials were used? Did the supply and quality of raw material determine the technology used for treating flint? How was raw material distributed: as blanks, preforms, or finished artefacts?

- What was made? Was there any form of specialized manufacture? What technological flint-knapping tradition occurred?

- Can the tools or the residue from their manufacture give information about the activities that were carried on?

Studying raw material is of great significance when it comes to gaining some idea of the origin of the material. In addition, deeper insight can be obtained about differences in quality between different types of flint and whether this was the reason for the choice of raw material for the manufacture of a specific kind of tool. From the crust on flakes it is possible to assess which phases of flint production are present in the material and to what extent whole flint nodules were used or not (Andrefsky 1998:96ff.).

Through technological studies of flint craft one can learn more about what was actually made on a site, even if the finished products have been deposited elsewhere. The knapped material has been divided through morphologically identifiable attributes into the following categories: bipolar, anvil, and platform flakes. All knapped material including blades and microblades has also been analysed to ascertain which impactors were used for the reduction process. Through experiments in flint knapping with different impactors, platform diagnosis has been developed by studying attributes of the knapped material. (Knarrström & Wrentner 1996). The cores have been sorted into the following categories: platform, anvil, and bipolar cores. The microblade cores have been divided into: bipolar cores, conical cores, handle cores, and other microblade cores.

Use-wear analysis has been carried out to give insight into the activities performed on the site. The analysis was performed by the author with the guidance and assistance of Dr Bo Knarrström of the Southern Excavations Division of the National Heritage Board in Lund. The equipment for the analysis was a metal microscope with 50–200 magnification. The method can be explained briefly as a search for structural changes on the use surface of the tool, after which an interpretation can be made of the purposes for which the object was employed and the material that was worked with it. The method can detect physical changes when the material is fragmented in a special way when used, or chemical transformations when the material in the tool has reacted with the processed material and resulted in a sheen which is reflected in the light in the microscope. The sheen differs depending on the hardness and moisture content of the worked material (Juel Jensen 1994).

One problem was the composition and colour of the flint, which entailed difficulties in exactly identifying use wear. The Cambrian flint was so coarse in its structure that assessment was impossible. For the quartz and ultramylonite material, casts were made with plastic film, which worked very well.

Raw material

A relatively large share of the flint is badly fragmented, which makes it difficult to determine the provenance ocularly. The most common raw material on the site is Cambrian flint (table 1), which comes from the areas around Mount Kinnekulle beside Lake Vättern in Västergötland, occurring in clefts or as loose blocks relatively near the ground surface, then being found in gullies and scree slopes etc. (Kindgren 1991:35ff.). Different kinds of south Scandinavian flint and Kristianstad flint are also present. By far the least frequent kind of flint was bryozoan flint, which originally comes from Sjælland in Denmark. Crust occurred relatively often on the Cambrian the flint but not on the south Scandinavian type. Prevailing crust conditions on the Cambrian flint are interpreted as showing that whole flint nodules were distributed to the site. In the few registered items of Kristianstad flint, the tendency is slightly different from that of the other south Scandinavian flint. As with the Cambrian flint, there are relatively large flakes in the material

Area 1	Knapped	Microblades	Blades	Cores	Total	Of which tools	
Cambrian flint	713	205	2	97	1017	41	4%
Senonian flint	278	46	3	41	368	49	13%
Danian flint	168	12	–	18	198	24	12%
Bryozoan flint	17	–	–	1	18	3	17%
Kristianstad flint	8	–	–	4	12	7	58%
Total House 1	**1184**	**263**	**5**	**168**	**1613**	**124**	**8%**
Area 2	Knapped	Microblades	Blades	Cores	Total	Of which tools	
Cambrian flint	313	39	1 frag.	27	380	10	2.6%
Senonian flint	212	24	–	15	251	23	9.2%
Danian flint	144	8	1 frag.	9	162	8	5%
Bryozoan flint	21	–	–	1	22	2	9.1%
Kristianstad flint	9	3	–	2	14	1	7.1%
Total House 2	**699**	**74**	**2**	**54**	**829**	**44**	**5.3%**
Sum total	**1883**	**337**	**7**	**222**	**2442**	**168**	**6.9%**

Table 1. The provenances of the flint.

but it is rarer to find crust-covered Kristianstad flints. There is also only one flake core in this type of flint. The proportion of tools of Kristianstad flint is also relatively high, 8 items, out of a total of 12, which means that an interpretation suggesting that whole tools or preforms of Kristianstad flint were distributed to the site seems reasonable. Two fragments of conical microblade cores of Kristianstad flint could be refitted. One of the core fragments had been retouched after the original core was worn out, to be reused as a scraper. This is an example of how people related to their flint material. Further examples of reuse are that scrapers which were no longer functional were transformed into bipolar microblade cores. This fact applies to all the types of flint but is particularly noticeable when it comes to Senonian flint.

What the south Scandinavian flints have in common is that they are very small and have very little crust. There are exceptions, however. On a blade knife of Senonian flint, about 50% of the dorsal side was covered with chalk. Since no blade cores are registered from the site, it is most likely that blades were not made here but distributed, either as finished knives or as blades. Among the scrapers of south Scandinavian flint, relatively few have crust. Otherwise, the registered south Scandinavian flints do not include pieces with any crust to speak of.

Even though Cambrian flint was the most frequent type, most tools were made of Senonian flint. The proportion of tools made of Danian flint is also relatively large compared to the proportion of Cambrian flints which are tools. Of the registered twelve items of Kristianstad flint, seven are tools. If we count all the tools of the different south Scandinavian flint types and compare them with the proportion of tools among the

Cambrian flints, we see that tools of south Scandinavian flint are almost three times as frequent as among Cambrian flints. The people on the Motala site thus preferred tools of raw material from south Scandinavia or the west coast. Cambrian flint, however, was not generally considered suitable for producing big tools, partly because of the quality and partly because the nodules are not particularly large, but this type of flint was nevertheless used for the manufacture of microblades.

Although most microblades found in the excavated area were knapped from Cambrian flint, many of them were fragmented immediately after manufacture and could not be used for, say, projectiles; this is also revealed by a comparison of the number of microblades and microblade cores in each category of raw material (table 2 and 3). In addition, most Cambrian microblades were made using bipolar technique, which is the least controllable. It was nevertheless relatively common to use platform technique for microblade manufacture from this raw material, but chiefly using a hammerstone as an impactor.

If one compares areas 1 and 2, certain differences can be seen in the raw material. South Scandinavian flint occurred more copiously in area 2 than in area 1. In area 2 Cambrian flint was the single most frequent raw material, but the proportion relative to the other flint material differed from area 1, as south Scandinavian flint types together were more frequent than Cambrian in area 2. As stated above, crust occurred rarely on the south Scandinavian flint, but slightly more encrusted flakes of south Scandinavian flint were registered in area 2 than in area 1.

Technology

It should be pointed out to begin with that, since the amount of Kristianstad flint and bryozoan flint is very small, they are not included in the flake analysis. Areas 1 and 2 agree in that the most common reduction method reflected in the knapped flint was bipolar technique, while the anvil technique was scarcely found at all. As regards the cores, here too the bipolar technique predominates. There is only one flake core where the anvil technique was used, which correlates well with the few flakes produced by this technique. The difference between bipolar and platform technique is even greater in the cores than in the flakes. This is probably because many of the original platform cores, after they were no longer serviceable, were used as bipolar flake cores or microblade cores instead; this could also be discerned by the analysis of the material. Many of the bipolar cores are very small, only a centimetre or two, meaning that they generated small flakes or debitage. Debitage is defined as residual products or knapped material with a size under 1 cm. This assemblage may therefore conceal many flakes struck from the small bipolar cores. This could possibly explain the relatively small number of bipolar flakes in proportion to the copious bipolar cores, as compared to platform cores. The bipolar reduction method is also the least controllable when it comes to the shaping of the flakes that are produced, which could generate a large amount of useless residual products when knapping. Perhaps this can also explain the large share of unidentifiable flakes in the material. Bipolar flint technology has often been associated with shortage of raw material around a site, but it can probably be explained also in terms of technically simpler production which need not necessarily be connected with regional raw material conditions. Although bipolar knapping can be defined as the simplest method for working lithic material, it also has some advantages. At least when small cores are used, the underlying surface or support means that the knapping force penetrates the lithic material and thus results in a reduction that is easy to handle. Another advantage can be that bipolar flakes, when the force is transferred from both the hammerstone and the anvil, become flatter and thinner than platform flakes with their curved outline (Flenniken 1981:32).

As regards microblades, south Scandinavian flint is represented only by Senonian and Danian types, which are relatively few in number. They have therefore been grouped together to give more statistically correct material for comparison. Most microblades are relatively small, just a centimetre or two in length and a couple of millimetres wide, which can also be correlated with many of the microblade cores that were registered. It is also worth noting that the majority of the Cambrian microblades were fragmented medial and distal parts or so damaged that they could not be diagnosed. This applies chiefly to the microblades analysed from area 1. Some whose platforms are not morphologically identifiable also fall within the category of undiagnosable microblades. Microblades and microblade cores, as mentioned above, are most frequently of Cambrian flint, as many as 244 microblades (table 2) and 46 microblade cores (table 3) are registered from the excavated areas. The corresponding figures for south Scandinavian flint are 93 microblades and 36 microblade cores. Here, however, a larger share of microblades were documented, with a punch or pressure flaker used for manufacture. Microblades made using bipolar technique were mostly of Cambrian flint rather than south Scandinavian raw material, although the different reduction methods for Cambrian flint were evenly distributed.

Area 1	Bipolar	Platform		Not diagnosable	Total
		Hammerstone	Punch/Pressure flaker		
Cambrian	32	30	28	115	**205**
South Scandinavian	1	2	20	35	**58**
Total	**33**	**32**	**48**	**150**	263
Area 2	Bipolar	Platform		Not diagnosable	Total
		Hammerstone	Punch/Pressure flaker		
Cambrian	8	8	7	16	**39**
South Scandinavian	–	7	12	16	**35**
Total	**8**	**15**	**19**	**32**	**74**
Sum total	**41**	**47**	**67**	**182**	**337**

Table 2. Reduction technique for microblades.

Area 1

Raw material	Bipolar cores	Other platform cores	Handle cores	Conical cores	Total
Cambrian	21	17	–	4	**42**
Senonian	6	3	5	3	**17**
Danian	1	5	1	3	**10**
Kristianstad	–	1	–	2	**3**
Total	**28**	**26**	**6**	**12**	72
South Scandinavian total	**7**	**9**	**6**	**8**	30

Area 2

Raw material	Bipolar cores	Other platform cores	Handle cores	Conical cores	Total
Cambrian	1	–	3	–	**4**
Senonian	–	1	1	1	**3**
Danian	–	–	2	–	**2**
Kristianstad	–	–	–	1	**1**
Total	**1**	**1**	**6**	**2**	10
South Scandinavian Total	**–**	**1**	**3**	**2**	6

Table 3. Microblade cores.

Area 1

Raw material	Scrapers	Retouch	Use-retouch	Arrowheads	Drills	Knives	Chisels	Total
Cambrian	7	25	3	–	3	2	1	**41**
Senonian	17	19	6	–	3	3	1	**49**
Danian	9	10	1	1	1	2	–	**24**
Bryozoan	1	2	–	–	–	–	–	**3**
Kristianstad	6	1	–	–	–	–	–	**7**
Total	**40**	**57**	**10**	**1**	**7**	**7**	**2**	124
South Scandinavian total	**33**	**32**	**7**	**1**	**4**	**5**	**1**	83

Area 2

Raw material	Scrapers	Retouch	Use-retouch	Arrowheads	Drills	Knives	Chisels	Total
Cambrian	4	6	–	–	–	–	–	**10**
Senonian	14	3	–	2	3	–	1	**23**
Danian	6	1	–	–	1	–	–	**8**
Bryozoan	2	–	–	–	–	–	–	**2**
Kristianstad	–	1	–	–	–	–	–	**1**
Total	**26**	**11**	**–**	**2**	**4**	**–**	**1**	44
South Scandinavian total	**22**	**5**	**–**	**2**	**4**	**–**	**1**	24
Cambrian total	**11**	**31**	**3**	**–**	**3**	**2**	**1**	51
South Scandinavian total	**55**	**63**	**7**	**3**	**8**	**5**	**2**	143

Table 4. Tools.

As with the microblades, most of the microblade cores were of Cambrian flint. The relative proportion of hard and soft technique corresponds very closely to what was found for the microblades. For the Cambrian flint it was mostly bipolar cores and platform cores made using a hammerstone, whereas just a handful of hammerstone-knapped cores of south Scandinavian flint were registered. It is also worth noting that three of the conical microblade cores of Cambrian flint do not have a prepared platform, which might suggest that a hammerstone was used for knapping.

There is no doubt that microblades were manufactured on the site, in view of all the microblades and microblade cores that were found. Another factor that supports this is that the analysis of the material revealed a large number of rejuvenation flakes from microblade cores, most of them from area 1. If one compares the entire flint material from the two areas, one finds a larger percentage of microblades and microblade cores in area 1. Microblade manufacture from south Scandinavian flint chiefly took the form of soft technique and dominated particularly in area 1, unlike area 2. It is noteworthy that many of the handle cores in area 1 were very small, only one centimetre across and half a centimetre high. It is difficult to imagine that microblades of this size were functional to use. Why did people go to the trouble of making these small microblades? Is this instead an indicator of what an important part the soft, indirect flint-knapping technique played in area 1?

Tools and use wear

Cambrian flint was the most frequently used raw material on the site. If one counts only the tools, however, a different picture is obtained. The south Scandinavian flint tools are almost three times more frequent than the Cambrian (table 4). Senonian flint was particularly common for tools. Scrapers or retouched flints are by far the most common tool forms, made from both flakes and cores. There are also numerous other core tools, for example, small triangular drills and chisels. Perhaps these tools are cultural substitutes for the core axes that were widespread in northern Halland and Bohuslän (Welinder 1975). Core drills were often retouched from worn-out microblade cores, where the remains of the platform are sometimes clearly visible, but there are also tools where bipolar cores were used.

Larger flint tools are represented by a number of blades and blade knives made of Senonian flint. Since there are no blade cores or rejuvenation flakes, the blades cannot have been made at Strandvägen and were probably instead transported from areas with more flint to the south or west. There are also some transverse arrowheads in the material, clear markers of influences from the south. It is worth noting a projectile which can best be compared to an Early Mesolithic lancet microlith (fig. 1). Perhaps this element in the material is a sign of early colonization of the Motala area where sporadic visits were made for hunting and fishing. Other Early Mesolithic settlement sites in Östergötland and an early radiocarbon dating (8795 ± 65 BP) from Motala support this thesis.

What distinguishes area 1 from area 2 in the toolkit is mainly that area 2 completely lacks cutting tools of flint while a total of seven knives were found in area 1. This is also seen in the flake material showing use retouch. Another difference was that the proportion

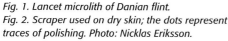

Fig. 1. Lancet microlith of Danian flint.
Fig. 2. Scraper used on dry skin; the dots represent traces of polishing. Photo: Nicklas Eriksson.

Fig. 3. Blade knife; the V on its side indicates double-sided microspalling.
Photo: Nicklas Eriksson.

of tools was higher in area 1, which can be interpreted as a sign that more intensive tool manufacture took place in area 2, resulting in more waste from the flint craft. Some of the flint has been subjected to use-wear analysis, to find out what materials the tools were used on and thus gain better insight into the economy of the site, while also shedding more light on the different activity areas on the site.

Generally speaking, use wear that arose from working organic materials can be divided into three different classes: (1) Microspalling and rounding or abrasion of edges. (2) Striations which can be seen as narrow traces or lines, often around the edge section. (3) Micropolishing leading to a change in the surface structure of the flint after contact with different materials. In this analysis there was a particular frequency of double-sided microspalling and rounded edges, but polishing of different kinds also occurred. Double-sided microspalling arises on the edge of the tool when it has been used as a cutting tool. Scrapers with polishing along the edges or where the edges are worn round can be said to have been used on skins which were dry, while round-worn edges with striations indicate that the scraper was used on fresh or soft skins. These are examples of how the method is employed to diagnose use wear on tools. Different combinations of traces can thus arise depending on the material that is worked. The references used in the analysis came from literature by archaeologists such as Juel Jensen 1994; Knarrström 2000a, 2001, 2003; Knutsson 1988.

The results of the use-wear analysis of the selected material showed that the scrapers were mainly used for working skins. Only one of the investigated scrapers showed any signs of having been used for bone or antler. The analysis of this scraper also showed that it had had a cutting function on one of the short sides. A common denominator for the scrapers is that they were very small and before the analysis they were assumed to have been shafted. At least two of the scrapers showed traces of shafting, and one even had remains of resin with wood fibres preserved on one side. The other scrapers may also be assumed to have been shafted, although no shafting traces were visible. Their small size would have made them impossible to use without shafting, but they were also almost identical in form to the two scrapers that showed signs of shafting. Initially the scrapers were presumably larger and stuck out a bit from the shafting, but as the edges became unusable they were repaired with new retouches until they were too small for use. Instead of replacing the scrapers in the shaft with new ones when the edges no longer functioned, they were resharpened, which might suggest that flint was in short supply and people used the raw material economically. The scrapers of quartz and ultramylonite are larger than the flint scrapers, but use-wear analysis of some of these scrapers also shows that they were mainly used on skins. What distinguishes the scrapers from the two excavated areas is that scrapers used on fresh or soft skin could be observed in the material from area 2, whereas one of the skin scrapers from area 1 was used on dry skin (fig. 2).

Another difference was that a burin and a planing tool were represented in area 2, while only cutting and scraping functions were present in the material from area 1. On one of the retouched quartz flakes there were traces of use as a burin on bone, possibly to make one of the many leister points that were registered. A wood plane of ultra-mylonite could also be diagnosed, with microspalling at the edges and striations at right angles a bit above the edges.

Use-wear analysis was also performed on some flakes, blades, and retouched flints, which confirmed, as we saw above, that no cutting tools were registered from area 2. Based on the analysed material from area 1, traces of cutting activity (fig. 3) could be detected on five different flints which were not registered as knives by the ocular inspection, so they must be added to the category of knives in the list of finds. If we count all the flints with a cutting function as revealed by the use-wear analysis together with the knives and the use-retouched material, the total we obtain is 22. For only one of these has it been possible to determine the exact function, a quartz flake used as a cutting tool on antler, bone, or wood.

Conclusions

The flint from Motala shows clear indications that different Mesolithic traditions or influences met and blended here. The Mesolithic inhabitants were active in regional and local contact networks where there was considerable exchange of goods and hence ideas, which created an affinity between different lithic traditions, linked together, for example, by microblades and handle cores. Although quartz was the most frequent raw material on the Motala site, it nevertheless seems as if the tools were proportionately more common in various types of flint (Carlsson 2004a). Motala and its surroundings was no doubt part of a larger complex area where influences arrived from several different directions. A population was established with its own material culture which was distinct from the sets of material in southern, western, and central Sweden, yet there are elements in the toolkit which hint at an affinity between the people from the different regions. The quartz and the bipolar knapping technique are elements indicating influences from the north and east, but two flaying knives of rock were also found at the Motala site, to which parallels have also been found in Södertörn in the Stockholm region (ibid.).

The flint shows different provenances, with Cambrian flint being most frequent. Cambrian flint occurs in the region and would have been collected or brought to the settlement site as whole nodules. The microblade cores and the larger objects of flint from southern or western Sweden, and also the knapped bryozoan flint from Denmark, show that this flint material was involved in different systems of exchange. The flint from the south presumably did not reach the site as blanks but as finished tools or preforms for further processing. It is also conceivable that it was brought to or ended up on the site through intermediaries in the distribution. In the Early Mesolithic there was a pattern of north–south movement along the Lagan, which rises south of Vättern and flows into the Laholm Bay, north of Öresund. During this period flint had presumably reached the Mörby site in Östergötland via the inland settlement sites of Småland at Hamneda and Lövås, near the Lagan (Knarrström 2000b:29ff.). A find from the settlement site in Motala, a projectile greatly resembling the Early Mesolithic lancet microliths in southern Scandinavia, and some early radiocarbon datings indicate that Motala too was part of a network of contacts with the south at an early stage, perhaps along the Lagan. Is it possible that people in the Late Mesolithic also travelled along the Lagan to exchange goods and ideas with their Mesolithic friends to the south? There were also contacts with people from western Sweden, as corroborated by the many small triangular core tools which were also common on the west coast, but there perhaps as slightly larger tools, for example, core axes (Welinder 1975).

The order of the flint craft on the Motala site may reflect a society with strict rules whereby homes were arranged in different ways. The bipolar technique was present all over the site, whereas microblade manufacture by the soft, indirect technique was pursued in places which were more spatially demarcated. The flint from area 1 undoubtedly shows high technological know-how, among other things with microblade manufacture. In particular, manufacture with the aid of pressure flakers or punches can with great probability be interpreted as a sign that a few individuals on the settlement site with special technical skills performed their craft in or near the house. This microblade craft using soft technique could possibly also be seen as a socially created need linked to status; there was a desire to display skills in microblade manufacture using the soft technique, which can chiefly be traced back to friends on the west coast and in southern Scandinavia. The very smallest microblades and microblade cores in area 1 support this assumption, since many of the finished products could scarcely have functioned as projectiles or bone points. Although there was a good supply of other materials such as quartz and ultramylonite, which are also suitable for microblade manufacture using soft technique, people nevertheless chose to use microblade cores of flint until they could not produce anything better than microblades no more than 1 cm long.

There are also other indications of how the settlement site was arranged in different ways. The many cutting tools and cooking pits and the hearths (Carlsson 2004a) from area 1 can be interpreted as an activity area where cooking was done just beside the larger two-aisled house. The great quantity of skin scrapers from here, one of which was used on dry skin, is also a result of activities which cannot be detected with certainty in area 2. If area 1 can be associated on the basis of the toolkit with specialized microblade manufacture, cooking, and possibly clothes making, the results of the use-wear analysis also show that the scraping of soft or fresh skins was done in area 2, a little bit away from the dwelling house. Area 2 does not display any really specialized activities, which should instead be interpreted as indicating a workshop area where various activities took place, but also everyday flint craft, above all with bipolar technique. Finds of a large number of hammerstones, axes, axe flakes, heavy hammerstones, and grindstones also suggest varied and intensive activities inside the smaller workshop building (ibid.).

Appendix
Use-wear analysis

Flint

Type	Find no.	Material	Wear	Function	Notes
House 1					
Blade fragment scraper	F09108	Flint Senonian	No wear	–	–
Scraper	F08992	Flint Danian	Resin remains with wood fibre, traces of shafting	Scraper	Edge certainly used but no traces of wear, perhaps because of the coarse structure of the flint.
Blade fragment	F08938	Flint Senonian	DSM, generic polishing	Cutting tool	–
Scraper	F10660	Flint Senonian	No wear	–	–
Scraper	F09697	Flint Senonian	Generic polishing	Scraper	–
Scraper	F09030	Flint Danian	Polishing along the edge	Scraper for dry skin	Cast
Knapped	F09193	Flint Danian	DSM	Cutting tool	–
Scraper	F09263	Flint Senonian	Traces of shafting, generic polishing	Scraper	–
Scraper	F09675	Flint Kristianstad	No wear	–	–
Bipolar core retouch	F09065	Flint Senonian	No wear	Scraper, previously core	Bipolar core, since negative scar of spalling came after older scraper retouch.
Retouch	F09940	Flint Senonian	DSM on the short side, no traces of retouch on the long side	Cutting tool	Has presumably been bigger, since the tool is fragmented.
Scraper	F10030	Flint Senonian	Generic polishing	Scraper	–
Bipolar core retouch	F08874	Flint Senonian	Generic polishing, rounded edge	Skin scraper	Bipolar core after scraper function ceased.
Knapped	F09566	Flint Senonian	No wear	–	–
Scraper	F08992	Flint Danian	Generic polishing, rounded edge	Skin scraper	Presumably shafted, since there are similar scrapers in the material with traces of shafting.
Knapped	F09652	Flint Senonian	DSM	Cutting tool	–
Bipolar core fragment retouch	F09588	Flint Senonian	No wear	–	–
Bipolar core scraper	F09262	Flint Senonian	Generic polishing, rounded edge	Skin scraper, previously core	Bipolar core, since negative scar after spalling came after earlier scraper retouch. The scraper was used until it could no longer function as a tool. It was presumably shafted.
Scraper	F10484	Flint Senonian	Slight polishing, microspalling on one retouched side. DSM on one short side	Combined tool, bone scraper, cutting tool	Presumably shafted, since there are similar scrapers in the material with traces of shafting.

Type	Find no.	Material	Wear	Function	Note
House 2					
Bipolar core scraper	F17259	Flint Danian	No wear	Scraper, previously core	Bipolar core, since negative scar of spalling came after earlier scraper retouch.
Microblade fragment	F17375	Flint Cambrian	No wear	–	–
Knapped	F17425	Flint Cambrian	No wear	–	–
Knapped	F17142	Flint Senonian	No wear	–	–
Knapped bipolar	F17806	Flint Cambrian	No wear	–	–
Bipolar scraper	F16604	Flint Danian	Rounded edge, vertical striations	Skin scraper for soft or fresch skin	Presumable shafted, since there are scrapers in the material with traces of shafting.
Projectile	F16519	Flint Danian	No wear	Projectile	–
Retouch	F17111	Flint Senonian	No wear	–	–
Retouch	F16873	Flint Senonian fire-damaged	No wear	–	–
Scraper	F17755	Flint Senonian	Abrasion, rounded edge	Skin scraper	–
Scraper	F16873	Flint Senonian	Rounded edge, vertical striations	Skin scraper for soft or fresh skin	–
Scraper	F18065	Flint Senonian	No wear	–	Presumably a rejuvenation flake instead of a scraper.
Scraper	F19811	Flint Danian	Rounded edge	Skin scraper	Presumably shafted, since there are scrapers in the material with traces of shafting.
Scraper	F18073	Flint Senonian	No wear	–	–
Scraper fragment	F17079	Flint Senonian	No wear	–	–
Other retouched point	F16545	Flint Senonian	No wear		

Quartz and ultramylonite

Type	Find no.	Material	Wear	Function	Note
Retouch	F09083	Quartz	Slight rounded abrasion of edge, sand-blasted	Scraper	Cast
Bipolar core retouch	F09340	Quartz	No wear	–	Cast
Retouch	F09601	Ultramylonite (quartzite)	No wear	–	Cast
Knapped	F10061	Quartz	Microspalling	Cutting tool for hard material (bone, antler, or wood)	Cast
Knapped	F10108	Quartz	No wear	–	Cast
Use-retouch	F10150	Ultramylonite (quartzite)	Striations along the edge, rounded abrasion on edge	Cutting tool	Cast
Scraper	F16568	Ultramylonite (quartzite)	Four areas with rounded edge	Skin Scraper	Cast
Bipolar core retouch	F16772	Quartz	Slight polishing, rounded abrasion	Skin scraper	Cast
Knapped scraper	F16806	Ultramylonite (quartzite)	Rounded abrasion of the edge	Skin scraper	Cast
Retouch	F16861	Ultramylonite (quartzite)	Rounded abrasion	Skin scraper	Cast
Retouch	F16972		Pitted striations at right angles towards the edge, rounded abrasion of the edge, microspalling, polishing	Bone-working tool/Burin	Cast. Retained by Bo Knarrström, UV Syd.
Retouch	F17847	Ultramylonite (quarzite)	Mircospalling at the edge, striations at right angles a bit above the edge	Wood plane	Cast

A more human society
Aspects of Mesolithic research

Magnus Rolöf

Mesolithic research often discusses culture and social formation on the basis of lithic technology and ecological factors. A site like Motala offers an opportunity for much more. For example, one can problematize many "truths" about sedentariness and territoriality, and ultimately how deep the roots of the so-called Neolithization really are.

All quiet on the eastern front?

With the excavations in Motala, research has been given something new, in more senses than one. The site undoubtedly changes our view of the Mesolithic in Östergötland. Its inhabitants demonstrably had far-reaching contacts in all directions, which means that not just Östergötland's Mesolithic research is influenced by this new source material. The site will be incorporated in Mesolithic research consciousness and will have repercussions for it. What is said about Strandvägen will have consequences for what is said about many other places.

It is not without problems to place Motala on the Mesolithic map and to assess its geographical or chronological relations with other sites. No such map exists; moreover, far too few sites have been excavated, or even discovered. Yet even if the source material from the period still shows huge lacunae, in the Motala site one can clearly see that it was a place in an active landscape. Its inhabitants were much more than small groups of isolated nomads and they lived in a large, developed society.

If one wants to discuss the society behind a site like Motala, one is in the field of fire between several grand and long-lived research traditions. One has to get involved in discussions about sedentariness and mobility, regionality and material cultural affiliation, and

Fig. 1. The Motala site from above, wedged in between roads, the railway, and Motala Ström. Photo: NHB.

The Motala site

one has to reflect on social structure and ethnicity. In many senses these discussions are unique for Stone Age research. One can be led to believe that the earliest people at our latitudes were essentially different from their farming successors. It is the same with their societies: they did not function – *could* not have functioned – according to the same principles as those in later periods which are more recognizable to us.

The main phase of use of the Motala site was during the Scandinavian Middle Mesolithic. The character and development of the period are rather controversial; broadly speaking, the debate concerns its position between the "colonization" of the area and Neolithization. Following several other writers, I adopt the stance that the classical picture of Neolithization as a sudden social upheaval is not plausible. Instead Neolithization can be viewed as a result of social processes during the Late Mesolithic time (Kaliff 1999:30ff.; Knutsson *et al.* 1999:116). The transition to agriculture in a traditional sense seems sudden in the archaeological record, but it can more likely be ascribed to a closing phase when the society finally accepted agriculture as the basis of the economy and typically "Neolithic" phenomena began to dominate. When this happened, the members of the society were already well prepared (Kaliff 1999:31; Karsten & Knarrström 2003:231f.).

Although many scholars count this "pre-Neolithization" as the second half of the Late Mesolithic (Lindgren 1997:30; Karsten & Knarrström 2003:231), the perspective can be extended back to even earlier periods. Certain processes shaping society could, in theory, have been operating throughout the Mesolithic. One such process, which will be discussed in this article, is the emergence of defined landscape spaces, incorporated into Mesolithic life.

The mobile, the sedentary, and all the others

The question whether the population of the Motala site were sedentary or not is as natural as it is inevitable. It is a simple question, but virtually impossible to answer unambiguously. Different aspects of the evidence can be cited to prove or disprove either stance.

The literature provides a number of criteria for what may be envisaged as characterizing a higher degree of sedentariness on a site. It is worth noting here that the same criteria that are considered to apply to a permanently occupied settlement are often applied also to frequently revisited places which could then be a part of a mobile social system.

Archaeological indications of a higher degree of sedentariness include:

a) *Economy*. Sedentariness is always viewed as being intimately associated with what is designated as a broad-spectrum economy. Wide utilization of many ecozones and their resources is necessary to be able to liberate oneself from a mobile life, which is typified by few sources of livelihood and hence is wholly dependent on the season. The localization of a settlement close to many biotopes is therefore crucial (Kaliff 1999:26; Nordquist 2001:73). Karsten & Knarrström (2003:216ff.) provide an exhaustive example of the

Fig. 2. A selection of the axes found at the Motala site. Only one example of local production. Photo: National Heritage Board.

calculation of sedentary population and ecological carrying capacity, and they argue that an increased intensification of food production should be visible in the archaeological record (ibid.:212). Further indications could be more permanent trapping installations, such as fixed fishing devices (Pedersen 1995; Nordquist 2001:76; Karsten & Knarrström 2003:212). The storage of food is also important in this connection. The osteological material is one of the obvious sources for a discussion of this (see also Åberg, this volume).

b) *Site character*. Sedentariness implies more people on the site than envisaged for more mobile forms of occupation. It is therefore suggested that a sedentary settlement should be larger in area and show traces of manifest buildings in the form of houses or at least huts (Kaliff 1999:26; Nordquist 2001:72; Karsten & Knarrström 2003:212; Larsson 1996:39, 2003:35). Lasting and continuous settlement should also have left more distinct occupation layers (Nordquist 2001:78) and, we may suppose, a larger amount of features.

c) *Composition of material*. Whereas mobile groups to a greater extent are thought to have selected sites for different functions, permanent settlers are expected to assemble their craft activities on the site. The accumulation of finds should therefore be large and above all varied, since the waste from a temporarily visited special site is rather monotonous by comparison. The evidence should also show distinct traces of tool manufacture (Nilsson 1995:184; Kaliff 1999:26; Karsten & Knarrström 2003:120).

d) *Social factors*. Implicit in the notion of sedentariness is the idea of the structured, more complex society (cf. Gräslund 1974:1). Increased sedentariness leads one's thought to things such as increased territoriality, the development of specialized craft, increased long-distance trade, status differentiation, and increased social inequality (Karsten & Knarrström 2003:213). Burial places near the dwelling site, for example, tend to be viewed as a sign of sedentariness (Nordquist 2001:78; Karsten & Knarrström 2003:212).

There is of course a great deal of value in these criteria, although they do not seem quite as certain when subjected to careful scrutiny. Source criticism and methodological and theoretical objections can always be raised. As an extremely sporadic example we may consider the seasonal interpretation of the Mörby site on the basis of the absence of a large amount of finds and in particular the lack of traces of tool manufacture (Kaliff 1999:26). Kaliff points out weaknesses in his own arguments: that the cleaning of the site could have minimized the amount of lithic material; that tool manufacture did not necessarily take place in the habitation area – it could have been done hundreds of metres away, which would leave it invisible in today's rescue excavations (ibid.:29). Another example is that a high degree of sedentariness need not always mean distinct house structures; in the case of Tågerup the use of small, in principle movable dwellings which could easily be re-established on site (Karsten & Knarrström 2003:120).

The criteria for sedentariness are a starting point for interpretations, but nothing more. A site need not just be either a place for temporary visits or else for constant occupation; it can be more or less of either. There is a large grey zone of settlement forms that can be used, and one can be open to alternative interpretations by taking into consideration the complexity of individual sites.

Sedentary, settled

The current model of settlement structure during this period is that people moved between different natural environments on a seasonal basis. In the winter half of the year they assembled in large groups at base sites on the coast, and then in the summer they divided into smaller groups and moved between smaller, more specialized sites beside lakes in the interior (see e.g. Larsson 1996:39; Carlsson *et al.* 1999:64f.; Kaliff 1999:26, 28). The model is based to a very large extent on Welinder's studies (Knutsson *et al.* 1999:91). Recent years' studies, however, have shown that it is perfectly possible that forms of settlement varied much more locally and were more complex than this (Hallgren cites examples from Gästrikland, Forsberg from Norrland, Åkerlund from eastern central Sweden, and Nordquist from the west Swedish archipelago; from Holm 2003a:25ff.; cf. Knutsson *et al.* 1999:93f.). Each Mesolithic site has a depth and complexity that risks vanishing if one automatically labels it according to one general model or another (cf. Ahlbeck *et al.* 2003:10).

Sedentariness has generally been associated with the establishment of agriculture. This almost paradigmatic linkage has become less rigid, however, and now a more fluid scale is envisaged. Several scholars have, more or less explicitly, suggested that certain populations were more stationary much earlier than previously assumed. Kaliff (1999:26) claims that there is no evidence to contradict the permanent occupation of the Early and Middle Mesolithic sites of Högby and Mörby. Karsten & Knarrström (2003:121, 212) argue that the Middle Mesolithic (Kongemose) population of Tågerup were more stationary than mobile, and that the Late Mesolithic (Ertebølle) population were definitely sedentary. Others take a more cautious stance, believing that the population may have been sedentary *within a particular area*, as in the case of the archipelago of eastern central Sweden (Knutsson *et al.* 1999:93). The question that should be asked is perhaps not whether a site had a permanent population or not, but rather what degree of permanence the site had.

If we look at the Motala site, we see a great deal of evidence in favour of a high degree of sedentariness. There is no room here for a detailed account of the findings (see Carlsson 2004a). Among the factors indicating high sedentariness we may reckon the varied economic activities (Åberg, this volume), the closeness to several biotopes, a very good location for communications, the large size of the site with fixed structures such as houses and workshops, and local tool manufacture. The population at Motala could probably have survived the whole year round in this place. If we then envisage a strategy whereby only parts of the population made excursions while others remained on the dwelling site, we must ask how this differs in principle from permanent occupation.

Finds and people

The next question is as simple as the one about sedentariness: Who were these people at Motala during the Mesolithic? Apart from the fact that they were probably a coherent group, how did they relate to their neighbours? Mesolithic research turns to the finds to look for an answer. The most common method – according to many scholars the only possible method – for studying Mesolithic cultural affiliation is through the lithic material above all. By meticulous studies and classifications of key artefacts, technologies, and raw material, it ought to be possible to say something about the cultural identity of different populations. From already established typologies and chronologies one can detect archaeological regions, defined according to variations in material culture (Knutsson *et al.* 1999:99ff.; Carlsson 2002:133). In this connection it is usually stressed that Östergötland occupies a kind of intermediate position between the flint- and quartz-dominated regions to the west and east. This will not be discussed here, since it is treated in greater detail elsewhere in this volume (cf. Carlsson).

Studies of material cultures and regions range from analyses of individual key artefacts (e.g. the distribution of transverse arrowheads) to entire technocomplexes (which incorporate many more technological aspects than just artefact category) (Larsson 1996:37f.; Carlsson *et al.* 1999:47f., 66f.; Knutsson *et al.* 1999:112; Bergsvik 2003:290; Karsten & Knarrström 2003:19). The basic idea is that the material, in every respect, constitutes social markers, that is to say, to some extent reflects and defines the people who used the things. By mapping the objects we capture the Mesolithic groups.

It is more problematic, however, to know exactly what kind of groups are captured merely by studying distribution maps of microliths or quartz technology. Karsten & Knarrström (2003:228) point out that material culture is an extension of the social norm rather than a direct reflection of it. The social framework that affected stone craft also affected all other material aspects of life. If we want to study this, we need to compare more categories than stone smithing.

If one is forced to think about what these spatial and chronological distribution maps of material variations represent if human beings are added to the equation, we may wonder what it is we see. It could be claimed that the archaeological regions we see are purely analytical constructions, yet this cannot be entirely correct either (Bergsvik 2003:297). After all, the transverse arrowheads ended up there as a result of human action, through

Fig. 3. Everyday Mesolithic research. Registration of knapped quartz. Photo: National Heritage Board.

actual social processes, and they reflect *something*. However, they do not reflect a "transverse arrowhead people". For every category of material one chooses to study, one obtains a new distribution picture (or region), often overlapping (Carlsson 2002:133). On a fundamental and concrete level, what we see is just the distribution of the use of the particular material category under study.

To put it crudely, the distribution of a category of material (or the distribution of a technology) reflects a craft tradition which extends over and beyond the boundaries of local populations. The regionality that they describe is not an ethnic division, but the spread of ideas and skills connected with these crafts. It virtually goes without saying that an exchange of this kind is not confined to individual raw materials or an axe type; it concerns all aspects of the life of people in this period, and thus should affect many parts of our source material (Bergsvik 2003:297). Craft is an important aspect of the life of Mesolithic people and of our analytical base. It is just one piece of the jigsaw puzzle, however, not the whole truth.

Mesolithic groups with similar material culture can of course be said to be united in some sense. To ascertain whether this unity meant that they had direct exchange or not, or whether they even knew of each other, requires studying the material from a different direction. We need to try to answer the question of how people organized themselves. Research offers a range of terms and concepts, with everything from family to supra-regional culture. Society includes everything from little to large, and one needs to know what level one wants to work with. In the case of the Motala site, it is fully possible thanks to the material to work with "down-to-earth" questions, questions about the actual life and history of the local population, about their landscape and hinterland. It is still not easy to speak about their neighbours in the same way, once again because of lacunae in the source material.

On the other hand, we may assume that the Motala site and its population did not come into existence in economic and ideological isolation. The entire society of which the Motala site was a part had probably already had thousands of years in which to develop (Carlsson 2002:127). In my opinion, there is nothing to suggest that this society was particularly "uncomplicated" compared to those of later periods. In the source material from Strandvägen we get many clues, but not only about the population that lived there; behind the material is a larger society, a whole network of social relations and societal processes.

Bergsvik (2003) has an interesting discussion which hints at how one can regard social organization. He talks of intra-group and extra-group identification on different levels. Very briefly, this refers to the way in which individuals and groups position themselves in society, by defining what is inside and outside, or if you like defining "us" and "them". This identification may be said to take place on two intra-group levels; in the little community it centres on aspects of life such as kinship, ancestry, political organization, and territoriality. Yet people were also part of a larger society, a different level of intra-group identification which is more concerned with social networks, alliance systems, language, history, and mythology. As a counter to these there are the people who are identified as being outside the group, the Others, who serve in equal measure to define the in-group (Bergsvik 2003:296).

The key point is that social organization – the identification of one's own group or population – does not arise by chance or by itself. It builds on palpable social instruments, such as solidarity through kinship, leadership, or history. It arises and is negotiated – in highly concrete terms – in the encounter between people and groups. Meetings and contacts are the driving force in social systems and the arena for the identification process, in which material culture also plays a part. Encounters contain the seeds of change; contacts between groups changes their perspectives and their traditions (Bergsvik 2003:298; Larsson 2003:29). The material boundaries that we see are social rather than ecological or economic (Knutsson *et al.* 1999:115). Material culture should be regarded as a vital instrument in the process, but it is people meeting people who build societies.

Mesolithic territoriality

Actual movements and travels in the landscape thus play an indispensable part in the construction of society. This is more than just a banal statement. The landscape is more than ecological carrying capacity, a source of raw material, or a series of sites where people chose to stay. The landscape is at least as important in the identification process

Fig. 4. The settlement site at Motala viewed from the bank of the river. Motala Ström was by far the most important communication route in this period. Photo: National Heritage Board.

as relations between people and the material culture they represent. There is no doubt that people had a good knowledge of their physical surroundings, but the social aspects of the landscape are at least as important; one's own place in the landscape, the neighbours' place, and the places that are shared with the neighbours (cf. Larsson 1996:42).

The landscape perspective does not occur as commonly in Mesolithic research as in the study of later periods. Scholars have not been accustomed to acknowledging that the mental and social landscape (as opposed to the purely economic landscape) was one of the most important aspects for prehistoric societies. This can be detected, for example, in the comment that people "perhaps" even had names for certain significant places (Larsson 1996:42). It is surely more likely that people named not just their own settlement or important meeting places but that through widespread naming they were aware of all the parts of the landscape in which they moved. In both the large-scale surroundings and the small settlement site, spatial division was an essential part of life. It was a part of the world-view and an element in the group identification (Carlsson *et al.* 1999:49; Knutsson *et al.* 1999:113).

This local spatiality has its counterpart in the distribution of craft traditions or the territorial social unit that is suggested to have comprised Denmark, south-east Norway, and south and central Sweden (Knutsson *et al.* 1999:117). This is the spatiality of ordinary life, the way in which people relate to the landscape and divide it into manageable and meaningful pieces.

If spatiality is perceived as being too vague a concept, perhaps territoriality is too narrow. It implies ownership structures and control over physical areas, which is not imagined to have existed in this period but is associated with Neolithization and the sedentary agricultural economy (Nordquist 2001:83f.). It is nevertheless difficult to conceive that this widespread network – all the alliances, all the travelling, meeting, and cultural exchange, and the definition of one's group and society – could have existed in an "open landscape". It is hardly reasonable that it did not seem as important to organize the landscape as it was to organize, say, the exchange of goods. Although it cannot be a matter of our modern attitude to land ownership and boundary drawing, it is still a territorial approach. Based on ethnographical examples, it is suggested that hunter-gatherers associated certain places with certain groups, but that a kind of common right to use landscape resources could be applied so long as one knew the proper attitude to the group in question (Nordquist 2001:85f). The difference is perhaps just one of degree; it may be a soft wersion, but it is still territoriality.

Spatiality of this kind does not presuppose sedentariness. Even if we envisage a society with a mobile settlement structure in which all sites reflect temporary visits, it is implicitly the same people who inhabit the same area. Larsson (1996:41) proposes the Tåkern area as a *base area* for the population during the Mesolithic. He does not say in detail what this would have meant in concrete terms, but the principle of the social division of the physical landscape is there. Territoriality/spatiality, in my view, can be seen as a social phenomenon going back much earlier than permanent settlements and an agricultural economy. In fact, I find it difficult to imagine that people did *not* meet and negotiate their places, areas, roads, and landscapes – whether in peaceful or hostile forms – during thousands of years of neighbourhood.

Identity in landscape

Landscape was a vital social instrument, indispensable and inevitable in the group-identi-fication process. Economic aspects of the landscape in the form of resources and assets were handled through social processes, if one does not envisage a society consisting solely of wandering nomads who just happened to meet now and then (cf. Larsson 2003:35). It is easy to over-emphasize the ecological landscape conditions in models of settlement structure and economy (see e.g. Nordquist 2001:73). Societies do not change because people become sedentary; people become sedentary because societies change, and that change is mainly due to social processes. At the same time, a great deal of the explanation for social change lies precisely in the relationship between people and the physical landscape. Survival is adjusted to needs, and ecological or demographical changes entail an almost constant need for renegotiation of the landscape.

In landscape negotiations, areas and boundaries are defined. This need not imply land ownership and physical boundaries as we are accustomed to thinking of them, but it is still a matter of defining landscape spaces. Several social instruments such as history and mythology, references to ancestors and events and naming were used. They became deeply rooted in the world in which people moved, becoming the cement that held the landscape together for everyone involved. In some sense the landscape is fixed through a public and collective formalization of how one is related to other groups around one. Bergsvik (2003:299) discusses this process in connection with sedentariness, but in my opinion the same principles are equally applicable to more mobile societies. An increasing stress on the defining of landscape spaces means a greater sense of what is one's own and other people's, and this may lead to limitations in how much one can move in the landscape and when and where one can meet.

The complexity of this social process and of these societies is also the reason why the spiral continues. The more complex these societies become as regards their inhabitants, their mutual relations, and everything that ties them together, the greater is the dynamism and the need for flexibility.

Mörby – the oldest settlement site in Östergötland

Anders Kaliff

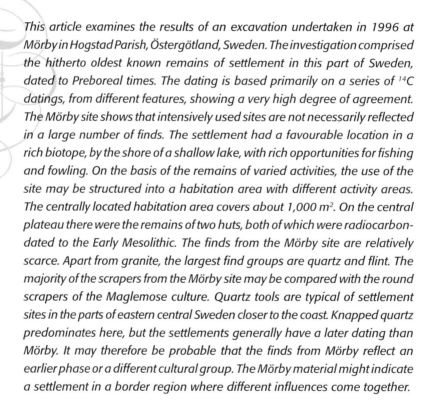
This article examines the results of an excavation undertaken in 1996 at Mörby in Hogstad Parish, Östergötland, Sweden. The investigation comprised the hitherto oldest known remains of settlement in this part of Sweden, dated to Preboreal times. The dating is based primarily on a series of ^{14}C datings, from different features, showing a very high degree of agreement. The Mörby site shows that intensively used sites are not necessarily reflected in a large number of finds. The settlement had a favourable location in a rich biotope, by the shore of a shallow lake, with rich opportunities for fishing and fowling. On the basis of the remains of varied activities, the use of the site may be structured into a habitation area with different activity areas. The centrally located habitation area covers about 1,000 m². On the central plateau there were the remains of two huts, both of which were radiocarbon-dated to the Early Mesolithic. The finds from the Mörby site are relatively scarce. Apart from granite, the largest find groups are quartz and flint. The majority of the scrapers from the Mörby site may be compared with the round scrapers of the Maglemose culture. Quartz tools are typical of settlement sites in the parts of eastern central Sweden closer to the coast. Knapped quartz predominates here, but the settlements generally have a later dating than Mörby. It may therefore be probable that the finds from Mörby reflect an earlier phase or a different cultural group. The Mörby material might indicate a settlement in a border region where different influences come together.

Not long ago, Early Mesolithic settlement sites were unknown in central Sweden. In recent years, however, early ^{14}C datings have been obtained at a few places in Östergötland. This article examines the results of an excavation undertaken in 1996 of site RAM 168 at Mörby in Hogstad Parish, Östergötland. The investigation comprised the hitherto oldest known remains of settlement in this part of Sweden, dated to Preboreal times. The certainty of this early date is based primarily on a series of ^{14}C datings showing a very high degree of agreement. The dating is also supported by the finds, which are in part extremely enigmatic, probably because few fully comparable sites have been investigated. The size of the area gave a unique opportunity to study an Early Mesolithic settlement site, as regards both its physical environment and internal structure and the distribution of finds in relation to features and structures.

The majority of research into the Mesolithic in Scandinavia in recent decades has concentrated on the latter part of the period. It is therefore urgent to publish and study material from the earliest phase of the Mesolithic, especially when it comes from regions which have not been studied in detail before. In Östergötland only a very few large-scale excavations focusing on Early Mesolithic settlement have previously been undertaken. A probable explanation for the failure to notice Early Mesolithic settlements is the difficulty in localizing the sites, unless they are characterized by large quantities of stray finds. The Mörby site shows that intensively used sites are not necessarily reflected in a large number of finds. Probable settlement locations must be assessed on the basis of the topography and soil type.

The aim of the present article is to present the Mörby site in its chronological and cultural context. The ^{14}C datings are very important for the argument, and the dating of the site will receive special treatment. The presentation of the features and finds is interwoven with a discussion of cultural affiliation and type of settlement. For a detailed presentation of the results, the reader is referred to the excavation report (Kaliff *et al.* 1997, with an English summary).

The postglacial development of the area

For Sweden the retreat of the ice sheet sets the *terminus post quem* for postglacial settlement. There is debate as to whether immigration to Scandinavia took place immediately after deglaciation or was more protracted in time. The traditional picture of Late Palaeolithic and Early Mesolithic colonization of Scandinavia is that the people followed the herds of reindeer in the wake of the retreating ice sheet. For the first population, however, there were two boundaries in the landscape: the edge of the ice sheet to the north and the surrounding sea. The picture of the reindeer hunters is beginning to change today, and it is now considered at least as probable that fishing and other coastal forms of livelihood were equally important factors for survival (Fischer 1996:157ff.).

The ice receded from southern Skåne around 13,500 BP (uncalibrated ^{14}C years). The Swedish West Coast also became ice-free fairly quickly and can show traces of older settlement sites than eastern Sweden. In the latter part of the Bølling period in particular (until *c.* 12,200 BP) the deglaciation was rapid, up to 50 km per century (L. Larsson 1996:141f.). The Younger Dryas thus sets a theoretical *terminus post quem* at *c.* 11,000 BP (*c.* 10,950 BC calibrated calendar years) for the postglacial presence of humans in the area where the Mörby site is located. The oldest datings today are around 9000 BP, but these are from find spots under the Highest Coastline of the Baltic Ice Sea.

In 1992 a settlement site was excavated at Högby near Mjölby, located beside a pre-historic lake or bog. The remains were found in two habitation areas and the features consisted of pits, hearths, hearth pits, and post-holes. A relatively small number of artefacts were found, including cores, debitage, and scrapers. A total of 16 features were dated to the Mesolithic, ranging from 8070 to 5590 BC. Two different concentrations of post-holes formed two small round-to-oval structures with openings towards the west. They had a width of about 3.5–4.0 m and were probably huts with their doors facing the nearby shore. Only one post-hole belonging to one of the huts was dated, to 7005–6666 BC (M. Larsson 1996).

Both the Mörby and the Högby sites have similarities in datings and in the site structure to the well-preserved Storlyckan site, just a few kilometres to the south of Mörby. Close to a dried-up river a small hut, sparse artefacts made of flint and quartz mark the limited space of the settlement (Molin 1999; Molin & Larsson 2000; M. Larsson 2003).

The topographical location of the Mörby site

The Mörby site is located in a transition zone between open plains and undulating wooded areas, about 7.5 km south-west of the Högby site mentioned above. To the north the terrain develops into a flat arable landscape at a height of about 125 m above sea level, with rocky outcrops here and there. The area to the south is undulating, with hills reaching 150 m above sea level. The site is naturally delimited to the west, east, and north. Just south of the settlement site, the landscape rises to become highland. To the north the shore of the former lake borders the site. On the west, too, there are areas of wetland. Right beside the eastern part of the site there is a noticeable rock formation, about 140 m above sea level. To the south the area was somewhat disturbed by the previous course of the E4, and parts of the settlement site were probably destroyed in connection with the building of the old road in the 1950s.

The excavated area comprised a total of about 18,000 m^2 in the form of a long, narrow area running east–west. The eastern part was highest, almost 130 m above sea level. From there the land slopes down to the west towards a sandy plateau, 125–126 m above sea level. The soil on the eastern slope consists of gravel mixed with till but otherwise consists mainly of sand. To the far west the soil is rich in blocks, on the edge of a wet wooded area. The settlement was mostly in ploughed land, which affected the preservation conditions. Several modern-day channels had been dug in the excavated area, flowing into an overgrown and drained area of wetland north of the excavated area. This was no doubt a shallow lake in prehistoric times.

On the basis of the remains of varied activities, the use of the area in Mesolithic times may be structured into a habitation area with activity areas to the east and west of it. The centrally located habitation area, located on a sandy plateau surrounded by streams (now dried up), was the most intensively used area, covering about 1,000 m^2. At the centre of the plateau, the remains of two distinct huts were excavated. Two other concentrations of post-holes may be traces of more huts, or they could be remains of structures such as drying frames. Between the two hut-remains there was an area that was free of features and finds, possibly a deliberately planned open area kept clear at the centre of the settlement. The habitation area was right beside the lake, with only a few metres to the shoreline as it was then.

Radiocarbon datings and source criticism

The excavation revealed features differing greatly in character and belonging to two distinct phases. Radiocarbon analyses from different types of features confirmed a division into two phases, with a hearth area from the Late Bronze Age and Pre-Roman Iron Age and a large Mesolithic habitation area with surprisingly early and concordant datings. The article deals only with the Mesolithic phase of settlement, which was also the most intensive.

The dating of the Mörby site is based chiefly on a large number, 18 in all, of ^{14}C datings to the Early Mesolithic, with the oldest dating to 9200 ± 85 BP and the youngest to 8030 ± 80 BP. Calibrated with a standard deviation of 1 sigma, all the datings lie within the range 8326–6751 BC, thus showing great concordance. The analysed samples with Early Mesolithic datings come from all the types of feature occurring on the site: post-holes, wall trenches, cooking pits, hearths, hearth pits, and pits of more uncertain function. All charcoal samples were taken from carefully selected areas in each feature. The Svedberg Laboratory performed the datings at Uppsala University. The datings are calculated according to the half-life of 5,568 years (Stuiver & Becker 1993).

Schild (1985 and 1998) has discussed the complexity of interpreting Mesolithic open sandy sites in order to overcome the problems with ^{14}C results that do not correspond to assemblages. The concordance of the datings at Mörby and the fact that the samples were taken from different types of feature are of great significance for their reliability. Isolated samples, or samples taken in the same type of feature, may always be feared to date another context than the feature itself. This may reflect traces of forest fires, which could have ended up in the soil through the roots of windfallen trees, digging, or the like (Browall 1999). In Mörby there are concordant samples from the bottom of hearth pits filled with cracked stone and from clear post-holes and wall structures. If the features had later been dug through a layer of charcoal, for example, from a forest fire that took place in Preboreal times, one would have reason to expect a spread in the datings through varying mixtures of later material. It is extremely improbable that all types of features located in a relatively large area could have been contaminated with Preboreal charcoal with no mixing. The later phase of activity from the transition between the Bronze Age and the Pre-Roman Iron Age consists of very distinct types of feature, easily distinguishable from the Mesolithic remains. The ^{14}C datings from the Mörby site may thus be said to be highly reliable.

Fig. 1. The ancient shoreline at the Mörby site. The photograph illustrates the location of the Early Mesolithic settlement sites in western Östergötland, which were mainly on sandy soil beside water systems and wetlands. Photo: National Heritage Board.

Huts and activity areas

On the central habitation plateau there were the remains of two huts, both of which were dated by ^{14}C to the Early Mesolithic. Hut I consisted of seven large post-holes without stone lining, which made up a horseshoe-shaped structure opening to the south-west. No hearth was found in or near the hut. No colouring from any floor level or adjacent occupation layer was preserved, probably because of ploughing. The width of the hut was 2.7 m from north-east to south-west and 2.54 m in the other direction, and the internal area was about 5 m^2. The post-holes were relatively large with depths of between 0.07 and 0.22 m. They were round to oval, with a diameter of 0.2–0.8 m. The filling in the post-holes was grey and leached, with elements of soot and isolated fragments of charcoal, which gave the impression that the hut had been destroyed by fire. The posts at the south-east of the entrance formed a double post-hole and could possibly be seen as a replacement post or a post added for extra support at the opening. The hut has been dated by charcoal from two of the post-holes to 9200 ± 85 BP (8326–8115 BC) and 8260 ± 80 BP (7391–7117 BC).

Hut II consisted of a round-to-oval structure in the form of a trench and two unlined post-holes, the latter located in what has been interpreted as the opening of the hut. The hut may have been a tent-like structure with the sides dug into the ground. Unlike hut I, this hut opened towards the former lake. Hut II had no trace of a hearth or a floor level either. The width from north to south was 3.3 m and from east to west 2.2 m, the internal area being about 6 m². The post-holes in the opening were large but unlined, approx. 0.3–0.4 m in diameter and dug down about 0.15 m from the excavated surface. The trenches formed three oblong, slightly bowed features, 0.14–0.3 m deep. The filling in all the trenches gave a greyish, leached impression but nevertheless contained soot and occasional pieces of charcoal. A ^{14}C sample from one of the wall trenches yielded the dating 8360 ± 90 BP (7470–7239 BC). The datings of huts I and II are together among the very oldest from any settlement remains in Sweden. The older dating from hut I is by far the earliest such dating.

Besides the post-holes that make up huts I and II, there were two further assemblages of post-holes in area C. It has not proved possible to group these in definite interpretable structures, but they suggest that more huts and other structures were located in the area. Four of these post-holes form a semicircle and may be envisaged as having belonged to a hut structure with its opening towards the south-west, that is, the same direction as hut I. One of these post-holes was dated to 8695 ± 85 BP (7863–7608 BC).

The western part of the habitation area at Mörby consisted of a clear activity area with a number of hearths and hearth pits. The features were similar in appearance and grouped in two concentrations. The role of the hearths at Mesolithic sites is debated. Besides cooking, there is evidence that a number of other activities were performed around the hearth, such as working stone, hides, or antler (cf. M. Larsson 1994:244f.). Beside the hearths at the Mörby site there were occasional post-holes whose function should be associated with activities to do with the hearths. The hearths also coincide with a find-bearing layer of sand and gravel, and beside this was the brook channel in which the largest amounts of finds from the actual habitation were discovered. Scrapers and cores, debitage, and an anvil were represented in the activity area. This may indicate that, for example, some tool-making and hide preparation was done close to the working area.

In the activity area there were seven hearths and hearth pits, containing cracked stone. Two features were dated to 8030 ± 80 BP (7031–6751 BC) and 8155 ± 80 BP (7270–7030 BC). By far the biggest single group of features at the site consisted of a couple of pits scattered in different groups. The pits varied a great deal in size, from about 0.25 to 1.8 m in diameter and with depths ranging from a few centimetres to as much as 0.4 m. The filling also varied from very sooty to grey and leached. It is difficult to interpret the function of most of the pits, but the majority belong to the Mesolithic phase of settlement. A few can be interpreted as cooking pits, one of them, yielding a ^{14}C dating of 8795 ± 90 BP (7950–7700 BC). Yet another six pits were radiocarbon-dated to the Early Mesolithic.

The finds from the Mörby site

The finds from the Mörby site are relatively scarce, most of them being found within a few limited areas. Of a total of 628 items, 70% come from a working area beside a worked quartzite block. Of the other material, 20 items can be associated with features, while the majority of the finds were discovered in squares of 1 m² excavated in certain areas and water-sieved. The proportion of finished tools is small. Apart from granite, the largest find groups are quartz and flint. The distribution of these two rock types is 62% quartz items and 38% flint items. In terms of weight, the distribution is even more lopsided, with 95% quartz to only 5% flint, which shows that the flint mostly consisted of small fragments.

The flint consisted of debitage, blades, and debris. The flints vary in appearance, and the raw material probably comes from three different regions, most likely Skåne and the west coast of Sweden. The Mesolithic blades consist of microblades. No whole flint cores were found, but certain residual products of microblade cores. Nine finds of worked *hälleflinta* were found in the form of debitage, cores, and scrapers. The *hälleflinta* occurred locally in the area. All cores and core fragments can be defined as blade cores. Two small scrapers of *hälleflinta* both have clear marks of use damage.

In the excavated area there were many small nodules of red *mosten*, a very hard metamorphic sandstone. Evidence of tool-making using *mosten* has previously been found in Dalarna (Lannerbro 1976:25ff.) and elsewhere. A small group of finds of worked *mosten* was discovered at the Mörby site: debitage, cores, and a scraper. The cores consisted of blade cores, of which two were microblade cores. Granite was also used as material for tools at the Mörby site, and this material is not totally unknown for tool-making (Lannerbro 1976; Welinder 1977; Gurstad-Nilsson 1995). The granite material from Mörby consists of cores, debitage, and a probable scraper. Finds of worked quartz: debitage, blades, cores, and waste. Altogether ten cores or fragments of cores were found, four of them microblade cores. A fragment of a microblade of quartz was also found.

The quartzite finds from Mörby are of special interest. This material was poorly represented at the actual habitation areas but was found to a large extent round a quartzite block on the western edge of the habitation area. The block was about 1.3 by 1.5 m, with a height of roughly 1.4 m. It bore clear traces of splitting surfaces where large pieces had been struck loose. The debitage was scattered over a limited area, which was excavated in squares of a half-metre size. A total of 883 fragments were retrieved, with a total weight of over 12 kg, not counting four large bits of the block. The finds consist of medium-sized crushed pieces of quartz and very thin, smaller fragments. The only identifiable tool at the place was a quartzite blade in two fragments. Two knapping stones were found among the waste material around the quartzite block, giving the place the impression of having been abandoned while work was in progress. Both the knapping stones were of solid red porphyry-like rock with clear crushing damage and well suited to the further

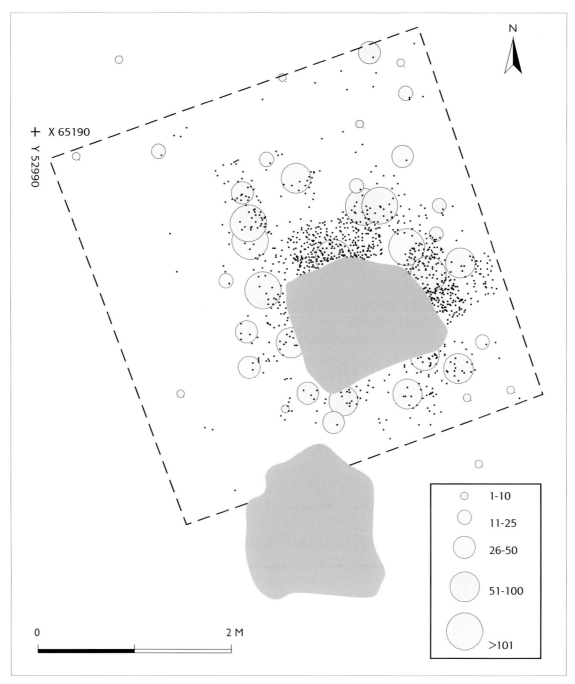

Fig. 2. Quartzite quarry and distribution of quartzite waste. The rings mark the number of pieces of waste collected from all the excavated 0.5 m squares. Dots show isolated waste found by surface cleaning. Graphics: Lars Östlin.

cutting of the quartzite. A total of seven knapping stones were found at the Mörby site, three of them with a faceted surface. Oval faceted knapping stones with wear surfaces at the ends are considered typical of working with the platform method, both with free-hand technique and with the use of an anvil (Callahan 1987:45).

Quartzite is a metamorphic sandstone with properties that lend itself to both knapping and pressure-flaking techniques (Broadbent 1982:78,). The quartzite from the block may have been intended for blade production. If so, this was carried out in a different place, since there was no residual material from any such production. The area should not be interpreted as a knapping place but was probably a raw material quarry where the blanks were rough-cut. The blade finds could then be interpreted as discarded tests, perhaps resulting from attempts to assess the quality of the material. The interpretation of remains of this type as places for working raw material has been discussed in several works (cf. Broadbent 1979:99ff., 1982:78f.; Lannerbro Norell 1987:21ff.; Lindgren 1996b).

Finds of organic material were very poorly represented, which can probably best be explained by the bad preservation conditions. Two unburned bones could possibly belong to the Mesolithic settlement phase: a breastbone from a hen and a metatarsal from a hare. The Mesolithic hearths yielded only very small burned bone fragments, which could not be identified (Sigvallius 1997).

Cultural affiliation and the function of the site

The huts from the Mörby site are both among the oldest dated settlement remains in Sweden. This makes comparisons with other find places difficult. Too few hut remains from the Early Mesolithic have been investigated as yet for us to be able to say what a typical dwelling was. There are, however, examples of huts, some of which are of a character similar to one or other of the Mörby huts and with partly comparable datings. In southern Scandinavia a small number of sites have been excavated with traces of hut structures from the Early Mesolithic. They are often characterized by a location beside a lake or bog. Examples of such sites are Ageröd and Bare Mosse in Skåne or Ulkestrup and Lundby in Sjælland. These places show fairly similar housing with small huts located close to open water (L. Larsson 1978a; Andersen et al. 1982). Excavated Danish sites from the Magle-mose period show hut structures with a rather similar appearance. The shape is round-to-oval or rectangular, and they are generally slightly bigger than the Mörby huts (cf. Blankholm 1985:65f.).

Only a few Mesolithic hut remains are known from Sweden, most of them from the latter part of the period. The majority of these have been found in Skåne, for example, a hut from Ageröd, dated c. 7100 BC (Larsson 1978a) and another one from Hagestad near Löderup, dated 7890–7540 BC (Strömberg 1986:61). In 1994 three uncertain huts were excavated at Valje outside Sölvesborg, with ^{14}C datings in the interval 6640–6040 BC (Biwall et al. 1997:195). With the exception of the Ageröd hut, which was bigger, the size of these huts corresponds to that of the huts from Mörby. There are also examples of Mesolithic huts with a trench, but these are not from the Early Mesolithic (M. Larsson 1986; Hallgren *et al.* 1995:13ff.; Biwall *et al.* 1997:195f.). A controversial structure was found at Tingby outside Kalmar, a rectangular building with sides measuring 8.8 by 3.5 m, dated by means of an artefact to the period 6500–5200 BC (Rajala & Westergren 1990:22). The structure is not like other excavated Mesolithic huts. The age of the Tingby house has been questioned, since it could be a younger structure built on an older site. A number of ^{14}C datings from various periods are the basis for this criticism (Grøn 1995:87; Johansson 1993:121ff.).

The two huts excavated at Mörby show two different structural solutions. Hut I was built with a structure of roof-bearing posts and no wall trench. The post-holes are relatively large and the hut must have been a stable structure. Comparable hut structures have been found at a Mesolithic site at Limsjön in Leksand Parish, Dalarna. The Leksand huts were built in a similar way, round-to-oval in shape and with roof-bearing posts, which indicates a frame of relatively stout posts. The internal area in the Leksand huts was bigger, however, 23–54 m^2. The Leksand site is later than the Mörby site, and dated to the period 6000–5000 BC (M. Larsson 1994:248).

On the basis of the material culture, the Early Mesolithic sites from southern Scandinavia are generally named Maglemose culture. The highly limited finds from the Mörby site partly fit this pattern. The quartz, however, is a discrepant feature which makes the cultural affiliation less certain. Otherwise it seems reasonable to assume that the sites in Östergötland in Preboreal times were a northern outpost of the Early Mesolithic cultures of southern and western Scandinavia. The coast of present-day central Sweden was mostly under water, and the pronounced quartz cultures that predominate in this area belong to a slightly later phase (cf. Åkerlund 1996a).

The majority of the scrapers from the Mörby site may be compared with the round scrapers of the Maglemose culture. The scrapers of *hälleflinta*, *mosten*, and granite are small, 14–22 mm in size, and almost round in shape. Small round flake scrapers of flint are characteristic of the Maglemose culture (cf. Althin 1954; Becker 1952:143). Similar scrapers have been found at the Högby site and as stray finds around Tåkern in Östergötland (Browall 1980:54; M. Larsson 1996:22). The cores of *hälleflinta* from Mörby are all microblade cores, most of them being conical. Conical microblade cores were also found in *mosten* and quartz. Two small cores of fine-grained granite are likewise conical in shape. The size of the conical microblade cores varies somewhat, with a height of 10–27 mm and a platform diameter of 7–19 mm.

The accepted chronological placing of conical microblade cores generally agrees with the finds from Mörby. The conical core appears to belong to an older phase than the handle core tradition which, according to Mats Larsson (1996), in Östergötland embraces the period *c.* 6500–5760 BC. No handle cores are found in the material from Mörby, which agrees well with the dating scheme suggested by the ^{14}C analyses. The dating of handle cores in Scandinavia is admittedly debated, but the conical microblade cores appear to have preceded the handle cores and can be derived from both the early and late Maglemose period (Olofsson 1995:106). C. J. Becker (1952:142ff.) used the introduction of the handle core to mark a boundary between early and late Maglemose culture. During the early Maglemose period, conical microblade cores are the most frequent element in material found at habitation sites. In western Sweden the cores are characteristic of the Sandarna culture, but coarse conical blade cores occur as early as Hensbacka times (Nordqvist 1997:16). Likewise, on the southern coast of Småland and in the inland, the conical microblade cores appear to be typologically older than the handle cores (Gurstad-Nilsson 1995:16f.).

The quartz material from Mörby relates the site to the Mesolithic in central Sweden, but the finds of flint simultaneously show affiliation with Early Mesolithic find places in southern and western Sweden. Nearby examples of these are the sites around Lake Hornborgarsjön in Västergötland, which date from the Hensbacka-Sandarna period (*c.* 8000–6000 BC). Flint is the most common material for tools at these sites (Åkerlund 1996a:37f.). Yet another nearby example is the site at Anderstorp in western Småland, with clearly Maglemose-influenced artefact forms (Pagoldh 1995). The relatively frequent finds of worked local raw material at the Mörby site are a feature that distinguish it from the southern and western Swedish settlement sites. Instead, the use of local raw material has parallels at certain Mesolithic settlement sites in Småland, where it is not unusual to find local raw material, especially quartz and *hälleflinta* (Gurstad-Nilsson 1993, 1995).

Quartz tools are typical of settlement sites in Södermanland, in the archipelago of eastern central Sweden. Knapped quartz predominates here, but the settlements also show a smaller element of microblades of flint (Lindgren 1997:11; Åkerlund 1996a:37f.). The absence of quartz with traces of the bipolar reduction method at the Mörby site distinguishes it from sites in the eastern coastal region, where this method is considered frequent (Lindgren 1994, 1996). The sites generally have a later dating than Mörby. Coastal settlements from Preboreal times may occur in the area (Gustafsson 1998), although this cannot yet be attested by sure datings. It may therefore be probable that the finds from Mörby reflect the very earliest phase. The Mörby materials indicate a settlement in a border region where different influences come together.

The Mörby settlement had a favourable location in a rich biotope, by the shore of a shallow lake. In the eastern part the site was sheltered by a height which could also function as a lookout point when hunting. To the south of the site, the highland area gave good protection against the wind, and there were probably good hunting grounds there. To the north was the lake or wetland, with rich opportunities for fishing and fowling. The lower parts in the immediate surroundings probably constituted a system of lakes in the process of being clogged by vegetation. Part of this lake system survived until historical times in the form of bogs and wetlands. Mesolithic settlement sites close to lake and water systems are well known, particularly from Skåne. From Lake Finjasjön in north-east Skåne there are examples of Late Palaeolithic and Early Mesolithic finds from a delta-like landscape. At Finjasjön there are also prominent hills which could have served as lookout places and for hunting (L. Larsson 1996:145).

There is nothing to say that the Mörby site was not used permanently over periods or as a part in a pattern of seasonal movements, or both. The surroundings ought to have been rich enough to provide a varied range of food in different seasons. While the Mörby site was in use, the shore of the Ancylus Lake was only 20–30 km to the east. The coast could thus easily have been reached in a day's march. It is therefore debatable whether it is reasonable to imagine seasonal moves of the habitation, when there was such great variation in biotopes within reasonable distance of the Mörby site. The model of seasonal mobility between different biotopes is in any case just a hypothesis. The Mörby site is an important piece in the jigsaw puzzle for interpreting whether people were permanently settled for long periods or moved seasonally. Even though there is a spread of over a thousand years in the total of 18 Mesolithic ^{14}C dates from Mörby, the series is comparatively coherent, especially in view of the statistical uncertainty of each individual test. The concordant datings together with the density of features at the site and the stable hut structures rather speak in favour of relatively permanent occupation.

Between Ancient Vättern and the Ancylus Lake
Early Mesolithic settlement in the Motala district in western Östergötland

Fredrik Molin

This article presents coastal Mesolithic sites from the Ancylus period in the Motala region in western Östergötland. The background is the large Mesolithic site recently excavated on the banks of Motala Ström. During the Early Mesolithic the water level in the Ancient Vättern (Fornvättern) was several metres higher than it is today, and in places there were well-formed shoreline formations. Several Mesolithic settlement sites have recently been discovered in the vicinity along the shore of the ancient lake. Lake Boren, about three kilometres downstream, was the inner part of a narrow bay of the sea. Today there are clearly formed wave-cut terraces and slopes which can be connected to the shoreline of the Ancylus Lake, where a couple of interesting sites have also been discovered recently. The text concentrates on presenting the composition of the find assemblages and providing a summary account of the location of the sites in the landscape.

It has previously been pointed out that the Mesolithic evidence from western Östergötland is eminently suitable for studies on topics such as colonization and establishment, material composition, and resource utilization (Molin 2000). Today, however, we know more about the inland environments in the Early Mesolithic in Östergötland than about settlements on the coast. Here too, studies of western Östergötland seem appropriate. During the Ancylus period, 9400–8200 ^{14}C-years BP, the area was geographically delimited by the large Lake Vättern to the west and by extensive areas of forest to the south and north. The Ancylus Lake frames the area to the east.

The aim of the following article is to present coastal Mesolithic settlement sites from the Ancylus period in the area around Motala in western Östergötland. The background consists of the large Stone Age site recently excavated beside the river Motala Ström in central Motala, close to the shore of Vättern (Carlsson *et al.* 2003; Carlsson 2004a), a settlement site dated to the transition from the Middle Mesolithic to the end of the Late Mesolithic (*c.* 7000–5000 BP). A survey of recently discovered Mesolithic material, and a specially directed inventory based on the landscape conditions prevailing during the

Ancylus period show that the location of the Motala site was also advantageous long before its main chronological centre of gravity. This is confirmed by a single ^{14}C dating of the site to the Ancylus period, 8795 ± 65 BP (Ua-26921).

This study presents only the immediate surroundings of Motala. In the Early Mesolithic the water level of Vättern was several metres higher than today, and there are places with well developed shoreline formations. Several recently discovered Mesolithic settlement sites lie along the former shore in the vicinity. Lake Boren, about three kilometres down Motala Ström, was the inner part of a narrow bay of the sea. Even today there are distinctly formed wave-cut terraces and slopes which can be associated with the shoreline of the Ancylus Lake, where a couple of interesting settlement sites have also been found recently. The emphasis in this article is on the composition of the finds and a summary presentation of the location of settlement sites in the landscape.

The physical conditions

Östergötland has been divided since historical times into four physiographical parts: the southern forests, the plain, the northern forests, and the archipelago. The city of Linköping is virtually at the centre of the province, dividing the plain into two parts, the western and the eastern Östgöta plain.

The southern forest is an outlier of the southern Swedish highlands and is characterized topographically by fissure valleys running in different directions. The valleys are often elongated, containing a large number of lakes and watercourses. The most common type of soil is till, which is generally sandy and coarse silty, at times with a large content of boulders. In the border zone between the southern forest and the plain, a transition belt can be discerned, characterized by varied landscape, undulating in places and with a rich element of old meadows and pastures and patches of deciduous forest. This transition belt has been shown to have been important as early as the Mesolithic. Several settlement sites and reflections of human activity have been documented on the edge of the southern forests since the 1990s (see Molin 2000 and works cited there). The attractiveness of this country may be due to an early adaptation to a broad-spectrum economy, which was a precondition for being able to spend entire seasons here. The carrying capacity of the forest, offering big game to hunt, plants to gather, and fishing, was probably of the utmost significance. To ensure a supply of food from several different ecological niches, settlement sites were located in areas where the marginal effect could be used to the full (cf. Knarrström 2000b).

The northern forests, including the areas around Kolmården and the forests north of Motala, are limited to the south by a large fault system. This extends from the Baltic Sea with the bay of Bråviken in the east, via Lakes Glan and Roxen at Norrköping and Linköping, and on to Lake Boren and finally to Vättern in the western part of the province. The terrain largely consists of fissure valleys and, like the southern forests, has a rich water system with lakes of varying size (Liman & Eriksson 1986:15f.). Motala is situated on the shore of Vättern, in the transition zone between the forest and the western plains.

The formation of the western plain

The plains extend all the way across the province, thus separating the two forested areas. The fault line constitutes its northern limit while in the south there is a more diffuse transition to the southern forests. The western parts of the southern and northern forests and the lakes Vättern and Roxen frame what is generally called the western plains, a gently undulating Cambro-Silurian plain which today mainly consists of fully cultivated land, but still with areas of fen and steppe meadows. The bedrock is seldom exposed, and the soil is mainly calcareous, humic clay till and glacial clay. Omberg on the shore of Vättern is a mountain rising just over 263 metres above sea level. It is a Precambrian horst with a base mainly of granite covered with calcareous, sandy till.

The lakes throughout the plains are few in number but large. The west is dominated by Lake Tåkern, which provides an unusually rich biotope for animals and plants. Well into historical times the plains held much more wetlands and small shallow lakes than today. Comparisons with maps from the eighteenth century, for example, show clearly that the number of wetlands has fallen sharply. This landscape has thus vanished, mainly as a result of drainage, to become arable and pasture land. Several streams and rivers drain the southern forests and the plains, flowing from the south towards the north and north-east. Svartån and Motala Ström are the largest and most important water routes. Svartån with its tributaries flows into Roxen north of Linköping. Motala Ström links Vättern with lakes including Boren below the fault line to the north and then finally discharges into Roxen.

The climate period of the Younger Dryas, at the end of the Late Glacial *c.* 11,000–10,000 BP, was characterized by heavy fluctuations and changes in climate. It probably started very cold, which had the consequence that the retreat of the ice sheet halted over Scandinavia and the ice at times advanced again. Until about 10,500 BP the edge of the ice was virtually still across central Östergötland, running over today's Linköping and on to Omberg, which was already ice-free beside Vättern. This led to large glaciofluvial formations on the plains and in the adjacent forests, for example, the Djurkälla field north of Motala. At every long pause in the retreat of the ice, glaciofluvial material was deposited in the form of deltas and transverse ridges along the ice front. In forward thrusts the ice pushed together moraine ramparts which took on a west–east direction. These formations are called the Middle Swedish Marginal Zone (Lundqvist 1998:66f.).

Around 10,300 BP there was a noticeable rise in temperature. This caused the ice front to recede relatively quickly, and parts of central Sweden including Östergötland became ice-free. The course of the deglaciation was thus very complicated, due to constant fluctuations in climate. In places the ice sheet was also broken into smaller pieces, forming

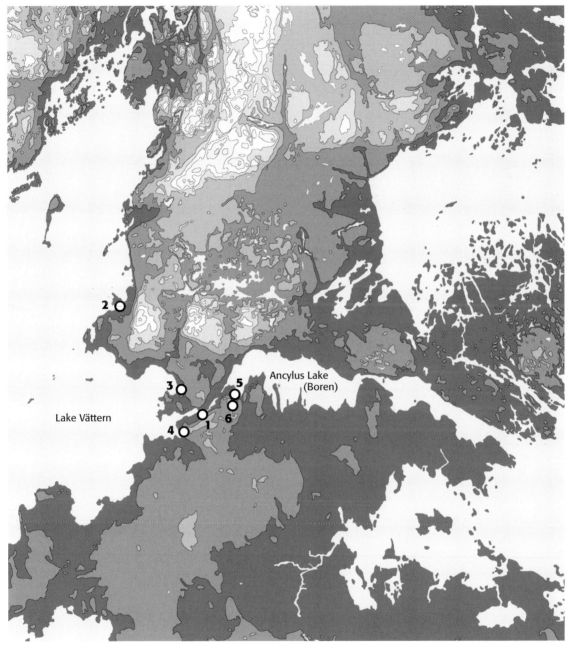

Fig. 1. Mesolithic sites in the Motala district in western Östergötland. Palaeogeographical map illustrating the relationship between land and water during the Ancylus period. The Ancylus Lake on the map corresponds to 75 metres above today's sea level. Lake Boren was the inner part of a narrow bay of the sea.
1 Motala, 2 Näs, 3 Varamon, 4 Södra Freberga, 5 Hultet I, and 6 Hultet II–III.

areas of dead ice which were later transformed into fens and small lakes. The Younger Dryas, at *c.* 11,000 BP, is thus the *terminus post quem* for the Late Glacial presence of humans in central Östergötland. At this time find sites can only be sought around locations that were free of ice in the areas around the Highest Coastline in southern Östergötland.

In recent years a pattern of small Early Mesolithic (*c.* 9000–6900 BP) inland settlement sites beside water systems and small in-filling lakes has been documented in the western plains. Several large-scale excavations have been conducted, giving great potential for increasing our knowledge, which partly had the character of basic research. The settlement sites have been interpreted as seasonal sites for small groups, places to which they returned in a repetitive cyclic pattern at certain times during the year. In several cases the settlements were established in the Preboreal and Early Boreal. Recurrent visits resulted in long site continuity, with the latest remains often being datable to the Atlantic period. Several of the settlement sites display clear internal structures, with hut remains and interpretable activity areas (see Molin 2000 and works cited there).

The plains around Lake Tåkern were discovered at an early stage in research – at the end of the nineteenth century – to have been significant in the Mesolithic, with several stray finds of artefacts such as core axes and an early large-toothed bone harpoon. Surveys since the 1980s have discovered no less than thirty Stone Age sites around the lake, many of which have material from the Mesolithic. The fertile soil of the plain and the many wetlands created a rich natural environment which probably allowed settlement to be more sedentary. The area around Tåkern is as yet the only part of Östergötland with confirmed Mesolithic burials and has thus been regarded as a core area during the Mesolithic period (Browall 1980, 1999, 2003).

The Ancylus Lake in Östergötland

The melting of the ice sheet had the consequence that meltwater was released and the earth's crust began to rise again after having been pressed down by the weight of the ice. The rapid course of land rise, in conjunction with deglaciation, created different stages in the development of the Baltic Sea (e.g. Risberg 2003). This in turn had dramatic effects on flora and fauna and on the early people who settled here in the constantly changing environment. Within a relatively short space of time the conditions could be completely transformed as the landscape was reshaped; this applied in particular to the coastal zones and the extensive and ongoing displacement of the shoreline (e.g. Björck 1995; Åkerlund 1996a; Hedenström & Risberg 1999; Pettersson & Wikell 2004).

The oldest observed settlement sites in Östergötland date to *c.* 9000–7500 ^{14}C-years BP (8300–6500 BC), that is, from a phase when the ice had long since vanished. The period is characterized by the transition from the Ancylus Lake to the preliminary stage of the Littorina Sea. Initially the Ancylus Lake covered much of the province, forming a wide bay that cut in across the plains and along the edge of the fault system via Boren towards Vättern. The first outlets of the Ancylus Lake were drained *c*. 9200 BP, which meant a land connection between southern and northern Sweden and the isolation of Vänern from the sea. This also resulted in a transgression phase around 9200 BP, with gradually changing conditions for coastal settlements (Björck 1995:31; Risberg 2003).

In the Linköping region a raised beach formation from the Ancylus period has been found, corresponding to the Ancylus limit around 75 m above sea level; at several places it can be discerned as a large erosion brink 2–3 m high, with the beach level lying below. In the south-eastern parts of the province the Ancylus limit likewise forms distinct shorelines around 70 m above sea level (Fromm 1976:53f.; Agrell 1980:230). Just outside Linköping a transgression phase can be detected in the stratigraphy of the beach formation. The beach ridge here overlies a thin layer of peat, indicating a rise in the water level. The peat has been ^{14}C-dated to *c*. 8600 BP (Fromm 1976:53f., 69). Along with the lake systems, at the edge of the northern forests, there are places with well-formed raised beach slopes and wave-cut terraces at levels between 75 and 80 m above sea level. Beach formation within this altitude range can be assumed to belong to the Ancylus Lake in western Östergötland.

The next major phase in the history of the Baltic Sea starts *c*. 8200 BP: the Littorina Sea. The initial phase here is also called the Mastogloia Sea (*c*. 8200–6800 BP), which is a brackish stage before the Littorina Sea proper, with its higher salinity (e.g. Risberg 1991:19ff.; Donner 1995:149f.). The continued displacement of the shoreline from the Ancylus period to the Littorina also had the result that Lake Roxen finally became a narrow, confined bay of the Littorina Sea, before the lake was finally cut off.

Settlement sites along Fornvättern

At the end of the 1990s archaeologists discovered the first Mesolithic settlement site that can be definitely associated with the shore of Vättern in Östergötland. It had previously been claimed that Vättern was not considered very interesting for settlement because its environment lacked sources of nutrition (Kindgren 1991:51ff.). Workers laying cables at Näs, north-west of Motala, uncovered a Mesolithic settlement site in arable land (Helander & Zetterlund 1998). The settlement site was indicated by worked quartz and by occasional fire-cracked stones on the field surface. When a trench was dug for the cable, a relatively large amount of finds – for the period and for Östergötland – were collected. They consisted almost entirely of worked quartz, but also small quantities of flint and quartzite.

The quartz objects were identified as having been reduced by both the platform method and the bipolar method. Several platform cores and bipolar cores were collected by surface surveys of the field and as stray finds in the trench. Excavated squares yielded several platform flakes and characteristic bipolar flakes with a straight flaking morphology, or the typical triangular splinters that arise from bipolar reduction. An end scraper of

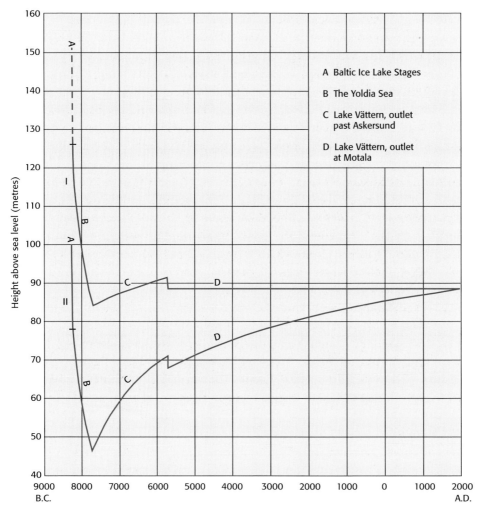

Fig. 2. General trend of the water-level changes in the Vättern basin from 8300 BC (uncalibrated age) to the present time: (I) at the latitude of Motala; (II) at Jönköping. After Norrman 1964.

quartz was found, made from a platform flake with retouches. The flints were all reduced to small pieces about a centimetre in size. They were all identified as platform flakes, one of which was blade-like.

A number of features of settlement site character were excavated, including hearths and sooty pits. Two charcoal samples date the settlement site to 7955–7725 BP (Ua-8951, Ua-8952), the early Littorina. The remains were located at the highest part of the investigation area, at a height of 95 m above sea level. The underlying soil consisted mostly of sand. The settlement site was thus on a sandy promontory extending into Lake Vättern, at the highest point between two bays. Today, however, the area is about 300 metres from the shore.

The history of Vättern since the lake was cut off from the Yoldia Sea around 9600 BP is relatively well known (Norrman 1964; Nilsson 1968). Studies have shown that the lake, under the designation *Fornvättern* (Ancient Vättern), was formed just before the transformation of the Yoldia stage to the Ancylus Lake. At this time Vättern was at its lowest water level, which varied greatly from its southern end at Jönköping, 46 m above sea level, and at its former outflow at Askersund, about 102 m above sea level. As a result of the higher uplift in the north, the lake overflowed to the south, which meant that the lowest pass threshold towards the plainlands was flooded and a new outlet was created in the vicinity of Motala.

Two calculations date the formation of the river Motala Ström to 8450–7700 BP, which marks the end of the Fornvättern stage. As a consequence of this, there was a continual transgression south of the outflow and a regression in the water level north of Motala (Norrman 1964:31f.; Nilsson 1968:76ff.; Donner 1995:151f.). At the time of the settlement site at Näs, just north of Motala soon after 8000 BP, the water was 90–92 m above sea level. This means that the settlement site was virtually on the shore. Following an altitude optimum of 95 m above sea level, the settlement site even forms an island near the mainland shoreline.

Worked quartz has also been observed recently in arable land just north of the settlement site at Näs, near the farm of Kavelbäck. An inventory retrieved a larger flake of quartz, worked using the platform method. The site is close to a stream flowing in a ravine into Vättern. The flake was found in sandy sloping soil just below a ledge. The place could possibly represent an earlier settlement site by the shore (Wikell, pers. com.).

Motala on the shore of Vättern

The oldest ^{14}C dating from the settlement site in Motala, around 8800 BP, is a strong indication that people were using the site as early as the Fornvättern stage, before the formation of Motala Ström and the new outflow of Vättern. There was probably a settlement site here similar to the one at Näs. Before the river broke its way through the sandy till soil, the water of Vättern reached a couple of metres above today's level. The settlement site was then on the shore, beside a flat rise, just over 90 m above sea level. We may envisage a small watercourse preceding the river, flowing from Vättern down towards the Ancylus Lake, only three kilometres to the north-east. At this time, then, the settlement site must have been at the end of the short valley that joined the two lakes, probably a frequently used communication route. Since no study has yet been undertaken of the very large assemblage of finds from Motala, based on questions about the Ancylus stage, this must for the time being be considered hypothetical. We do know, however, that there are tendencies in the material towards finds of earlier origin, for example, known cores for microblade manufacture, which take on almost conical shapes.

Something which corroborates the assumption of an earlier settlement phase in Motala is the fact that, while the excavation was in progress, yet another settlement site was found in Motala at the same time, at Varamon near the shore of Vättern. As with the other sites, the location is obviously connected to the Fornvättern stage. The finds were discovered during a survey of a field, when several pieces of worked quartz, including a scraper and a hammerstone, were collected (Eklund & Hennius 2004; Roger Wikell, pers. com.).

The scraper is made from a bipolar flake with a large number of distinct retouches. The other quartz objects – a core fragment and a flake – were worked with both bipolar and platform methods. In connection with the survey, a local historian handed in a small amount of finds from the place, consisting of worked quartz and a single flake of Cambrian flint.

The settlement site is situated on a flat sandy plateau just over 90 m above sea level. Today it is almost 500 metres down to the water. As late as the eighteenth century, however, there were wet meadows near the arable field, as maps of the area show. This means that the settlement site earlier in the Fornvättern stage was on a point surrounded by water. In 2002 the place was the subject of a limited excavation occasioned by the construction of a new road. Machine excavation uncovered prehistoric remains in the sand, including several hearths and pits. The remains could not be exactly dated but were assumed to be connected to the area with Stone Age finds (Carlsson 2003).

The most recently discovered settlement site is just south of Motala, at Södra Freberga. It was discovered in 2004 as a result of work rebuilding a stretch of railway line (see Elfstrand 2000). The settlement site is on a distinct ledge along a sea cliff in an otherwise steep west-facing slope, 95 m above sea level, right above a bathing place deep in a bay of Vättern. The ledge is built up of calcareous clay, with occasional large blocks. The bathing place below the settlement site is covered by the finest washed sand deposited in the earlier Fornvättern stage.

A preliminary archaeological investigation showed that both finds and settlement site remains are scattered over the ledge. An interesting thing is that the finds are mostly south Scandinavian flint, the majority of it burnt. Most of the flints are worked using direct technique, presumably with a hammerstone. The material shows a preponderance of platform flakes of differing size. There are also small flakes which are probably traces of core preparation and retouching, or else sharpening, of all kinds of artefacts. A flake scraper with clear retouches was collected. Among the flints is a flake of Cambrian flint.

The rest of the material contains a small quantity of bipolar-struck quartz and several larger quartz nodules, or workpieces, which are a preliminary stage for large quartz cores. It has not been possible to classify any tools among the quartz finds. From the settlement site there is also a small amount of knapped quartzite and probably locally collected *hälleflinta*. The only find that gives any hint of the chronology of the material is a broken microblade of south Scandinavian flint, which is likely to be from the Mesolithic. The settlement site remains have not been ^{14}C-dated, but the topographical location beside the former shore suggests a dating to the Early Mesolithic.

The settlement sites at Knäppeviken

In 2000 an amateur researcher handed in a fascinating collection of finds from a previously unknown settlement site close to the shore of Lake Boren. During a walk in the woods on the edge of a nature reserve, along the edge of the former Ancylus shore, he noticed worked quartz which had appeared by erosion in a newly dug ditch for a stream. A number of selected finds were collected, and the material, after classification, turned out to contain quartz worked with a soft technique, which had only been observed sporadically before that on Mesolithic settlement sites in Östergötland. The find was the incentive for a specially focused survey of the vicinity, which resulted in the discovery of two more nearby settlement sites.

Hultet I

The settlement site today is beside a sheltered fen near the croft of Hultet in the inner part of a bay called Knäppeviken. In this area the Ancylus Lake formed distinct wave-cut shorelines in the calcareous till, often with several ledges above each other. The levels vary between 75 and 80 m above sea level. The settlement site, called Hultet I, was on the lower of two ledges protruding like a small point into the Ancylus Lake. Today mixed forest grows along the edge of the fen, with stout conifers among the trees. A test dig in a large uprooted tree stump revealed large flakes, worked using platform technique. The upper ledge probably represents the oldest phase of the settlement site, or else a completely independent earlier stay in the same area.

A total of about sixty pieces of worked quartz were collected from the lower ledge. The material consists exclusively of milk quartz of high quality. Only a few pieces have retained the crust, which might indicate that the people used quartz nodules rounded by wear or nodules of quartz-rich till. The remaining quartz may very well be pure cleaved quartz, broken off some nearby vein of quartz (cf. Lindgren 1996b:359). In Östergötland, as in the rest of central Sweden, quartz occurs profusely as an element both in loose till and in the bedrock.

The finds can mainly be classified as flakes and flake fragments, but the material also includes cores, core fragments, a point, and part of a cutting tool, probably a segment knife. The proportion of identifiable tools is thus small, as is usual in quartz-based finds. The reduction methods used for working the quartz can be studied on the basis of the cores and the flakes. Both bipolar knapping and reduction by means of the platform method are represented (cf. Callahan 1987; Callahan *et al.* 1992). They probably constitute different stages in the working. Bipolar technology predominates, evidently with

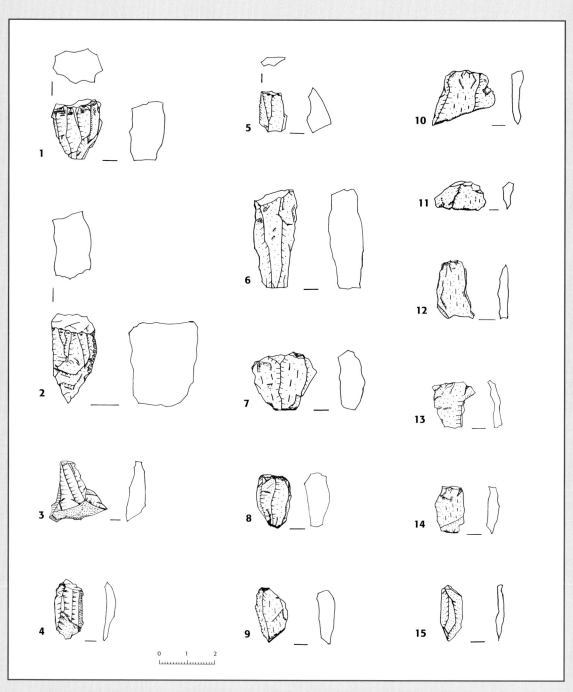

*Fig. 3. Quartz artefacts from Hultet I. **1–2** Microblade cores. **3–5** Rejuvenation flakes from microblade cores. **6–9** Bipolar cores. **10–14** Bipolar flakes. **15** Point made from a bipolar flake. Drawing: Fredrik Molin.*

the aim of making small, sharp flakes with cutting edges. The bipolar flakes are mostly small, thin, and straight, often looking like blades with a thin "crushed" platform.

Among the finds there are two microblade cores and a further three rejuvenation flakes showing the distinct negative of earlier microblades. The cores are small, 2–2.5 centimetres in height, with deliberately struck platforms which are flat or slightly concave. The material is pure milk quartz and the form of the core resembles the front part of small handle cores. From the negatives one can see that the microblades were about 3–5 mm wide and up to 2 cm long. The rejuvenation flakes are all taken from the platform in order to clean a core and create new flaking surfaces. The cores and flakes display a conscious microblade technology and are evidence of microblade production on the site. There are as yet no finds of partial or intact microblades from the site, however. The point that was found is 2 cm long and 9 mm wide and probably made from a bipolar blade-like flake and not a microblade. There is a hint of a crushed platform at the proximal end. There are also hints that the long sides were deliberately retouched.

The finds as a whole can be dated to the Mesolithic, with a large proportion of bipolar reduced quartz and a well-developed microblade technology. The production of bipolar flakes and microblades can plausibly be related to the completion of points and barbs for different composite tools and projectiles (see Lindgren 1994; Knarrström 2000b:19ff.). Everything suggests that the site was on the shore of the Ancylus Lake, in the inner part of the bay. If the assumption about the shoreline location is correct, the settlement site should be dated to before 8400 BP.

Hultet II and III

In autumn 2004 there was a specially geared survey of the immediate surroundings of the newly discovered settlement site. The landscape around Knäppeviken has alternating arable fields, fens, and mixed forest, both coniferous and deciduous. The fens are open with ample grass and reeds, and in summer they are grazed by cattle. Several streams drain higher-lying areas, flowing down towards the fen. Along the eastern shore of the bay there are several modern sites with boat berths and holiday cottages. The forests in the area as a rule have a relatively thick, calcareous layer of grey brown podzol, which covers the underlying calcareous till.

The survey was deliberately conducted at an altitude from the shore of Boren, around 74 m above sea level, up to 100 m above sea level, where the terrain is flatter. A general feature of the area is the well-formed cliffs between 75 and 85 m above sea level, which can probably be associated with the former shore of Ancylus. Small test pits were dug with hoes at all spots which were thought likely to contain concealed remains in the forest. All the stumps of windfallen tree were likewise searched systematically with hoes.

A further two settlement sites were found close to the croft, designated Hultet II and III. Hultet II is on a ledge on a steep east-facing slope 80–90 m above sea level. The site

Fig. 4. The location of the Hultet II site on a ledge on a steep east-facing slope. The water of the Ancylus Lake covered the bottom of the earlier valley. Photo: National Heritage Board.

consists of arable which at the time of the survey had just been ploughed but unfortunately not harrowed. The finds were collected in the arable soil within an area of about 50 x 50 metres along the ledge and just below it. In the past the fen (the former bay of Ancylus) extended all the way to the foot of the slope, but today a large part of the wetland is cultivated.

The finds consist exclusively of quartz, apart from one platform core of red porphyry. The quartz is generally of poorer quality than that from Hultet I, and the majority probably come from loose collected nodules. Several of the pieces have probably been damaged by ploughing. Among the finds are cores, flakes, and flake fragments. Virtually all the cores are bipolar with clear crush marks at the poles. Several have a "cushion-like" appearance. One platform core is irregularly knapped from several different platforms. The material includes two identifiable tools. One is a scraper shaped from a large platform flake. The edge measures 4.5 cm and shows large, widely spaced retouches and probable traces of use wear visible to the naked eye. The other object is an intact segment knife consisting of a platform flake just over 4 cm long with a straight side along which there are obvious wear marks, but no deliberate retouches.

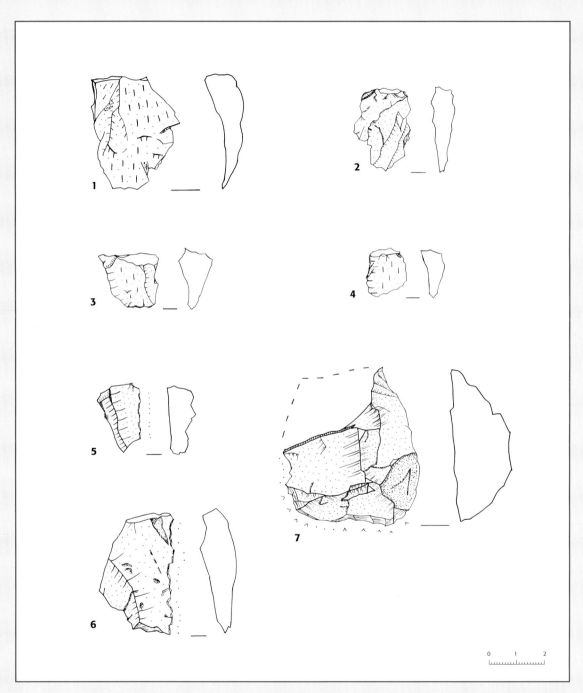

*Fig. 5. Quartz artefacts from Hultet I and Hultet II. **1–4** Platform flakes (Hultet I). **5** Cutting tool, probably a knife with use wear (Hultet I). **6** Knife with use wear (Hultet II). **7** Scraper with retouches and use wear (Hultet II). Drawing: Fredrik Molin.*

About 70 metres to the west, higher up the increasingly flat slope, the next concentration of material was found, called Hultet III. The finds were in ploughed soil beside a distinct hill, 95 m above sea level. Scattered pieces of knapped quartz were collected within an area of about 20 x 20 metres. The material consists of flake fragments and a bipolar core of modest size. The quartz is of similar quality to that found further down the slope. Together with the quartz, a damaged hammerstone of a heavier dense rock was found.

It is more difficult to draw any sure chronological conclusions on the basis of the evidence from Hultet II and III. The methods used to reduce the quartz are common to a large part of prehistoric times (Callahan 1987). It has been pointed out, however, that a high proportion of objects worked using the bipolar reduction method is often found on Mesolithic sites in eastern central Sweden (Lindgren 1994, 1996, 2004). Hultet II, on the other hand, is connected to the former shore of Ancylus, in view of the location along a pronounced cliff, which strengthens the assumption of a Mesolithic dating.

Conclusion

Around 10,000 years ago Lake Boren was the innermost bay of the Ancylus Lake in Östergötland. The lake cut across the province all the way to Motala, on the shore of *Fornvättern* (Ancient Vättern), at the edge of the western plains. The plains were thus framed, which means that for the people in the Motala district there was a close relationship between lakeside, coast, and the rich soils and wetlands of the plains. At several places the Ancylus Lake left clear shoreline formations which are visible today as wave-cut terraces or ridges between 75 and 80 m above sea level. Later, during the transition to the Littorina period, the sea withdrew towards the east on account of the ongoing uplift. Lake Roxen at Linköping remained for a long time as a narrow bay of the sea. At the same time as the Ancylus Lake, Fornvättern reached levels of 90–95 m above sea level in the area around Motala. Its first outflow was at the north end of the lake. Before *c.* 7700 BP, however, a new outflow was created at Motala, causing the formation of Motala Ström and the end of the Fornvättern stage.

The present study has shown that there were several Mesolithic settlement sites in the immediate surroundings of Motala, and there are good reasons for associating them with the Ancylus Lake and the shores of Fornvättern. The settlement sites can thus be dated to the Early Mesolithic, assuming that they were once shorebound. Along the shores of Vättern at least three settlement sites have been observed and subjected to small-scale archaeological investigation: the settlement sites at Näs, Varamon, and Södra Freberga. They all have preserved features, for example, in the form of hearths and finds, mainly of worked quartz and flint. Only the settlement site at Näs has been ^{14}C-dated, to a maximum age of 7955 BP, which connects the site to the shore of Fornvättern.

From the recently excavated settlement site beside Motala Ström in Motala, mainly dated to the Late Mesolithic, there is also a ^{14}C dating to the Ancylus period, around

8800 BP. Based on the other settlement sites in the vicinity, one can argue that there was also a settlement on the site during the Ancylus period. The geographical location seems highly favourable, on the shore of the lake at the end of a valley through which one could easily reach the nearby sea. An older Early Mesolithic settlement would almost certainly be "drowned", becoming virtually invisible in the large amount of later settlement site material. No studies of this hypothetical stage have been conducted, however.

A further three assemblages of early settlement site material have been found close by, at Hultet near Lake Boren, beside the former Ancylus shore. The settlement sites have been observed as a result of collected stray finds as part of a specially focused survey. One of the sites, Hultet I, shows traces of microblade manufacture from quartz, including finds of a couple of microblade cores and rejuvenation flakes. The finds date the remains to the Mesolithic, and the topographical location suggests that the site was on the shore of the Ancylus Lake during the Early Mesolithic. The settlement site at Hultet II was in a comparable position, above an erosion bluff along the former seashore.

It has previously been observed that the plains display a well-developed pattern of small inland settlement sites from the Early Mesolithic. Several settlement sites have been excavated in the last ten years. The surroundings of Lake Tåkern have also been described as an incipient central area, with Mesolithic burials and other features. Much of the material around Tåkern has been found by specially focused surveys. Everything suggests that our picture of the Mesolithic settlement pattern along the early coastal areas can be filled out in greater detail by more such focused studies. Similar work has been done in other parts of Östergötland, at Kolmården, Vikbolandet, and Valdemarsvik, with results that are at least as good (see Ericsson & Wikell and Wikell in this volume).

A simple conclusion is thus that priority must be given to focused surveys. Only a concerted picture of settlement patterns, both inland and along the coasts, can provide a sufficiently tenable foundation on which to draw far-reaching conclusions about problem areas such as demography, resource utilization, and social organization during the Mesolithic in Östergötland.

Many Mesolithic sites along the shores
Some results from surveys in Kolmården and Vikbolandet, Östergötland in eastern central Sweden

Roger Wikell

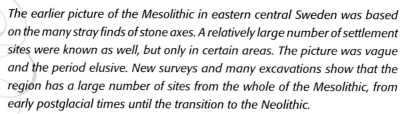
The earlier picture of the Mesolithic in eastern central Sweden was based on the many stray finds of stone axes. A relatively large number of settlement sites were known as well, but only in certain areas. The picture was vague and the period elusive. New surveys and many excavations show that the region has a large number of sites from the whole of the Mesolithic, from early postglacial times until the transition to the Neolithic.

The landscape of eastern central Sweden is distinctive, with its fissure valleys which have in principle been lifted completely out of the sea to form large archipelagos. Close cooperation with Quaternary geologists provides the key to reading the landscape. Fishing and seal hunting were important in this archipelago world. The shores were thus important places to choose for settlements. The tendency in the newly discovered material shows that the archipelagos of the whole of eastern central Sweden were claimed, as land uplift made them accessible. The number of sites is thus very large. The sites reflect a mobile society, where life was based on a constant readiness to travel between natural and social resources.

Introduction

Generally speaking, very little is known about the Mesolithic cultural landscape in eastern central Sweden. It is true that quite a lot of settlement sites are known, and even more stray finds of stone axes (Forsberg & Larsson 1994:10; Hermansson & Welinder 1997; Groop & Guinard forthcoming). Yet what we see is just the tip of the iceberg when it comes to the Mesolithic cultural landscape.

Surveys specially focused on the Mesolithic can yield very good results. In the 1990s and up to the present day, several surveys have been conducted in Kolmården and Vikbolandet in easternmost Östergötland, and in eastern central Sweden as well. This has led to the discovery of a large number of previously unknown Stone Age sites, chiefly indicated by knapped quartz. Most of the sites are of Mesolithic character, and if they were once on the shore, the course of colonization in early postglacial times can be sketched, and patterns of settlement can be followed up until Neolithization. It is a rich cultural landscape with countless sites – everything from large, find-rich axe sites to small places poor in finds. These correspond to different parts of Mesolithic society and are thus important for building up our knowledge.

This article presents some reflections based on these and other surveys, chiefly from Södertörn (Hanveden-Tyresta), concerning the Mesolithic cultural landscape in the coastal areas of eastern central Sweden.

Background

The traditional inventory of ancient monuments has chiefly been geared to the visible cultural landscape. For Östergötland and also eastern central Sweden this primarily means the Iron Age and Bronze Age (Kaliff 1999). The large numbers of visible antiquities, such as graves, hill-forts, and rune stones, have claimed all the resources. Settlement sites which were not visible above ground, except when signalled through finds in arable land, have been neglected. They were difficult to see or perceive, and their characteristic features were diffuse. Moreover, a ploughed settlement site is, if not destroyed then at least disturbed. It was thus more important to register the antiquities that had still not yet been sacrificed to the expansive land hunger of the late nineteenth and early twentieth centuries. It was probably considered problematic to demarcate settlement sites: How many finds are required if one is to dare classify the place as an ancient site? The centralized nationwide inventory produced for the economic map was not really prepared for a general search for settlement sites from the Stone Age. Stone axes and sites with copious finds were nevertheless registered (Selinge 1989:19). Thanks to the efforts of early scholars, individual sites were highlighted, and also settings or complete landscapes, with the Pitted Ware sites of Kolmården (Middle Neolithic) as examples. Because of the uneven spread of this work, we had contexts which were rich in finds and others which were seemingly empty, blank spaces on the archaeological map. The Stone Age was well represented in areas with a high degree of cultivation, and with an early presence of archaeologists curious about the Stone Age. Distinct find categories such as axes, formal tools of flint, and pottery facilitated this interest. There were also topics that captured all the interest, such as typology and chronology.

Whereas the west coast seemed to be very rich in Mesolithic remains, thanks to early and persevering survey work, the east coast was for a long time more sparsely represented (Alin 1953, 1955; Cullberg 1973). Southern Scandinavia was likewise richly represented (Larsson 2003). At first it seemed doubtful whether eastern central Sweden had any settlement at all, but the amount of stray finds (stone axes) indicated that it had (Montelius 1873). Work was systematized through a drive started by Knut Stjerna (Nerman 1965), surveying different landscapes in the region. Kolmården in Östergötland was surveyed by Birger Nerman (1911). In Södermanland, the province just north of Östergötland,

Ivar Schnell completed parts of the work by publishing the rich finds from the western side of the Södertörn peninsula (Schnell 1930). Kolmården and Södertörn, among other areas, stood out at an early stage as core areas for Stone Age settlement on the east coast. It was chiefly the Middle Neolithic ceramic sites with their wealth of finds that characterized these areas, but there was also a rich presence of stone axes, primarily pecked axes and also closely related forms at higher levels in the province. The first colonization was believed to have occurred 7,000 years ago, on the shores of the Littorina Sea (Schnell 1930; Welinder 1977; Olsson & Åkerlund 1987).

Kjel Knutsson, in his survey of research 1986–1990, has described the situation thus: "the east Swedish Mesolithic … is basically a blank page in Swedish archaeology" (Knutsson, K. 1995:15). This picture was valid until quite recently, when specially focused surveys and many rescue excavations gave us a more detailed view of the Mesolithic in eastern central Sweden.

This development was clearly foreseen by Carl Cullberg in 1980: "The settlement sites of Atlantic time are probably spread over this entire region. Only faint traces suggest their presence in the South Swedish Upland and the areas to the north. However, more intensive research would almost certainly bring to light a large number of sites where there are now blank spaces on the map" (Cullberg 1980:431).

As the results of the last two decades' work have been published, a new picture has emerged of the Mesolithic in eastern central Sweden (Hammar & Wikell 1994; Åkerlund 1996a; 2001; Lindgren 1997; 2004; Knutsson et al. 1999; Åkerlund et al. 2003; Pettersson & Wikell 2004, to name just a few recent works). In fact, all the axes had already indicated this (Forsberg & Larsson 1994:10; Hermansson & Welinder 1997; Groop & Guinard forthcoming).

Focused surveys have contributed in large measure to the new picture of the Mesolithic. A group of archaeologists, Dag Hammar, Mattias Pettersson, and myself, wondered in 1991 whether the prevailing picture of the Mesolithic remains was correct. We did most of our work on the eastern side of Södertörn (Hanveden-Tyresta), where few finds were known compared with the western side (Schnell 1930; Åkerlund 1996b; Broström 1996; Hammar & Wikell 1994, 1996: Pettersson 1994). The uneven distribution map seemed problematic. Similar settings for the Stone Age could be found on the eastern side (and at other places along the entire coast of eastern central Sweden), but with the important exception that there was no arable land (or archaeologists) at the levels that were relevant during the Stone Age. Eastern Södertörn is an upland, wooded area with a low degree of cultivation. Could the absence be the result of insufficient surveying? Extensive surveys since the 1990s have resulted in a large number of sites in an area that was formerly almost without finds. The good results of the surveys inspired continued efforts in other areas along the coast, as well as in Kolmården, Vikbolandet, and Valdemarsvik in Östergötland. Special surveys looking for Stone Age traces achieved good

Fig. 1. Henrik Munthe, 1921, was here researching the Highest Coastline, loaded with his geologist's bag and levelling equipment, auger, and spade, riding his old bicycle. Photo G. Lundqvist, 5 June 1921 at the croft of Krogsfall, Tjärstad parish, Östergötland. Picture and caption from Lundqvist 1965:575.

results, and it seemed perfectly possible that the idea from Södertörn could be applied elsewhere (see Ericsson & Wikell, this volume).

A history of research

Stone Age research in north-east Östergötland began around 1900, when the Middle Neolithic settlement with rich finds of Pitted Ware material attracted attention. Birger Nerman, a native of Östergötland, did pioneering studies in Kolmården. On the basis of pottery styles on different settlement sites and their height above sea level he was able to propose a relative chronology for the pottery, at the Säter site (Nerman 1911, 1927). From Fagervik a similar sequence was put forward, Fagervik I–IV (Bagge 1951). More and more sites were discovered along the long, straight coast once archaeologists had learned which topographical locations were favourable for settlement. Today many Pitted Ware sites are known along the straight Kolmården coast. Pitted Ware sites are presumably just as numerous along the whole east coast of Sweden, as recent surveys have shown (Björck 1999, 2000; Björck & Guinard 2003; Niclas Björck pers. com.).

An important effort for the localization and publication of Stone Age sites in Kolmården was the work of the archaeologist Torsten Engström, who collaborated with the geologist Harald Thomasson. They found several of the sites known today (Engström 1932, 1934). They performed systematic investigations with test pits. An important part of the work entailed carefully assessing the height of the settlement sites above sea level. Several higher aceramic sites were discovered, characterized by stone axes. The rich occurrence of quartz was also noticed. Quartz was found at lower levels and could sometimes be explained as remains from tempering of pottery. On the higher sites, presumed to be older and formerly in littoral locations, this explanation could not be correct. They suggested that the numerous pieces of quartz were tools or remains of tool manufacture: "If quartz does not seem suitable for the retouch treatment of flint technology, this was not necessary, since razor-sharp edges could be obtained by knapping. A piece of quartz from which splinters were struck seems to suggest that this may have occurred on the site. The large number of sherds on the settlement sites may mean merely that dull tools were discarded, since the supply of raw material was copious" (Engström 1935:36). They make comparisons with the quartz-dominated Stone Age in Finland (Ailio 1909).

A longer passage from Engström's work on the Mesolithic settlement site at Majstorp, Krokek parish, deserves to be quoted in its entirety, since it shows what a fine ability to assess the landscape and interpret the terrain they acquired during their fieldwork: "The location in the innermost part of the north shore of a former bay of the sea was ideal. The height to the north afforded protection, and areas of rock to the west and east framed a shallow beach. There was a good supply of fresh water, as two streams had their outflow in the area" (Engström 1935:22).

An important theory on which scholars in eastern central Sweden, have long based their work is that settlement sites were mostly shore-bound (De Geer 1896; Hollender 1901). Both disciplines, archaeology and Quaternary geology, have cooperated closely right up until the present day because of their points of contact (Olsson 1992; Olsson & Risberg 1996; Åkerlund 1996a; Hammar & Risberg 2002).

In 1916 Uno Sundelin conducted Quaternary geological studies of levels and of the Stone Age in the south part of Östergötland's east coast (Ericsson & Wikell, this volume). The collaboration between the archaeologist Engström and the geologist Thomasson was fruitful (Engström & Thomasson 1932). The Quaternary geologist Henrik Munthe was assiduous in mapping different phases in the history of the Baltic Sea. He did work in Östergötland, where he devoted studies to his pet interest, the Ancylus Lake (Munthe 1940), fig. 1. The Quaternary geologist Erik Nilsson likewise mapped different shore levels in the field, including Kolmården, where the Ancylus limit was placed at just over 80 m above sea level (Nilsson 1953, see fig. 4). Sten and Maj-Britt Florin, archaeologist and geologist respectively, were a husband and wife team; they were most active in Södermanland, working a great deal with the levels of the Littorina Sea (Florin, S. 1944). A model of shoreline displacement for Östergötland has been drawn up by Persson and Svantesson (1972), based on material from Kolmården. The problem of shoreline displacement and the coastal location of settlement sites were important questions in Agneta Åkerlund's doctoral dissertation (1996a), which had Kolmården and Vikbolandet among the case studies. Recent efforts include the project "Man in the Early Landscape" (Åkerlund *et al.* 2002). This also involved a preliminary Quaternary geological study by the archaeologist Dag Hammar and the Quaternary geologist Jan Risberg (2002), focusing on levels of the Ancylus Lake in Kolmården.

There has been criticism that a one-sided concentration on the landscape could be essentialist, that is, an unreflecting attitude to research, forgetting the actual object of study: human beings (Lindgren 2004:84ff.). The risk is obvious if scholars content themselves with studying the landscape but, as Lindgren also states, the environment is important for our understanding of the Mesolithic. It can otherwise be incomprehensible why we see the settlement pattern we see, if we do not know the main features in the development of the landscape and climate. The shore displacement in eastern central Sweden is part of this fundamental and essential knowledge. The natural landscape is the scene on which society acted, influenced by a multitude of factors. The cultural landscape depends on a series of active choices made by the Mesolithic societies (Åkerlund 1996a). As we shall see in the following, shoreline displacement is highly significant, since Mesolithic man lived close to the waterside in a maritime economy and culture. We can imagine not knowing anything about Holocene landscape development. How would the finds be interpreted then? Stone axes were believed long ago to be Thor's thunderbolts – atmospheric phenomena which could give protection against lightning strikes, and quartz was not seen at all. We now know that this was wrong, but it was considered "true" in its day.

Palaeogeography

Eastern central Sweden consists of a lowland, today's Östergötland and the Mälaren valley. It is surrounded by forested areas which are quite elevated for the region, such as Holaveden in south, Tiveden and Kilsbergen in the west. In the north the forests of Bergslagen start. Even in the lowland zone there are occasional areas of elevated forests, Kolmården being one of the distinctive examples. These landscape features are the scene constituted by eastern central Sweden. The shoreline displacement after the Ice Age created an incredibly rich and constantly changing landscape, an archipelago of many islands.

The investigation area in north-east Östergötland takes its character from the fissure valleys that break it up. There are both small and large valleys. The dramatic features include the striking fault slopes, of which there are several in eastern central Sweden. Gigantic "plates" of the crystalline basement have become imbalanced, with the result that the edge of one plate sticks up higher than another. The result is elevated areas of rock and steep slopes – today's inaccessible forested areas in easternmost central Sweden. They are visible as long, straight "walls" in the landscape. The large blocks of crystalline basement are cut in several directions by the fissure valleys. The landscape is dramatic despite the fact that, geologically speaking, it is a wholly eroded bedrock plain. The frequent variations in altitude on a small scale have formed a labyrinth of spaces from a human perspective.

Kolmården is dramatic by the standards of central Sweden. The south wall of the fault is particularly noticeable, today reaching about 120 m above sea level, almost directly out of the sea. It is rare to find such differences in height anywhere else in eastern central Sweden. This east–west "wall" is cut by a series of valleys, mostly filled with washed sand from former shores. This is also where the streams are found. Vikbolandet is more low-key in character. The differences in altitude are not so large. The area has constituted a well-formed archipelago. We are actually in the middle of a plate of crystalline basement, which because of its low elevation is completely filled with loose washed sediment. The greatest heights are found at the fault in the south, which slopes steeply down to the Slätbaken bay. Vikbolandet is a less dramatic copy of the Kolmården area.

The mosaic of heights and valleys is an essential feature of the archipelago landscape that eastern Östergötland has been since the earliest times. Since the last glaciation relinquished its hold on eastern central Sweden, there has been a continuous displacement of the shoreline. The high fracture level and the uplift are the reasons for the changing and constantly expanding archipelago landscape. Thousands of islands, rocks, and skerries have come into being, and the waters around them – fjords, straits, and bays – have changed their shape.

The people who lived in this landscape had access to a rich coastal environment, where sheltered shores along bays and long straits along the steep Kolmården side offered good locations for settlement sites. In the south Vikbolandet was a rich archipelago.

Implementation of the survey

The focused surveys that we conducted in Kolmården and Vikbolandet took place in different stages during the 1990s and continued until recently. The author, together with Dag Hammar, has done most of the surveys. There was close collaboration with Agneta Åkerlund as part of the work on her doctoral dissertation (1996a), which was carried out in 1993 and 1994 (Åkerlund 1994; 1996a). This was followed up by the project "Man in the Early Landscape", where the archaeologist Helena Andersson also participated (Andersson & Hammar 2002). The latest, but certainly not the last, effort was in the late autumn of 2004. This was a category survey by two excavation departments of the National Heritage Board, UV Mitt and UV Öst, before the construction of the Ostlänken railway line, conducted by the author and Fredrik Molin (Beckman-Thoor et al. 2003; Kihlstedt & Wikell in prep).

The surveys were preceded by a run-through of available archives such as the Register of Ancient Monuments, the Antiquarian Topographical Archives, and museum catalogues. Relevant literature on the area was acquired, along with topographical and economic maps and, where possible, orienteering maps. Geological maps with their accompanying descriptions were also studied, mainly to learn about the distribution of soils.

The method used in the field was the one we applied in Södertörn: intensive field survey by bicycle, and sleeping in tents. The advantage of this close-to-the-landscape approach is: "you can make your way, for example, on paths and roads even if they are blocked by bars. Being close to the landscape also makes it easier to interpret" (Andersson & Hammar 2002:31), fig. 2. The most recent survey was done by car because of external circumstances. The short time, at most three weeks in a row, did not permit any all-embracing area surveys. Instead we selected different settings, on the basis of the existing picture of antiquities, soils, and topography, and in particular the questions asked by Åkerlund (1996a). Places with ground damage were sought out: windfallen trees, paths, road cuts, tracks left by forestry machines, ploughed clearings, gravel quarries, and – where possible – open arable land. Test pits were not dug except in exceptional cases.

Fig. 2. In the field in Kolmården, 1993. From left to right: Picture 1. The author is crossing the stream Pinneström, the medieval border between Södermanland and Östergötland. Along Pinneström there are five settlement sites. Picture 2. Dag Hammar mends a puncture at the base camp. Photos: National Heritage Board.

Trowels were brought along for small-scale cleaning of ground damage. At the latest survey a pickaxe was used and test pits were dug, a very efficient method (Kihlstedt 1993; Bondesson 2002; Björck & Guinard 2003). The finds were marked on maps, described, and reported to the Register of Ancient Monuments.

The working hypothesis was that sites were mainly on the sea shore. Experience of previous investigations indicated that most sites were close to the shore (Åkerlund 1996a, b). Of course there are many exceptions, especially in view of the fact that Kolmården was a large peninsula during much of the Mesolithic. It would be strange if there had not been any activity further inland, away from the coast (Färjare 1999; Molin manuscript; see also Ericsson & Wikell, this volume).

A total of two months' surveying was done in Kolmården, and two weeks in Vikbolandet. The emphasis in Kolmården was on the northern shore of the Bråviken bay. In the course of the survey we also established good contacts with the local people, who were able to tell us about places where stone axes had been found, both supplementary details about already known finds and previously unknown information. People in the district remembered Torsten Engström (1935). He had shown potsherds and talked about the Stone Age in the school in Krokek. An old gentleman with a good memory also recalled "the Nerman boys" (Nerman 1911). We were thus moving "in Torsten Engström's footprints", which was also the title of Åkerlund's first article from the work in Kolmården (Åkerlund 1994).

Results and discussion

The surveys resulted in the discovery of about 50 new sites of Mesolithic character in Kolmården and 13 in Vikbolandet. The finds on the presumed Mesolithic sites are dominated by quartz, followed by varying amounts of worked greenstone, sandstone, and rock. The artefacts in these categories are often axes, grindstones, and hammerstones. Among the axes we found both pecked axes and other axes of more occasional character, but very like pecked axes, in certain cases quadrilateral and fully polished examples.

Very little flint was found, chiefly at lower levels, during the Late Mesolithic and at Middle Neolithic levels. Slate has also been discovered on the latter levels. We found fire-cracked stone too, both together with other finds, mainly quartz, and also on its own, not in the context of other remains. Occurrences of just fire-cracked stone are not infrequently found in larger areas of sand, sometimes completely flat.

The focused surveys show that there is a rich Mesolithic cultural landscape in Kolmården and Vikbolandet, as in other elevated forests of eastern central Sweden. If these were archipelagos, there is a great likelihood of finding settlement site remains. Since people preferred to establish settlement sites by the water, they constantly moved to new locations as the shoreline moved downwards and the old site became unfavourable. This leaves a great many settlement sites, and in practice we do not have a single Mesolithic cultural landscape, but several successive ones. As the changing landscape expanded, new virgin archipelagos were claimed. It seems as if people were highly prepared to be mobile in this landscape. The colonization of new shores was an integral part of the society, a pattern of culture if you will (for further discussion see Knutsson H. 1995; Åkerlund et al. 1995; Åkerlund 1996a; Pettersson & Wikell 2004).

Quartz was an important part of everyday life in the region during the Mesolithic. Knapping quartz was part of the cultural pattern. Of course people had a constant need for good new tools, as the old ones became worn and were discarded. But we can suspect that it was more than just the function of sharp-edged flakes for scraping and cutting edges that people wanted. The copious, almost extravagant, amount of worked quartz is sometimes overwhelming.

In a life with seasonal mobility between natural resources and social contacts, many places in the landscape are visited. One may ask how many places a person managed to visit during one year. At how many places did they knap quartz during one year, or during a lifetime? There were many generations of quartz-smiths in eastern central Sweden during the 4,000 years when quartz was in frequent use. With a very low estimate, if we reckon that one person worked quartz once a year in a new place, we would thus hypothetically have 4,000 quartz sites in eastern central Sweden. New (settlement) sites were moreover created as new shores were formed. Since a culture is carried by many people, we may suspect that the number of sites in the landscape was very large.

A cultural landscape with many sites

The number of quartz sites in the Mesolithic archipelagos of eastern central Sweden is likely to be very large. Focused surveys, preliminary archaeological investigations and excavations in different areas have yielded the following figures, counting from south to north: Valdemarsvik 14 sites, Vikbolandet 13, Linköping 20, Motala 7, Kolmården 50, Ostlänken 50, Hälleforsnäs 30, south-eastern Närke 21, Åker 10, Ösmo 9, northwest Södertörn 50, Tullinge etc. 110, Käglan 20, Västmanland 300, Sala 5, and Stormossen 18. This is a total of 727 newly discovered sites in eastern central Sweden. This list does not claim to be complete, merely to indicate that as soon as efforts are directed towards the Stone Age, there is a very good chance of finding something. This is underlined by all the already known settlement sites. To this should also be added the large number of registered stone axes. As we saw above, the distribution of the old finds is uneven on account of the uneven archaeological work. An advantage of the new finds is that they have a more even coverage. They thus indicate (together with the axes) that the Stone Age can be expected in many places in the whole of eastern central Sweden.

The new findings confirm the focused surveys conducted in eastern Södertörn, where the systematic accumulation of knowledge about the Mesolithic cultural landscape has resulted in 1,000 new sites (Pettersson & Wikell 2004). Virtually all are found within one sheet of the topographical map, Stockholm SO. Moreover, this result is an underestimation. The severe forest fire in Tyresta National Park in 1999 burnt all the vegetation and litter. The mineral soil was exposed. After the autumn rain the white quartz was very clearly seen against the blackened ground. Some 130 sites were found within an area of about 2 km². Before this, only eight sites were known. Calculations of the density of settlement sites based on Tyresta and the above-mentioned places in Södertörn (Tullinge etc.), give us a figure of at least 2,000–10,000, indeed, perhaps as many as 20,000 sites in eastern Södertörn (Pettersson & Wikell 2004; this statement should be seen as a correction to the second last (incomplete) sentence in that work: 2004:467). See fig. 3. It must be stressed that these numbers are estimates based on only four sample areas. Perhaps the estimates are wrong in calculating km²; instead the available shoreline in a highly fractured landscape would be more appropriate. Anyhow, the hypothetical and roughly estimated number of sites is given to force and provoke the reader to be aware of the very site-rich settlement pattern in eastern central Sweden.

Pioneers

The large number of sites and the ample quantities of quartz are a challenge both for archaeologists and for the authorities in charge of cultural heritage management (Selinge 1989:19; Trotzig 1993). What we can already see in the material is that there is a great span. This applies to the localization in the landscape, the content and frequency of finds, the size of the habitable area. The divisions into large and small settlement sites that have

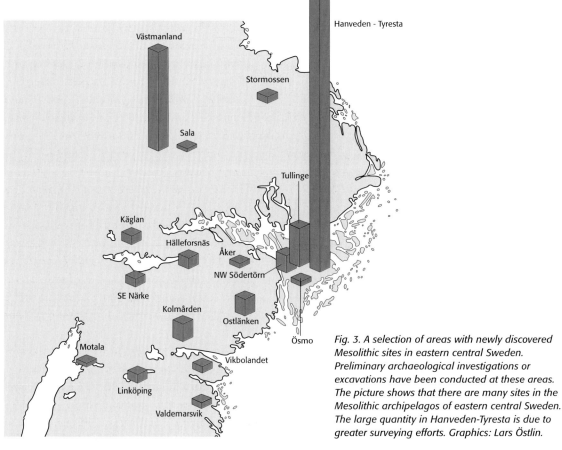

Fig. 3. A selection of areas with newly discovered Mesolithic sites in eastern central Sweden. Preliminary archaeological investigations or excavations have been conducted at these areas. The picture shows that there are many sites in the Mesolithic archipelagos of eastern central Sweden. The large quantity in Hanveden-Tyresta is due to greater surveying efforts. Graphics: Lars Östlin.

Valdemarsvik 14 (Ericsson & Wikell, this volume)
Vikbolandet 13 (Åkerlund 1996a)
Linköping 20 (Molin in prep. and pers. com.)
Motala 7 (Molin 2000 and this volume)
Kolmården 50 (Åkerlund 1996a; Andersson & Hammar 2002; Nilsson 2004; Rolöf 2005;
 Kihlstedt & Wikell in prep.; Fredrik Molin pers. com.)
Ostlänken 50 (Kihlstedt & Wikell in prep.)
SE Närke 21 (Luthander & Pettersson 2002)
Hälleforsnäs 30 (Asplund & Wikell 2002, Wikell in prep.)
Åker 10 (Patrik Gustafsson in prep. and pers. com.)
Ösmo 9 (Isaksson et al. 2003; Ahlbeck et al. 2005; Mattias Ahlbeck, pers. com.; Mikael Isaksson pers. com.)
NW Södertörn 50 (Broström 1996 and pers. com.)
Tullinge etc. in northern Södertörn 110 (Bondesson 2001, 2002, 2003, 2004; Granath Zillén 2001;
 Olsson & Runeson 1999; Kihlstedt 1993, 1992; Schierbeck 1996; Ahlbeck et al. 2004; Wivianne Bondesson pers. com.)
Hanveden-Tyresta 1,000 (Hammar & Wikell 1994, 1996; Pettersson 1996, 1999; Wikell 2002; Pettersson & Wikell 2004)
Käglan 20 (Apel et al. unpublished; Arthursson, M. unpublished; Edenmo 1997; Luthander & Holm 1999;
 Antilla & Holm in prep.; Graner & Luthander 2005; Jenny Holm pers. com.; Lars Sundström pers. com.)
Västmanland 300 (Löthman, L. 1993; Sven-Gunnar Broström pers. com.)
Sala 5 (Holm 2001; Ählström 2002; Skanser 2004)
Stormossen 18 (Björck & Guinard 2003; Guinard & Eriksson 2004, 2005 & pers. com.)

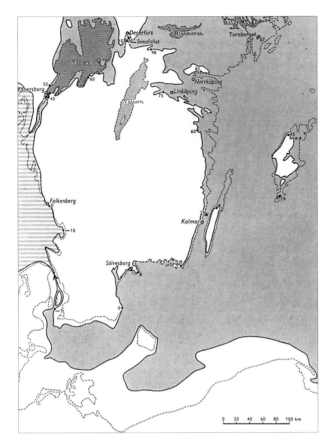

Fig. 4. The Ancylus Lake. The presumed first colonizers of eastern central Sweden arrived at this time (9000 BP), but it is likely that there are older traces. The map should be regarded as a model of one phase in the stages of the Baltic Sea. The Ancylus Lake has not yet been satisfactorily investigated, and many important questions remain to be resolved. The picture is thus somewhat out of date, but it still illustrates the situation, albeit with one serious defect: the rich archipelago landscape in the region is not shown. After Erik Nilsson 1953:209.

hitherto been suggested seem far too general. The Mesolithic in eastern central Sweden may at first sight seem abstract with the ever-present quartz. The different sites with their differing character suggest that we have here a dynamic cultural landscape, a landscape that was used for 4,000 years, from the presumed first colonizers in the early postglacial phase, to the transition to the Neolithic. Quartz is found abundantly in the area and was used right from the beginning. By the very beginning is meant the highest levels in the landscape where the newly discovered sites are. In Södertörn they are just over 80 m above sea level, in Kolmården at 85 m above sea level. When dated by means of the shoreline this means an age of 9000 BP in Södertörn (Risberg 2003:xlvi, fig. 2; Åkerlund *et al.* 1995). They are thus roughly comparable with the early sites of Mörby, Högby, and Lilla Åby in western Östergötland. These mainland sites have been dated to *c.* 9000 BP (Kaliff *et al.* 1997; Appelgren 1995; Carlsson and Molin, this volume). No finds have been encountered above these levels, despite repeated efforts (which does not mean that they do not exist). In Kolmården especially there are many suitable sites and areas which, if they had been at a lower level, would have yielded finds. The distribution of finds, material, etc. is another argument suggesting that the settlement sites as a rule are situated close to the shore. The level of the highest finds can perhaps be linked to the levels of the suggested Ancylus transgression (Munthe 1940; Nilsson 1953; Andersson & Hammar 2002; Risberg & Hammar 2002). Erik Nilsson describes the Ancylus limit thus: "The highest location adopted by the Ancylus Lake at this transgression is marked by an often very beautifully formed shoreline in the form of large shore cuts or huge beach ridges" (Nilsson 1953:205). See figs. 1 and 4. In Kolmården finds have been made beside a noticeable beach ridge at 85–90 m above sea level. These are the sites of Rothult and Skottsätter, Krokek parish (Objects 1 and 2, Andersson &

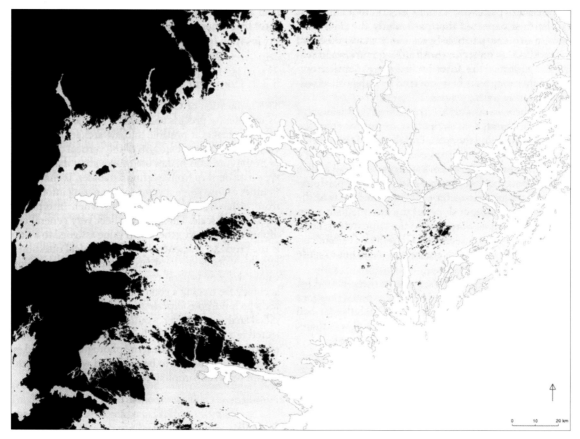

Fig. 5. The Ancylus Lake, 75 m above sea level. Map based on contour lines on modern maps. Note that the coastlines to the north and south as shown on the map are not contemporary because of differing uplift in the region. The contour 75 m above sea level represents the shoreline at c. 9000 BP in Södertörn, the Outermost Archipelago in the east. There are now maps which take into consideration the differences in uplift but they do not as yet have such high resolution. This map clearly shows the high fracture structure in the fissure valley landscape of eastern central Sweden. There are many shores in a landscape like this. Reading maps is a process of interpretation. (After Åkerlund 1996a:120.)

Hammar 2002:30–31). They are protected in withdrawn locations, resembling the situation in Hanveden and Tyresta, likewise occupied by presumed pioneers in an archipelago (Pettersson & Wikell 2004). In Hanveden this level is dated by means of the shoreline to *c.* 9000 BP (Risberg 2003:xlvi, fig. 2). See fig. 4.

The focus on the shore and the sea is a recurrent theme in the Mesolithic cultural landscape in easternmost central Sweden, that is, the parts that have been archipelago. Kolmården occupies an intermediate position in this respect. Since it is a large peninsula extending far into the then Littorina Sea, and earlier in the Ancylus period was an archipelago with large islands, the available inland area was considerable. Of course there are settlement sites in the interior of Kolmården which were not on the sea coast, the site at Gullvagnen being one example (Färjare 1999; Wikell 2002; see also Ericsson & Wikell, this volume). It is most likely that these can be found beside fresh water, such as lakes and streams. The surveying situation at the lakes in Kolmården was unfavourable. Vegetation often grows all the way down to the shores of the lake and there is thus little ground damage, so no finds can be made.

Conclusion

The newly discovered material from Kolmården and Vikbolandet, with the surrounding archipelagos, constitutes rich Mesolithic cultural landscapes. In the material can we study the course of colonization, right from the presumed first humans in early postglacial time to the continuous occupation of newly emerging archipelagos. The amount of sites, their varied content, both locally and regionally, will allow us in the future to study social organization and change in the long term. Thanks to the focused surveys a rich corpus of material has been obtained. In all the areas that we have surveyed, more Mesolithic sites have been discovered. It is obvious that the state of our sources suffers from a shortage of well-conducted surveys in large continuous areas throughout eastern central Sweden. Together with the fruitful results of recent years' excavations, there is good hope that the archaeological discussion of the Mesolithic in the region will be enhanced. The Mesolithic cultural landscape is rich, also when viewed in inter-regional or international perspective. In the elevated forests of eastern central Sweden, as in other areas around the coasts of the northern Baltic/Europe, there is a fossil marine cultural landscape from the Mesolithic, which is unusual in north-west Europe, where a great deal is under today's sea level.

Basically, we can say in reply to Kjel Knutsson's summary ten years ago: the east Swedish Mesolithic is no longer a blank page (Knutsson 1995:15). And Carl Cullberg was perfectly right in stating that more intensive research would bring to light a large number of sites (Cullberg 1980:431).

Newly discovered sites on the shores of the Littorina Sea

Alf Ericsson & Roger Wikell

The authors have conducted a focused survey of Stone Age sites in the Valdemarsvik district in Östergötland. The aim was to investigate whether flint or quartz dominates on the sites. It was possible to localize a number of settlements along the shores of the ancient Littorina Sea. The newly discovered sites are wholly dominated by knapped quartz, and several of them lay like small satellites around the Ämtöholm site, which has been known for a long time, with numerous finds of pecked stone axes. The Ämtö-holm site and several of the newly discovered small sites were presumably part of one and the same socio-economic system during the Mesolithic. The boundary between flint and quartz runs further south along the Baltic coast, probably between Oskarshamn and Kalmar.

Introduction

During one fine week in early September 1995, the authors and Dag Hammar conducted a special survey of Stone Age sites north and west of Valdemarsvik in Östergötland. The inspiration for the survey came from the specially focused surveys of Stone Age sites that was, and still is, in progress in Södertörn south of Stockholm.

Surveys in highland forested areas such as Hanveden and Tyresta in Södertörn have revealed many new Mesolithic sites. A rich and formerly unknown cultural landscape has thus been made visible. Provided that the sites are coastal, the pattern of settlement can be followed during the Mesolithic from early postglacial times to the transition to the Neolithic. A recurrent theme in this cultural landscape is the ever-present quartz. The quartz culture was well established already at the most elevated, and thereby presumably the earliest, settlement sites.

In southern Scandinavia and on the west coast flint was the predominant material throughout the Mesolithic. In Möre (the area around Kalmar) on the east coast, flint also occurs regularly on settlement sites. The aim of the survey was to investigate whether the boundary between flint and quartz ran in the Valdemarsvik district.

The Stone Age at Valdemarsvik

The picture of the Stone Age around Valdemarsvik was dominated early on by stray finds of stone axes (Gärme 1956; Hellman 1970:55ff.). These have often been found during farming work. Thanks to alert and interested people, the finds have then been made known to archaeologists. In many cases the stone axes can be the first thing that signals Mesolithic settlement sites since they are often at elevations above 25 m above sea level, which corresponds to the end of the Mesolithic. Several of the archaeologically known axes in Valdemarsvik are pecked stone axes, a type that chiefly occurs during the Mesolithic, but they are also well represented on Pitted Ware settlement sites in eastern central Sweden. The district around Valdemarsvik thus reveals a picture that we recognize from other areas along the east coast, such as Vikbolandet, Kolmården, and Södertörn (see also Wikell in this volume and works cited there).

A Mesolithic site that attracted attention early on is Ämtöholm in Ringarum parish (see fig 1, page 11, this volume) (Sundelin 1919; Hellman 1970:59ff.). The settlement site is located on the watershed in a fissure valley running north–south to the north of Valdemarsvik (fig. 1). Through ploughing and gravel quarrying in the late nineteenth century

Fig. 1. The Ämtöholm site is located on a glaciofluvial deposit (an esker) sticking out into a cultivated fen, formerly part of Lake Ämten. Photo from the north by Alf Ericsson.

and the twentieth century, many stone axes had been unearthed. When Uno Sundelin performed a Quaternary geological study in 1916 he observed in the gravel quarry a noticeable occupation layer of soot, charcoal, and fire-cracked stone overlayered with 0.2–0.5 m of sand. The settlement layer was between 36 and 37 m above sea level. Sundelin dug a trench below the settlement site, in the fen around the sunken lake of Ämten. Here he documented the profile of the layer sequence and performed pollen analyses which served as a basis for a discussion of changes in the Ancylus Lake and the Littorina Sea.

During its period of use the Ämtöholm site was in a highly favourable location for communications, between two narrow bays coming from north and south. The place resembles Middle and Late Mesolithic settlement sites in Södermanland. The Ämtöholm site, together with a fairly rich occurrence of pecked axes and Lihult and Limhamn axes in the vicinity (Hellman 1970:55ff.; Gärme 1956), indicated that there were good chances of finding more Mesolithic settlement sites here.

Earlier research also concentrated on the find-rich ceramic Neolithic sites, and the same applied to the area around Valdemarsvik. An excavation of the then newly discovered site at Lundby-Rosenlund in Gryt parish (Janse 1932) uncovered a rich assemblage of Pitted Ware, pecked axes, and other stone tools. The Middle Neolithic site is located between 18 and 23 m above sea level. When the settlement was in use it was on the northern mainland site of the Valdemarsviken fjord. On the opposite side, in Tryserum parish, there is a Pitted Ware settlement at Djurglo. Slightly further out in the archipelago, on the island of Stjärnö, which was much smaller then, there is yet another settlement from the same period (Hansson 1937; Einerstam 1957). About five kilometres to the south a Pitted Ware site was excavated in 1988 at Kurum (Gustafsson 1996). The settlement was on an island in what was then the inner archipelago. The Pitted Ware settlements are all on the coast, and their location suggests that much of the Mesolithic lifestyle persisted during the Neolithic (Guinard & Wikell 2003).

Palaeogeography

The specially surveyed area is wholly dominated by crystalline basement with narrow, clay-filled fissure valleys. The highest mountains reach just over 80 m above sea level. The investigation area is entirely under the Highest Coastline. The main fissure valleys run from north-west to south-east, but these are also crossed by smaller valleys. Where several fissure valleys meet there are small sediment basins. Along the valleys there is till and in places glaciofluvial deposits. At occasional spots there are larger areas of sand and fine sand, often washed from overlying till. There are also some eskers in the area, for instance in the above-mentioned north–south valley, which set their stamp on the area.

The fissure valleys sink gradually to the east, as a result of which the ongoing uplift has shifted the shore eastwards since the end of the Ice Age (fig. 2). The archipelago has constantly grown, moving eastwards. In all phases of prehistory the fissure valleys have formed a rich archipelago. Indeed, the fissure valley landscape is the very precondition for the extensive archipelago, with thousands of islands and skerries, and for all the long, narrow bays and fjords cutting deep into the land. The words of the archaeologist G. A. Hellman sum up the character of the landscape well: "Several small groups of islands occupied the area of the then coastline and thereby formed a rich archipelago with the huge Ancylus Lake as a fading horizon to the east" (Hellman 1970:53).

Scope and aim

The survey area covered 35 km^2 and was mostly located in the parish of Ringarum in Östergötland, but with an offshoot in the parish of Tryserum in Småland. According to today's administrative boundaries, the area lies wholly within the municipality of Valdemarsvik and the county of Östergötland.

The aim was thus to investigate whether the boundary between flint and quartz on the east coast could be found in the neighbourhood of Valdemarsvik. It is likely that the quartz/flint boundary runs somewhere between Kolmården/Vikbolandet in the north and Möre in the south (Åkerlund 1996a; Carlsson *et al.* 2003). Could it be discovered in the investigation area, or does it run a little further to the south? Quartz predominates in Vikbolandet, in Kolmården, and northwards along the coast of eastern central Sweden (Lindgren & Nordqvist 1997; Lindgren 2004; Hammar & Wikell 1994, 1996; Åkerlund *et al.* 1995, 2003; Pettersson & Wikell 2004). Flint, by contrast, is found in Möre, both as Ordovician flint from Öland, and to a certain extent as south Scandinavian flint. Otherwise there are also local rocks in the material, such as porphyry and quartzite (Alexandersson 2000; Hagberg 1979; Gurstad-Nilsson 1993; Knutsson 1998; Rosberg & Sarnäs 1992:34; Werthwein 2000; Westergren & Hansson 1987).

Since Stig Welinder's studies in the 1970s, the *flint group* and the *quartz group* that he discussed have been debated in research on the Mesolithic of eastern central Sweden. Welinder (1977:57–60) defines the flint group on the basis of material and technique. The most important characteristics are flint or local rocks that behave similarly when reduced. These were chiefly used for making microblades from handle cores. The flint group was dated to 5000–4000 BC and had contacts with the Lihult culture on the west coast. The quartz group, on the other hand, is wholly characterized by the locally available quartz. There are few tools in a formal sense. Handle cores and microblades are absent. The axes are typically pecked axes. The quartz group was assumed to have lacked a large network of contacts and was dated to 5000–2500 BC.

With the improved knowledge of recent decades, chiefly due to archaeological excavations, it has proved difficult to find pure settlement sites according to Welinder's definition (Lindgren & Nordqvist 1997:30–32). Hans Kindgren (1991:58) criticizes the division into two groups on the grounds that different areas on settlement sites show an uneven spread of material. Instead Kindgren thinks that the Mesolithic of eastern central

*Fig. 2. Valdemarsviken from Lejonberget in Valdemarsvik.
This is how the Mesolithic landscape in the investigation area
may have looked before the fissure valleys dried out.
Photo from the west by Alf Ericsson.*

Sweden is like that of western Sweden, but with the difference that quartz instead of flint is the foundation of the lithic culture. Agneta Åkerlund (1996a:37) finds it strange that both the flint group and the quartz group managed to occupy virtually the same places in Welinder's small corpus of just six sites.

The eastern archipelago area, chiefly the peninsula of Södertörn south of Stockholm, seems from the excavated material to belong to the quartz group in so far as quartz dominates there and no microblades were manufactured. Occasional microblades are found, but they were brought there as ready-made tools. Judging by the increased find material, the manufacture of microblades by means of handle cores seems largely to have taken place on what was then the mainland. The flint and quartz groups thus seem to have been geographically separate and could more appropriately be called the *mainland group* and the *archipelago group* (Lindgren 1997:30–32, 2003, 2004; Åkerlund 2000; Carlsson *et al.* 2003; Holm 2003b). In the extensive surveys conducted in Södertörn, handle cores and microblades are likewise notably absent.

The flint and quartz groups have thus gradually been replaced in research with a mainland group which regularly made microblades, and an archipelago group chiefly characterized by quartz. The distribution of the material is in part chronological. The quartz group is older and existed from at least 8000 BC. The handle cores have mostly been associated with Late Mesolithic settlement sites, partly based on what is known from research on the west coast. Recent finds suggest that handle cores are almost as early there as in southern Scandinavia (Larsson 2003:xxvii; Kindgren & Schaller Åhrberg 1999:231). In eastern central Sweden too there are finds indicating that handle cores were introduced early on (Knutsson *et al.* 1999; see also Molin, this volume).

The basis of the lithic culture, both on the mainland and in the archipelago, was nevertheless quartz. As a result, there have been few natural points of contact with Mesolithic research in southern Scandinavia and western Sweden. Scholars of southern Scandinavia have shown little understanding of the eastern Swedish quartz-based culture. The reception of Stone Age research in eastern central Sweden has suffered from the paucity of typological elements and – until recent years – from the lack of large-scale excavations and securely ^{14}C-dated settlement sites (Larsson 1990, 2003).

Method, definitions, and strategy

The survey was conducted during a week in September 1995. The participants camped in tents and made their way by car through the landscape in search of terrain suitable for fieldwalking. No test pits were dug, but trowels were brought along for simple cleaning operations in windfallen trees and road cuts.

Before the fieldwork started, an overall view of the topography of the investigation area was obtained from the economic and topographical maps. The soil map was also studied, along with the national Register of Ancient Monuments (RAM) maintained by the National Heritage Board and relevant literature. The strategy was to visit suitable site locations along the valleys, such as ledges and patches between rock. On the basis of the process of shoreline displacement it was considered that levels below 20 m above sea level were not relevant for the Stone Age. Since there is not much cultivated land in the investigation area, and what there is mainly consists of clay soils in valley bottoms, it was obvious that the survey could not be confined to open, low-lying arable land. Instead we had to systematically examine areas of land which were open for reasons other than tillage. Examples of these are gravel quarries, road cuts, paths with damage caused by wear and erosion, windfallen trees, scarified areas in forest, etc. There was high-lying arable land in the area, but for reasons of physical geography this was exceptional. The type of soil did not dictate the choice of places to survey, nor did the direction the places faced. Altitude above sea level is stated in terms of the contours on the economic map, which are five metres equidistant. Sites discovered were marked on the economic map, so the elevation above sea level in the following account cannot be stated more accurately than between the contours on the map.

A working hypothesis was that the settlement sites were mainly on the coast. A chrono-logical boundary for the possible presence of flint could then be obtained based on coastline datings. Certain levels, perhaps the highest ones, could contain flint, which can be interpreted as showing that the first colonizers primarily brought flint with them. Did they then stick to flint after they became established in the area, or did they later switch to quartz?

At the very highest levels in eastern central Sweden (Södertörn) the lithic material is wholly dominated by quartz. The highest settlement sites around 80–85 m above sea level are dated by the shoreline to just before 8000 BC (Risberg 2003). If the first humans came from the strictly flint-based cultures in the south and west, the transition in the material from flint to quartz could possibly be seen at Valdemarsvik. All the contour levels that were coastal during the Mesolithic were surveyed.

If a location was to be registered as a *Stone Age settlement site* (Swedish *boplats*) we had to discover at least five finds of Stone Age character in a good spot for a settlement site. The finds could consist of flakes, cores, artefacts, etc. A good spot for a settlement site means a favourable local environment in terms of land uplift and drainage. The occurrence of fire-cracked stone reinforced the assessment of a place as a Stone Age settlement site but was not an independent criterion. Places with single finds were classed as *find sites* (Swedish *fyndplats*). It can be an antiquarian problem that places with few finds are not given the status of settlement sites. There is an obvious risk that we miss an important aspect of the Mesolithic cultural landscape. Our experience from Södertörn is that places with few finds are numerous. In addition, the chances of discovering more than one find in a place are often highly limited, since ground damage in forest is not always of the kind that an archaeologist might wish.

During the 1990s there was discussion of how one should handle places with small quantities of finds, based on the content of the Mesolithic cultural landscape in Södertörn (Jakobsson & Kihlstedt 1995; Kihlstedt 1996). In several cases archaeologists in the 1990s followed the minimum criterion of at least two artefacts for a "settlement site" in the broadest sense of the term. This may seem small, but for anyone unfamiliar with the landscape in eastern central Sweden it may be useful to know that the Mesolithic finds are encountered in high-lying forested areas. These areas have had the character of outland since the Bronze Age. It does not seem likely that anyone in modern times would have scattered large quantities of quartz or flint. During the Mesolithic today's high-lying, rocky forests were extensive archipelagos. Since we often come across the finds in similar locations, albeit with great variation, it is not probable that we happened to discover an arrowhead (of little interest for research) in the place where it landed. The spots in the Mesolithic cultural landscape with small quantities of finds are important pieces in the jigsaw puzzle that we are trying to fit together (Pettersson & Wikell 2004).

Results

The investigation area was difficult to survey in places. Early September is not the optimal time, since the fields as a rule are not ploughed. Fieldwalking on arable land should preferably be done some time after the autumn ploughing, so that the rain has been able to wash clean any finds on the surface. Moreover, the summer vegetation is still growing in the forest, which impairs visibility. September can also be warm. The best conditions for surveying are instead late autumn and early spring, when the rain has done its job and vegetation is not an obstacle. We make no claims to have conducted a complete survey. On the contrary, we had too little time at our disposal to obtain a detailed picture. The results be regarded as a promising outline; more Mesolithic remains will no doubt be discovered in the future.

There were plenty of good settlement site locations, but few of them had ground damage or other open areas. Within the investigation area we registered 13 new sites (fig. 3). All of them have been entered in the RAM. Six of them are Stone Age settlement sites and seven are find sites with objects of Stone Age character. In addition, we discovered one Stone Age settlement site (RAM 210) outside the investigation area in connection with an excursion to the Pitted Ware settlement site at Lundby-Rosenlund in Gryt parish, excavated in the 1920s (Janse 1932). For a full account of the results of the survey the reader is referred to Ericsson & Wikell in preparation.

RAM 210 is located in Gluttskogen, about 1.5 km north of the Pitted Ware settlement site. The former settlement site is on a north-facing slope sheltered between two mountains (fig. 4). While RAM 210 is at 35–40 m above sea level, the Pitted Ware site is between 18 and 23 m above sea level. RAM 210 in Gluttskogen agrees well with the other newly discovered sites in the investigation area.

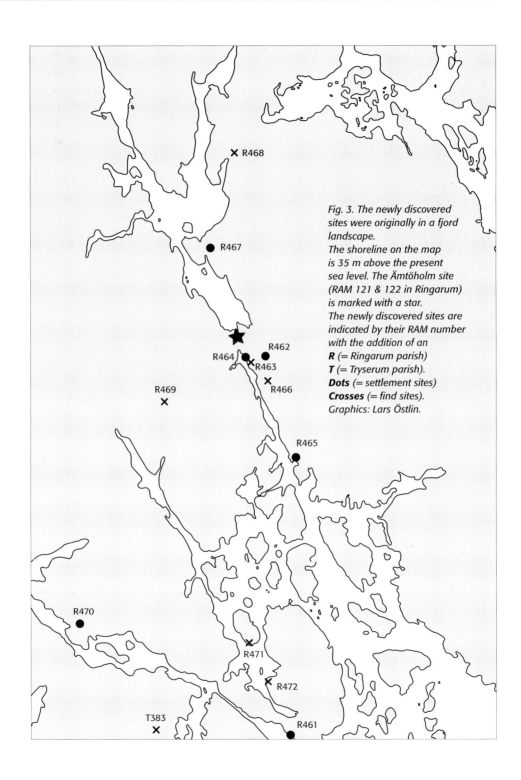

Fig. 3. The newly discovered sites were originally in a fjord landscape.
The shoreline on the map is 35 m above the present sea level. The Ämtöholm site (RAM 121 & 122 in Ringarum) is marked with a star.
The newly discovered sites are indicated by their RAM number with the addition of an
R (= Ringarum parish)
T (= Tryserum parish).
Dots (= settlement sites)
Crosses (= find sites).
Graphics: Lars Östlin.

Fig. 4. The settlement site RAM 210 in Gluttskogen, Gryt parish. In the road cut, in a windfallen tree, and in ground damage caused by a forestry machine the survey retrieved 18 finds of knapped quartz, including two cores. Photo from the north by Alf Ericsson.

A total of 93 finds were retrieved during the survey. These consist almost exclusively of knapped quartz. Exceptions are a flake of flint (south Scandinavian), three flakes or flake fragments of rock, and a grindstone fragment of sandstone. The major part (64%) of the quartz consists of debitage or debris. This is followed by flake fragments (16%) and flakes (11%). Cores account for the smallest share (9%).

For almost 40% of the objects (39 items) it has been possible to identify the method of reduction. The flint flake and one of the rock flakes were made using platform technique. Of the quartz flakes and flake fragments, twice as many (19) were made with platform technique as with bipolar technique (10). Of the eight cores, six were knapped with bipolar technique and two with platform technique. On all the sites except one (RAM 461 in Ringarum) both platform technique and bipolar technique are found. Four pieces of quartz have a rough surface and presumably come from nodules of till. Just one piece of quartz, a flake fragment, has retouches. The material thus resembles quartz from other areas in eastern central Sweden, that is to say, locally extracted quartz and few formal tools.

The sites are located between the contours 25–30 and 60–65 m above sea level (fig. 5). Most of them, however, are between 35–40 and 50–55 m above sea level, which corresponds well to the shore of the Littorina Sea in the Middle and Late Mesolithic. Exceptions to this pattern are the lowest and the highest sites. The former is the find spot (RAM 471 in Ringarum) of a grindstone fragment of sandstone. The low level (25–30 m above sea level) suggests that the find is not earlier than the Late Stone Age. The latter site is a place with fire-cracked stone (RAM 470 in Ringarum) located 60–65 m above sea level on a glaciofluvial deposit. The high level indicates either that it was a settlement on the shore of the Ancylus Lake or an inland site contemporary with the coastal sites of the Littorina Sea.

A reservation is in order here. On the Gullvagnen site in Kolmården quartz and fire-cracked stone ware found at 80 m above sea level (Färjare 1999; Wikell 2002). The ^{14}C dating gave an age corresponding to approximately 50 m above sea level. Gullvagnen is situated on a good ledge on a sandy slope above a lake. The location can perhaps be explained in terms of the proximity of the lake. In addition, we know from archaeological experience that eskers and sandy places have a tendency to be attractive in all periods. It is therefore not unusual that they were found attractive for various kinds of activities (Kihlstedt & Lindgren 1999; Granath Zillén 2001; Carlsson, this volume). A number of Early Mesolithic sites on sandy and gravelly ground in western Östergötland were revisited much later. The list of sites could be continued, but it is not necessary to name them here. The settlement site RAM 470 in Ringarum is enigmatic and alluring. How old could it be?

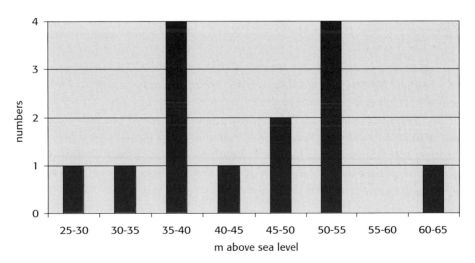

Fig. 5. The distribution of the sites at different levels (m above sea level). The distribution is bimodal with one peak around 35–40 and another around 50–55 m above sea level. Graphics: Lars Östlin.

If it was a coastal site it could represent a very old phase, and the small amount of material that was observed there consisted solely of quartz. Does this mean that the coastal area had already switched completely to quartz? Further west in Östergötland, at inland sites, there is a distinct element of flint, but quartz still dominates there (Carlsson in this volume and works cited there).

Regularly recurrent assemblages of finds at different levels can be explained on the basis of a hypothesis about coastal settlement sites. As the shoreline was displaced, settlement moved with it. This hypothesis has been an important tool in all the Stone Age research in eastern central Sweden (Åkerlund 1996a; Pettersson & Wikell 2004). The assumption has been essentially confirmed. It would otherwise be difficult to explain accumulations of finds, artefacts, and material at certain levels. There is really nothing in a modern forest-dominated landscape to reveal what height above sea level one is at. The large number of sites around the shores of the Littorina Sea in the investigation area agree very well with the results from Södertörn, Kolmården, and Vikbolandet. During the Atlantic period the Littorina Sea underwent a series of transgressions, or at least stopped its regression. Several settlement sites could then have been located at these levels, which is then reflected in the survey results. In Södertörn there are hundreds of sites at these levels, and the real figure could be several thousand (Pettersson & Wikell 2004).

It is not the case, however, that there are automatically many settlement sites just because the shore lay still at a particular level; there must also be people living near the coast and making copious use of quartz.

The majority of sites in the investigation area face south. There are some (3), however, oriented north. A position facing the sun was thus preferred but was not always the decisive factor in the choice of location. Glaciofluvial deposits are the most common foundation (58%), followed by washed sand (21%), and till (14%). There is only one find spot on clay. In view of how few glaciofluvial deposits there are in the investigation area, these must have been greatly preferred to other soil types. The north-facing sites RAM 462 in Ringarum and RAM 210 in Gryt are both on sand/fine sand. Alternative locations facing the sun were available on till soils but were evidently rejected. A reservation must be made here. Because of the short time and the season of the year, the survey was in no way all-embracing. In the quartz-dominated archipelago environments to the north along the Mesolithic coast there are many sites located on till soils (Pettersson & Wikell 2004).

Finally, let us consider our primary question: does the boundary between quartz and flint run in the neighbourhood of Valdemarsvik? The answer must be no. The boundary where flint begins to be used runs further south. The quartz sites that we found in the investigation area correspond well to the other quartz-dominated archipelago area further north on the east coast.

The inland settlement sites at Högby, Mörby, and Storlyckan in western Östergötland (Carlsson, this volume) have flint. Yet it is highly uncertain that they represent the start of the flint area. What is clear, however, is that they differ significantly from settlement sites in eastern Östergötland. The transition is perhaps vague, and it could have been different in different parts of the Mesolithic.

Recent surveys in the Oskarshamn district show that the boundary should be sought between that town and Kalmar (Michael Dahlin, pers. com.; see also Dahlin & Seward 2002; Dahlin 2004). A little further into the interior of Småland there is mixed lithic material, with quartz, porphyry, and flint (Gurstad-Nilsson 1993). In south-west Små-land (Finnveden) there are flint-dominated sites on the shore of the former Lake Bolmen. The flint objects found there are typical of the Maglemose culture (Pagoldh 1992, 1995; C. Persson 1997; J. Gustafsson manuscript). In some places some quartz has also been found, for example, at Nennesmo (J. Gustafsson manuscript). It is uncertain, however, whether the quartz belongs to the Mesolithic or a later period. Further south in Finnveden a site from the Early Mesolithic (later part) at Hamneda has been excavated and found to contain both quartz and flint. The flint was heavily exploited, which suggests a short-age. There is also a fragment of a conical core of quartz (Knarrström 2000b). Finally, at Lake Hjälmsjön in northern Skåne there is a quartz-dominated settlement site, which suggests that local groups towards the Småland highlands switched to quartz at an early stage (Karsten & Knarrström 1998).

Conclusion

The majority of the newly discovered sites at in the Valdemarsvik district can be associated with the shores of the Littorina Sea. The scale of settlement sites in the investigation area ranges from the large Ämtöholm site via small settlements to temporarily used places. Ämtöholm seems like a hub around which Stone Age life circled in the Littorina period. Ämtöholm appears to have been a central place of assembly. This is emphasized in particular by its optimal position on a watershed and by the quantity of finds, chiefly pecked axes. About 35 are known from reliable sources. In addition it is said that "a great many previous finds" have been scattered by the trade in antiquities (Sundelin 1919:15; Gärme 1956; Hellman 1970:60).

It would not be too bold to claim that at least 50 pecked axes have been found on the Ämtöholm site (fig. 6). This makes it one of the axe-rich settlement sites in eastern central Sweden from the Middle and Late Mesolithic (Lindgren & Nordqvist 1997; Lindgren 2004; Åkerlund *et al.* 2003). The Ämtöholm site thus also resembles to some extent the Late Mesolithic settlement site in Motala (various articles in this volume). Pecked axes in Södertörn often indicate an early dating, around 6000 BC (Lindgren 2004:48). This would agree well with the pecked axes from Ämtöholm, which have been dated by means of Sundelin's (1919) Quaternary geological study of shorelines to the

Fig. 6. Pecked stone axes from the Ämtöholm site. After Sundelin 1919.

early Littorina period. From this it follows that the sites we have found at higher levels (50–55 m above sea level) could very well have been situated at the Ancylus Lake.

A wide range of settlement sites from large to small, dominated by quartz and pecked axes in an archipelago environment, means that the Mesolithic around Valdemarsvik can be assigned to the *archipelago group* (formerly the quartz group) in eastern central Sweden. The find complex in a geographically limited area stands out as an independent "culture" characterized by a stubborn relationship to quartz. Pecked axes are likewise an indicator during much of the culture's existence, as are other axe types such as wholly polished axes with a narrow side (occurring during the Late Mesolithic), and a sporadic presence of Lihult axes and Limhamn axes (Lindgren 2004; Åkerlund *et al.* 2003). Also belonging to the picture are a large number of sites of varying size in archipelago environments.

The large number of sites at a particular level are probably dependent on the social organization. We can envisage several small groups moving within the area, where the small settlement sites correspond to some kind of working group or household. These groups assembled periodically at large settlement sites, centrally located with good communications and preferably rich resources to exploit (Larsson 1980:19; Lindgren 2004: 42ff.). These central settlement sites could possibly be viewed instead as more permanent hubs in the otherwise mobile life. It was here that people spent most of the year, and then made seasonal visits to the small sites in the surroundings. This classical question about the seasonality and functions of different sites is even more urgent. A well-founded answer, however, requires richer source material than we retrieved in our little survey. Above all, it is animal bones that can provide crucial information about which season a site was used in and for what purpose (Rowley-Conwy 1987).

Flint thus does not seem to have been essential material for tool manufacture in the hunting and fishing societies of the eastern central Swedish Mesolithic. Where exactly the transition between flint and quartz went along the east coast has not been ascertained, but we should probably search between Kalmar and Oskarshamn. A characteristic of the Mesolithic sites in Möre is that other rocks and minerals than flint, such as porphyry and quartzite, were used. On Early Mesolithic sites in western Östergötland there are quartz, flint, and local rocks. Local rocks also occur sometimes on the easterly quartz sites, but on a rather small scale. The Mesolithic in the Valdemarsvik district thus clearly belongs to the quartz-using coastal culture in eastern central Sweden.

Acknowledgements

The survey was carried out with the aid of a contribution from the Hildebrand Foundation; we would like to thank here the Swedish Antiquarian Society (Svenska fornminnesföreningen) for their benevolence.

References

A ___ **Aaris-Sørensen, K. 1988.** *Danmarks forhistoriske dyreverden: Fra istid til vikingetid.* Copenhagen.

Åberg, N. 1923. Kalmar läns förhistoria. *Södra Kalmar län* I. Kalmar.

Agrell, H. 1980. The Quaternary History of the Baltic. Sweden. In Gudelis, V. & Königsson, L.-K. (eds.), *The Quaternary History of the Baltic.* Acta Universitatis Upsaliensis. Symposia Universitatis Upsaliensis Annum Quingentesimum Celebrantis 1. Uppsala.

Ahlbeck, M. 1995. Kvartsiell afasi: Stenmaterialet från den gropkeramiska fyndplatsen Bollbacken utifrån ett processuellt kunskapsintresse. C-uppsats. Institutionen för Arkeologi, Uppsala universitet.

Ahlbeck, M., Blidmo, R., Holmgren, I. & Isaksson, M. 2003. *Undersökningsprogram för mesolitiska lämningar i östra Mellansverige.* Rapporter från Arkeologikonsult. Upplands Väsby. http://www.arkeologikonsult.se/.

Ahlbeck, M., Isaksson, M. & Fors, T. 2004. *Embryot 2: Mesolitiska aktivitetsytor i Flemingsberg.* Arkeologikonsult 2004:2002.

Ahlbeck, M., Isaksson, M., Fors, T. & Risberg. J. 2005. *Riksväg 73: Förundersökningar. Överförs–Västnora.* Rapporter från Arkeologikonsult 2005:10091, Arkeologiska förundersökningar längs Riksväg 73, Överfors–Västnora.

Ählström, J. 2002. *Väg 67/70, Förbifart Sala.* Västmanlands läns museum rapport 2002:A41. Västerås.

Ailio, J. 1909. *Die steinzeitlichen Wohnplatzfunde in Finnland* I–II. Helsinki.

Åkerlund, A. 1994. I Torsten Engströms fotspår – fler stenålderslokaler vid Bråvikens norra strand. *Arkeologi i Sverige*, Ny följd 3. Stockholm: Riksantikvarieämbetet.

Åkerlund, A. 1996a. *Human Responses to Shore Displacement: Living by the Sea in Eastern Middle Sweden during the Stone Age.* Riksantikvarieämbetet Arkeologiska Undersökningar Skrifter 16. Stockholm.

Åkerlund, A. 1996b. Testa strandförskjutningsmodeller och boplatsers strandbundenhet! In Bratt, P. (ed.), *Stenålder i Stockholms län: Två seminarier vid Stockholms läns museum.* Stockholm.

Åkerlund, A. 1999. "Som man ropar i skogen får man svar" ("As the question, so the answer"). In Andersson, K., Lagerlöf, A. & Åkerlund, A. (eds.), *Forskaren i fält: En vänbok till Kristina Lamm.* Riksantikvarieämbetet Arkeologiska Undersökningar Skrifter 27. Stockholm.

Åkerlund, A. 2000. Separate Worlds? Interpretation of the Different Material Patterns in the Archipelago and the Surrounding Mainlands of East-Central Sweden in the Stone Age. *European Journal of Archaeology* 3.

Åkerlund, A. 2001. Stenålder i Östra Mellansverige: undersökningar utförda under de senaste decennierna. In Bergenstråhle, I. & Hellerström, S. (eds.), *Stenåldersforskning i fokus.* Riksantikvarieämbetet Arkeologiska Undersökningar Skrifter 39. University of Lund, Institute of Archaeology. Report Series 77.

Åkerlund, A., Gustafsson, P., Hammar, D., Lindgren, C., Olsson, E. & Wikell, R. 2003. Peopling a Forgotten Landscape. In Larsson, L., Kindgren, H., Knutsson, K., Loeffler, D. & Åkerlund, A. (eds.), *Mesolithic on the Move: Papers Presented at the Sixth International Conference on the Mesolithic in Europe, Stockholm 2000.* Oxford: Oxbow Books.

Åkerlund, A., Hammar, D. & Wikell, R. 1995. Pioneers in the Archipelago of Eastern Middle Sweden 9000 BP. In Robertsson, A.-M., Hackens, T., Hicks, S., Risberg, J. & Åkerlund, A. (eds.), *Landscapes and Life: Studies in Honour of Urve Miller.* PACT 50. Rixensart.

Åkerlund, A., Risberg, J., Hammar, D., Wikell, R., Luthander, A., Pettersson, M., Andersson, H. & Asplund, M. *Projektet "Människan i det tidiga landskapet": Inventeringar i höglänta skogsområden i nordvästra Södermanland, sydöstra Närke och nordöstra Östergötland.* Stockholm Archaeological Reports. Field Studies 8.

Alexandersson, K. 2001. Möre i centrum: Mesolitikum i sydöstra Kalmar län. In Magnusson, G. (ed.), *Möre: historien om ett Småland.* Kalmar.

Alin, J. 1953. *Stenåldersforskningen i Bohuslän.* Göteborg.

Alin, J. 1955. *Förteckning över Stenåldersboplatser i norra Bohuslän.* Utgiven av Göteborgs och Bohusläns Fornminnesförening. Göteborg.

Almgren, O. 1906. Uppländska stenåldersboplatser II. *Fornvännen.*

Althin, C. A. 1954. *The Chronology of the Stone Age Settlement of Scania, Sweden 1. The Mesolithic Settlement.* Acta Archaeologica Lundensia, Series in 4°, 1. Lund.

Andersen, K. 1983. *Stenalderbebyggelse i den vestsjællandske Åmose.* Copenhagen: Fredningsstyrelsen.

Andersen, K., Jørgensen, S. & Richter J. 1982. *Magelemose hytterne ved Ulkestrup Lyng.* Nordiske Fortidsminder 7. Copenhagen.

Andersen, S. 1976. Nye harpunfynd. *KUML* 1975.

Andersen, S. H. 1972. Ertebøllekulturens harpuner. *KUML* 1971.

Andersen, S. H. 1995. Coastal adaption and marine exploitation in Late Mesolithic Denmark – with special emphasis on the Limfjord region. In Fischer, A. (ed.), *Man and Sea in the Mesolithic: Coastal Settlement above and below Present Sea Level. Proceedings of the International Symposium, Kalundborg, Denmark 1993.* Oxbow Monograph 53. Oxford.

Andersen, S. H. 1997. Ertebølleharpuner og spækhuggertænder: Aspekter af marin fangst i Ertebølletid. *KUML* 1995–96.

Andersson, H. & Carlsson, T. 2005. Ristat i rader: Två mesolitiska föremål funna i Motala. *Fornvännen* 2005:1.

Andersson, H. & Hammar, D. 2002. Arkeologisk inventering i västra Kolmården. In Åkerlund, A., Risberg, J., Hammar, D., Wikell, R., Luthander, A., Pettersson, M., Andersson, H. & Asplund, M., *Projektet "Människan i det tidiga landskapet": Inventeringar i höglänta skogsområden i nordvästra Södermanland, sydöstra Närke och nordöstra Östergötland.* Stockholm Archaeological Reports. Field Studies 8.

Andrefsky, W. 1998. *Lithics: Macroscopic Approaches to Analysis.* Cambridge Manuals in Archaeology. Cambridge.

Antilla, K. & Holm, J. In prep. Torpstång: Mesolitisk kvartsbearbetning på Kuphällaön i Käglanskärgården. Antikvarisk kontroll och förundersökning. RAÄ 339, Torpstång 1:3, 2:2, 2:1, Götlunda socken, Västmanlands län, Närke.

Apel, J. (ed.) Unpublished. Skumparberget 1 och 2: En mesolitisk aktivitetsyta och tidigneolitiska trattbägarlokaler vid Skumparberget i Glanshammars socken, Örebro län, Närke. För- och slutundersökningsrapport från Arkeologikonsult AB.

Apel, J., Falkenström, P., Guinard, M. & Nordin, M. 2004. *Lyttersta 2: En stenålderslokal i Västra Vingåker. Arkeologisk förundersökning RAÄ 448.* SAU rapport 2004:2.

Appelgren, K. 1995. *Lilla Åby: arkeologisk undersökning Lilla Åby 3:2 m fl., RAÄ 49 och del av RAÄ 50, Slaka socken, Östergötland.* RAÄ, Rapport 1995:19, UV Öst. Linköping.

Arne, T. J. 1905. Ett fynd från äldre stenåldern i Östergötland. *Meddelanden från Östergötlands fornminnesförening* 1905. Linköping.

Arthursson, M. Unpublished. Lysinge: Två mesolitiska boplatser i östra Mellansverige, Närke, Lillkyrka socken. För- och slutundersökningsrapport från Arkeologikonsult AB.

Arvidsson, G. 1923. Några ord om Motala ströms fiske. *Motala ström från Vättern till Boren: Ett minnesalbum utgivet av Motala museiförening.* Motala.

Asplund, M & Wikell, R. 2002. Arkeologisk inventering i västra Mälarmården. In Åkerlund, A., Risberg, J., Hammar, D., Wikell, R., Luthander, A., Pettersson, M., Andersson, H. & Asplund, M., *Projektet "Människan i det tidiga landskapet": Inventeringar i höglänta skogsområden i nordvästra Södermanland, sydöstra Närke och nordöstra Östergötland.* Stockholm Archaeological Reports. Field Studies 8.

B ⸺ **Bäckström, Y. 1996.** *Tafonomiska processer: Exemplet Fågelbacken, Hubbo Sn, Västmanland.* M.A. thesis. Institute of Archaeology, Uppsala University. Uppsala.

Bagge, A. 1951. Fagervik: Ein Rückrat für die Periodeneinteilung, der Ostschwedischen Wohnplatz- und Bootaxtkulturen aus dem Mittelneolithikum. *Acta Archaeologica* XXII.

Baudou, E. 1962. De arkeologiska undersökningarna vid Flemingsberg år 1960–61. *Huddinge Hembygdsförenings årsskrift* 1961–62.

Becker, C. J. 1952. Maglemosekultur paa Bornholm. *Aarbøger for nordisk Oldkyndighed og Historie* 1951.

Beckman-Thoor, K., Fast, T., Luthander, A. & Philipson, A. 2003. *Kulturhistoriskt underlag för Ostlänken. Exempel för Södermanland.* Stockholm: Riksantikvarieämbetet.

Berglund, B. E. 1982. *Vegetationsutvecklingen i Norden efter istiden.* Lund.

Bergstrand, T. 2004. *Mesolitikum i Motala ström: Utkastlager och fiskeplats vid Strandvägen 1 Östergötland, Motala socken, fastighet RAÄ 173. UV Öst Dokumentation av fältarbetsfasen 2004:2.* Riksantikvarieämbetet.

Bergsvik, K. A. 2003. Mesolithic Ethnicity – Too Hard to Handle? In Larsson, L., Kindgren, H., Knutsson, K., Loeffler, D. & Åkerlund, A. (eds.), *Mesolithic on the Move: Papers Presented at the Sixth International Conference on the Mesolithic in Europe, Stockholm 2000.* Oxford: Oxbow Books.

Bille Henriksen, B. 1976. *Sværdborg 1. Excavations 1943–44: Settlement of the Maglemose Culture.* Arkæologiske Studier III. Copenhagen.

Binford, L. R. 1978. *Nunamiut Ethnoarchaeology.* New York.

Biwall, A., Hernek, R., Kihlstedt, B., Larsson, M. & Torstensdotter Åhlin, I. 1997. Stenålderns hyddor och hus i Syd- och Mellansverige. In Larsson, M. & Olsson E. (eds.), *Regionalt och interregionalt: Stenåldersundersökningar i Syd- och Mellansverige.* Riksantikvarieämbetet Arkeologiska Undersökningar Skrifter 23. Stockholm.

Bjärvall, A. & Ullström, S. 1985. *Däggdjur: Alla Europas arter.* Stockholm.

Björck, N. 1999. *Gropkeramiska boplatser i norra Uppland – En inventering av neolitiska kustboplatser 1997.* Länsstyrelsen meddelandeserie 1999:11. Uppsala.

Björck, N. 2000. *Projektet "Yngre stenålderns kustboplatser": Inventering av neolitiska kustbosättningar i Gävleborgs län 1995–1998.* Gävle: Länsmuseet Gävleborg.

Björck, N. & Guinard, M. 2003. *Stenåldersboplatser längs den nya sträckningen för väg E4: Sträckan Uppsala-Mehedeby.* Riksantikvarieämbetet i samarbete med SAU. UV Gal, Rapport 2003:1. Stockholm.

Björck, S. 1995. Late Weichselian to Early Holocene Development of the Baltic Sea – with Implications for Coastal Settlements in the Southern Baltic Region. In Fischer, A. (ed.), *Man and Sea in the Mesolithic: Coastal Settlement above and below Present Sea Level. Proceedings of the International Symposium, Kalundborg, Denmark 1993*. Oxbow Monograph 53. Oxford.

Blankholm, H. P. 1985. Maglemosekulturens hyttegrundrids: En undersøgelse af bebyggelse og adfærdsmønstre i tidlig mesolitisk tid. *Aarbøger for nordisk Oldkyndighed og Historie* 1984.

Blankholm, H. P. 1995. *On the Track of a Prehistoric Economy: Maglemosian Subsistence in Early Postglacial South Scandinavia*. Aarhus: Aarhus University Press.

Boaz, J. 1999. The Mesolithic of Central Scandinavia: Status and Perspective. In Boaz, J. (ed.), *The Mesolithic of Central Scandinavia*. Universitetets Oldsaksamlings Skrifter, Ny rekke 22. Oslo.

Bokelmann, K. 1981. Duvensee, Wohnplatz 8: Neue Aspekten zur Sammelwirtschaft im Frühen Mesolithikum. *Offa* 38.

Bondesson, W. 2001. *Riksten: En golfbana på Södertörn*. RAÄ. UV Mitt, Rapport 2001:12. Stockholm.

Bondesson, W. 2002. *Tullinge flygplats*. RAÄ. UV Mitt 2002:13. Stockholm.

Bondesson, W. 2003. *Stenålderns skärgårdsliv i Tullinge*. RAÄ. UV Mitt, Rapport 2003:4. Stockholm.

Bondesson, W. 2004. *Vägen till stenåldern*. RAÄ. UV Mitt, Rapport, 2004:25. Stockholm.

Bonsall, C. Sutherland, D., Tipping, R. & Cherry, J. 1987. The Eskemeal Project: Late Mesolithic Settlement and Environment in North-West England. In Bonsall, C. (ed.), *The Mesolithic in Europe: Papers Presented at the Third International Symposium*. Edinburgh.

Bradley, R. 1998. *The Significance of Monuments: On the Shaping of Human Experience in Neolithic and Bronze Age Europe*. London.

Broadbent, N. 1979. *Coastal Resources and Settlement Stability: A Critical Study of a Mesolithic Site Complex in Northern Sweden*. Aun 3. Uppsala.

Broadbent, N. 1982. *Skelleftebygdens historia 3. Den förhistoriska utvecklingen under 7000 år*. Uppsala: Almqvist & Wiksell.

Brøndsted, J. 1938. *Danmarks oldtid 1. Stenalderen*. Copenhagen: Gyldendal.

Broström, S.-G. 1996. Inventering av stenåldersboplatser på västra Södertörn. In Bratt, P. (ed.), *Stenålder i Stockholms län: Två seminarier vid Stockholms läns museum*. Stockholm.

Browall, H. 1980. Mesolitisk stenålder vid Tåkern. *Östergötland: Meddelanden från Östergötlands och Linköpings Stads Museum*, 1980.

Browall, H. 1986. *Alvastra pålbyggnad, social och ekonomisk bas*. Theses and Papers in North-European Archaeology 15. Stockholm.

Browall, H. 1997. Broby vid Alvastra. In Åkerlund, A., Bergh, S., Nordbladh, J. & Taffinder, J. (eds.), *Till Gunborg: Arkeologiska samtal*. Stockholm Archaeological Reports 33. Stockholm.

Browall, H. 1999. Mesolitiska mellanhavanden i västra Östergötland. In Gustafsson, A. & Karlsson, H. (eds.), *Glyfer och arkeologiska rum – en vänbok till Jarl Nordbladh*. Gotarc Series A 3. Göteborg.

Browall, H. 2003. *Det forntida Alvastra*. Statens Historiska Museum. Monographs 6. Stockholm.

Burström, M. 1995. Gårdstankar. In Göthberg, H., Kyhlberg, O. & Vinberg, A. (eds.), *Hus & gård i det förurbana samhället*. Riksantikvarieämbetet Arkeologiska Undersökningar Skrifter 14. Stockholm.

C —— **Callahan, E. 1987.** *An Evaluation of the Lithic Technology in Middle Sweden During the Mesolithic and Neolithic*. Aun 8. Uppsala.

Callahan, E., Forsberg, L., Knutsson, K. & Lindgren, C. 1992. Frakturbilder: Kulturhistoriska kommentarer till det säregna sönderfallet vid bearbetning av kvarts. *Tor* 26.

Carlsson, T. 2002. Mesolithic Relations: Reflections on Ethnic Societies in Central Sweden during the Late Mesolithic. In Bergstøl, J. (ed.), *Scandinavian Archaeological Practice – in Theory: Proceedings from the 6th Nordic TAG, Oslo 2001.* Oslo Archaeological Series 1. Oslo.

Carlsson, T. 2003. *Skepparpinan, RV 50 och väg 1088.* Arkeologisk utredning, etapp 2. Riksantikvarieämbetet. Avdelningen för arkeologiska undersökningar. Rapport UV Öst 2003:10.

Carlsson, T. 2004a. *Mesolitikum och yngre järnålder på Strandvägen 1. Arkeologisk slutundersökning. Östergötland, Motala stad och kommun, RAÄ 173. Riksantikvarieämbetet, UV Öst.* Dokumentation av fältarbetsfasen (DAFF), Rapport 2004:2. Linköping.

Carlsson, T. 2004b. Skifferknivar. In Carlsson, T. (ed.), *Mötesplats Motala – de första 8000 åren.* Linköping: Riksantikvarieämbetet UV Öst.

Carlsson, T., Gruber, G., Molin, F. & Wikell, R. 2003. Between Quartz and Flint: Material Culture and Social Interaction. In Larsson, L., Kindgren, H., Knutsson, K., Loeffler, D. & Åkerlund, A. (eds.), *Mesolithic on the Move: Papers Presented at the Sixth International Conference on the Mesolithic in Europe, Stockholm 2000.* Oxford: Oxbow Books.

Carlsson, T., Kaliff, A. & Larsson, M. 1999. Man and the Landscape in the Mesolithic: Aspects of Mental and Physical Settlement Organization. In Boaz, J. (ed.), *The Mesolithic of Central Scandinavia.* Universitetets Oldsaksamlings Skrifter, Ny rekke 22. Oslo.

Cegielka, S., Eriksson, M., Ingvald, J., Magnell, O., Nilsson, K. & Nilsson, P. 1995. Jakten på det levande – En analys av det osteologiska materialet från den senmesolitiska boplatsen Bökeberg III. Photocopy. Arkeologiska Institutionen, Lunds Universitet.

Cronberg, C. 2001. Husesyn. In Karsten, P & Knarrström, B. (eds.), *Tågerup specialstudier.* Skånska spår – arkeologi längs Västkustbanan. Lund: Riksantikvarieämbetet, UV Syd.

Cullberg, C. 1973. Om boplatsinventering i Göteborgsområdet. Projektet: Stenåldersboplatser i Göteborgstrakten. Dupl. Göteborg.

Cullberg, C. 1980. The Mesolithic and its Research in the Southern Scandinavian Peninsula. *Veröffentlichungen des Museums für Ur- und Frühgeschichte Potsdam 1445.*

Cullberg, C. 1996. West Sweden: On the Earliest Settlements. In Larsson, L. (ed.), *The Earliest Settlement of Scandinavia, and its Relationship with Neighbouring Areas.* Acta Archaeologica Lundensia, Series in 4°, 24. Lund: Almqvist & Wiksell International.

D —— **Dahl, E. 1989.** *Lär känna kronhjorten.* Stockholm.

Dahlin, M. 2004. *Fåror i forntidens spår.* Oskarshamn.

Dahlin, M. & Seward, P. 2002. Hela bygden på jakt efter sin sten- och bronsålder. *Populär Arkeologi* 2002:4.

Damell, D. 1976. Linköpingsbygden under förhistorisk tid. In Kraft, S. (ed.), *Linköpings historia 1. Från äldsta tid till 1567.* Linköping.

De Geer, G. 1896. *Om Skandinaviens geografiska utveckling efter istiden.* SGU, ser. C no. 161a. Stockholm.

Donner, J. 1995. *The Quaternary History of Scandinavia.* Cambridge: Cambridge University Press.

E —— **Edenmo, R. 1997.** *En boplats från tidigmesolitikum vid Kuphälla.* RAÄ. UV Stockholm, Rapport 1997:35. Stockholm.

Edmonds, M. 1999. *Ancestral Geographies of the Neolithic: Landscapes, Monuments and Memory.* London.

Einerstam, B. 1957. Tryserum under forntiden. In Hofrén, M., *Några kapitel ur Tryserums och Fogelviks historia.* Västervik.

Eklund, S. & Hennius, A. 2004. En nyupptäckt stenåldersboplats. In Carlsson, T. (ed.), *Mötesplats Motala – de första 8000 åren.* Linköping: Riksantikvarieämbetet UV Öst.

Elfstrand, B. 2000. Område 2. Södra Freberga. In Carlsson, T., Elfstrand, B., Gruber, G., Larsson, L. Z., Molin, F. & Nielsen, A.-L., *Ett arkeologiskt linjeprojekt i västra Östergötland.* Riksantikvarieämbetet. Avdelningen för arkeologiska undersökningar. Rapport UV Öst 2000:12. Linköping.

Enghoff, I. B. 1995. Fishing in Denmark during the Mesolithic period. In Fischer, A. (ed.), *Man and Sea in the Mesolithic: Coastal Settlement above and below Present Sea Level. Proceedings of the International Symposium, Kalundborg, Denmark 1993.* Oxbow Monograph 53. Oxford.

Engström, T. 1932. *Nya stenåldersboplatser inom Kolmården.* KVHAA Handlingar 37:2. Stockholm.

Engström, T. 1934. Stenåldersboplatserna vid Bråviken: Kortfattad översikt i anslutning till boplatskeramiken i Östergötlands museum. *Meddelanden från Östergötlands fornminnes- och museiförening* 1933–1934. Linköping.

Engström, T. 1935. *Från stenålderns boplatskultur vid Bråviken.* KVHAA Handlingar 37:6. Stockholm.

Engström, T. 1936. Strandbundna fynd äldre än yngre Litorinamaximum (L II). In *Från stenålderns boplatskultur vid Bråviken.* KVHAA 37:6. Stockholm.

Engström, T. & Thomasson, H. 1932. *Stenåldersboplatser i Östergötland: Ett boplatsområde i Kvarsebo socken.* KVHAA Handlingar 37:4. Stockholm.

Ericsson, A. & Wikell, R. (manuscript). Nyupptäckta boplatser vid Litorinahavets stränder. In Ericsson, A. & Nilsson, P. (eds.), *Arkeologi och bebyggelsehistoria i Hammarkinds härad.* Riksantikvarieämbetet, Avdelningen för arkeologiska undersökningar, Skrifter.

Ericsson, P. 1985. Osteologisk rapport av ben från Almeöboplatsen vid Hornborgasjön i Västergötland. Unpublished report.

Eriksson, M. & Magnell, O. 2001a. Det djuriska Tågerup: Nya rön kring Kongemose- & Ertebøllekulturens jakt och fiske. In Karsten, P. & Knarrström, B. (eds.), *Tågerup specialstudier.* Skånska spår – arkeologi längs Västkustbanan. Lund: Riksantikvarieämbetet, UV Syd.

Eriksson, M. & Magnell, O. 2001b. Jakt och slakt. In Karsten, P., *Dansarna från Bökeberg: Om jakt, ritualer och inlandsbosättning vid jägarstenålderns slut.* Riksantikvarieämbetet Arkeologiska undersökningar Skrifter 37. Lund.

Erixon, S. 1913. Stenåldern i Blekinge. *Fornvännen.*

F — **Färjare, A. 1999.** *Gullvagnen, Arkeologisk förundersökning, Östergötland, Krokek socken, RAÄ 85.* Riksantikvarieämbetet, Avdelningen för arkeologiska undersökningar, UV Mitt, Rapport 1999:17. Stockholm.

Fischer, A. 1995. An Entrance to the Mesolithic World below the Ocean: Status of Ten Years' Work on the Danish Sea Floor. In Fischer, A. (ed.), *Man and Sea in the Mesolithic: Coastal Settlement above and below Present Sea Level. Proceedings of the International Symposium, Kalundborg, Denmark 1993.* Oxbow Monograph 53. Oxford.

Fischer, A. 1996. At the Border of Human Habitat: The Late Palaeolithic and Early Mesolithic in Scandinavia. In Larsson, L. (ed.), *The Earliest Settlement of Scandinavia, and its Relationship with Neighbouring Areas.* Acta Archaeologica Lundensia, Series in 8°, 24. Lund: Almqvist & Wiksell International.

Fischer, A., Vemming Hansen, P. & Rasmussen, P. 1984. Macro and Micro Wear Traces in Lithic Projectile Points: Experimental Results and Prehistoric Examples. *Journal of Danish Archaeology 2.*

Flenniken, J. 1981. *Replicative Systems Analysis: A Model Applied to the Vein Quartz Artifacts from the Hoko River Site.* Hoko River Archaeological Project. Contribution No. 2. Washington State University. Laboratory of Anthropology. Reports of Investigations 59. Washington.

Florin, S. 1944. Kustförskjutningen och bebyggelseutvecklingen i östra Mellansverige under sen-kvartär tid. In *Allmän översikt.* Geologiska föreningens förhandlingar 66. Stockholm.

Florin, S. 1948. *Kustförskjutningen och bebyggelseutvecklingen i östra mellansverige under senkvartär tid.* Stockholm.

Florin, S. 1955. Geologi och stenåldershistoria. In Schnell, I. (ed.), *Vingåkersboken* II. Vingåker: Vingåkers hembygdsförening.

Forsberg, L. & Larsson, L. 1994. Tidiga fångstkulturer. In Selinge, K.-G. (ed.), *Kulturminnen och kulturmiljövård.* Sveriges National Atlas. Stockholm

Fredsjö, Å. 1953. *Studier i Västsveriges äldre stenålder.* Skrifter utgivna av Göteborgs arkeologiska museum. Göteborg.

Fromm, E. 1976. Beskrivning till jordartskartan Linköping NO. *Jordartsgeologiska kartblad skala 1:50 000. Serie Ae* 19. Stockholm: Sveriges Geologiska Undersökning.

G —— **Gärme, E. 1956.** "Ringarum" bebott i 6–7000 år: Stenåldersyxor från Emtöholm spårlöst försvunna sedan 1920. *Östergötlands Dagblad,* 10 December 1956.

Gendel, P. A. 1984. *Mesolithic Social Territories in Northwestern Europe.* BAR International Series 218. Oxford.

Gill, A. 2003. *Stenålder i Mälardalen.* Stockholm Studies in Archaeology 26. Stockholm.

Göransson, G. 1987. *Lär känna vildsvinet.* Stockholm: Svenska jägarförbundet.

Göransson, H. 1989. Dags mosse: Östergötlands förhistoriska kalender. *Svensk botanisk tidskrift* 83.

Gosden, C. 1994. *Social Being and Time.* Oxford.

Granath Zillén, G. 2001. *Besökt och återbesökt: Arkeologisk undersökning, stenålders- och bronsåldersboplats vid Myrstugeberget, väg 259, Södermanland, Huddinge socken, Masmo 1:8 och Myrstugeberget 2, RAÄ 331.* UV Mitt Rapport 2001:8. Stockholm: Riksantikvarieämbetet.

Graner, G. & Luthander, A. 2005. *Kuphälla: senmesolitiska besök på en ö i Käglands skärgård, Närke, Götlunda socken, Torpstång 2:15, RAÄ 320. Arkeologisk undersökning och kompletterande inventering.* RAÄ, Rapport, UV Bergslagen 2003:12. Örebro.

Graner, G. & Luthander, A. Manuscript. Kuphälla. RAÄ, Rapport, UV Bergslagen.

Gräslund, B. 1974. Befolkning – bosättning – miljö: Några synpunkter på det forntida jägarsamhället i Norden. *Fornvännen* 69.

Grøn, O. & Kuznetsov, O. 2003. Ethno-archaeology among Evenkia Forest Hunters: Preliminary Results and a Different Approach to Reality. In Larsson, L., Kindgren, H., Knutsson, K., Loeffler, D. & Åkerlund, A. (eds.), *Mesolithic on the Move: Papers Presented at the Sixth International Conference on the Mesolithic in Europe, Stockholm 2000.* Oxford: Oxbow Books.

Grøn, O. 1995. *The Maglemose Culture: The Reconstruction of the Social Organization of a Mesolithic Culture in Northern Europe.* BAR International Series 616. Oxford.

Groop, N. & Guinard, M. Forthcoming. Stenyxor i Mälardalen: Produktion och reproduktion (working title). SAU.

Guinard, M. & Eriksson, M. 2004. Stormossen – boplatser i ytterskärgården under jägarstenåldern. In *Arkeologi E4: Årsberättelse 2003. Utgrävningar från Uppsala till Tierp.* Uppsala.

Guinard, M. & Eriksson, M. 2005. Stormossen 1 – en mesolitisk samlingsboplats. In *Arkeologi E4: årsberättelse 2004. Utgrävningar från Uppsala till Mehedeby.* Uppsala.

Guinard, M. & Wikell. R. 2003. Once the Shore – Always the Shore: Mesolithic and De-Neolithic Strategies in Eastern Middle Sweden: Cases from Södertörn in Södermanland and the Siljan Region in Dalarna. In Samuelsson, C. & Ytterberg, N. (eds.), *Uniting Sea: Stone Age Societies in the Baltic Sea Region.* Uppsala.

Gurstad-Nilsson, H. 1993. *Stenålder i Kalmar läns inland: Bebyggelseutveckling och bosättningsmönster i Hultsfreds kommun.* Kalmar: Kalmar läns museum.

Gurstad-Nilsson, H. 1995. *Stenålder i gränsbygd: En bebyggelsearkeologisk analys med utgångspunkt från specialinventeringen av Emmaboda kommun.* Kalmar Läns Museum. Rapport 1995:4. Kalmar.

Gustafsson, J. Manuscript. Stenåldern i Nennesmo (working title). Report from Jönköpings länsmuseum.

Gustafsson, P. 1996. *En gropkeramisk lokal i Kurum.* Riksantikvarieämbetet, Arkeologiska undersökningar, UV Stockholm Rapport 1996:106. Stockholm.

Gustafsson, P. 1998. The Earliest Stone Age Occupation of Eastern Middle Sweden. *Current Swedish Archaeology* 6.

Gustafsson, P. In prep. Mesolitikum i Åker.

H —— **Hagberg, U. E. 1979.** Den förhistoriska kalmarbygden. In Hammarström, I. (ed.), *Kalmar stads historia* 1. Kalmar.

Halén, O. 1994. *Sedentariness during the Stone Age of Northern Sweden: In the Light of the Alträsket Site, c. 5000 B.C., and the Comb Ware Site Lillberget, c. 3900 B.C. Source Critical Problems of Representativity in Archaeology.* Acta Archaeologica Lundensia, Series in 8°, 20. Stockholm.

Hallgren, F., Bergström Å. & Larsson Å. 1995. *Pärlängsberget: En kustboplats från övergången mellan senmesolitikum och tidigneolitikum.* Tryckta rapporter från Arkeologikonsult AB 13. Upplands Väsby.

Hammar, D. & Risberg, J. 2002. Litostratigrafiska undersökningar i västra Kolmården. In Åkerlund, A., Risberg, J., Hammar, D., Wikell, R., Luthander, A., Pettersson, M., Andersson, H. & Asplund, M., *Projektet "Människan i det tidiga landskapet": Inventeringar i höglänta skogsområden i nordvästra Södermanland, sydöstra Närke och nordöstra Östergötland.* Stockholm Archaeological Reports. Field Studies 8. Stockholm.

Hammar, D. & Wikell, R. 1994. Nyupptäckta stenåldersboplatser på Södertörn. *Arkeologi i Sverige.* Ny följd 3. Stockholm: Riksantikvarieämbetet.

Hammar, D. & Wikell, R. 1996. 250 nyupptäckta stenålderslokaler på Södertörn. In Bratt, P. (ed.), *Stenålder i Stockholms län: Två seminarier vid Stockholms läns museum.* Stockholm.

Hansson, H. 1897. En stenåldersboplats på Gotland. *Svenska Fornminnesföreningens Tidskrift* 28.

Hansson, H. 1937. Ny stenåldersboplats vid Valdemarsviken: Helt boplatskomplex finnes i bygden att döma av i dagarna gjorda fynd. *Östergötlands Dagblad,* 4 November 1937.

Hedenström, A. & Risberg, J. 1999. Early Holocene Shore-displacement in Southern Central Sweden as Recorded in Elevated Isolated Basins. *Boreas* 28.

Helander, A. & Zetterlund, P. 1998. *En mesolitisk boplats vid Nedra Lid.* Arkeologisk förundersökning. Näs, Nedra Lid, UV 1, Västra Ny socken. Motala kommun, Östergötland. Riksantikvarieämbetet. Avdelningen för arkeologiska undersökningar. Rapport UV Linköping 1997:24. Linköping.

Hellman, G. A. 1970. Ringarums forntida bosättning. In Gärme, E. (ed.), *Bondebygd och bruksbygd: Ringarums socken genom tiderna.* Söderköping.

Hermansson, R. & Welinder, S. 1997. *Norra Europas trindyxor.* Östersund: Mitthögskolan.

Hodder, I. 1999. *The Archaeological Process: An Introduction.* London.

Hollender, A. 1901. *Om Sveriges nivåförändringar efter menniskans invandring.* Geologiska föreningens förhandlingar 23. Stockholm.

Holm, J. 2003a. Handtagskärnor och kvarts. In Karlenby, L., *Mittens rike: Arkeologiska berättelser från Närke.* Riksantikvarieämbetet Arkeologiska Undersökningar Skrifter 50. Stockholm.

Holm, J. 2003b. Quartz, Microblades and the Meaning of Life. In Samuelsson, C. & Ytterberg, N. (eds.), *Uniting Sea: Stone Age Societies in the Baltic Sea Region.* Uppsala.

I —— **Ingold, T. 1999.** On the Social Relations of the Hunter-Gatherer Band. In Lee, R. B. & Daly, R. (eds.), *Hunters and Gatherers*. Cambridge.

Iregren, E. & Lepiksaar, J. 1993. The Mesolithic Site in Hög in a South Scandinavian Perspective: A Snap Shot from Early Kongemose Culture. *Zeitschrift für Archäologie* 27.

Isaksson, M., Holmgren. I., Fors, T., Ahlbeck, M. & Blidmo, R. 2003. *Riksväg 73, Alternativ E. Älgviken – Fors. Ösmo och Västerhaninge socknar, Södermanland: Särskild arkeologisk utredning.* Rapporter från Arkeologikonsult 2003:1082.

J —— **Jakobsson, M. & Kihlstedt, B. 1995.** Boplats eller fyndplats: Om fornlämningsbegreppets tillämpning. *Kulturmiljövård* 1995:4.

Janse, O. 1932. *En stenåldersboplats vid Valdemarsvikens strand, Stenåldersboplatser i Östergötland 1.* KVHAA Handlingar 37:5. Stockholm.

Jansson, P., Knöös, S., Larsson, F., Lövgren, A.-K., Mårtensson, J. & Rommerdahl, H. 1998. Osteologisk analys av den mesolitiska lokalen Ringsjöholm. Photocopy. Arkeologiska institutionen, Lunds Universitet.

Janzon, G. 1984. A Megalithic Grave at Alvastra in Östergötland, Sweden. In Burenhult, G. (ed.), *The Archaeology of Carrowmore.* Theses and Papers in North-European Archaeology 14. Stockholm.

Jennbert, K. 1984. *Den produktiva gåvan.* Acta Archaeologica Lundensia, Series in 4°, 16. Lund.

Jensen, O. L. 2001. Kongemose- og Ertebøllekultur ved den fossile Nivåfjord. In Jensen. O. L., Sørensen, S. A., Hansen, K. M. (eds.), *Danmarks jægerstenalder – status og perspektiver: Beretning fra symposiet "Status og perspektiver inden for dansk mesolitikum" afholdt i Vordingborg, september 1998.* Hørsholm.

Jochim, M. A. 1976. *Hunter-Gatherer Subsistence and Settlement: A Predictive Model.* New York.

Johansson, A. Degn 2000. *Ældre stenalder i Norden.* Farum.

Johansson, L. G. 1989. Var Tingbyhuset från järnåldern? *Populär Arkeologi* 7:2.

Johansson, L. G. 1993. Source Criticism or Dilettanti? Some Thoughts on "Scandinavia's Oldest House" in Tingby near Kalmar, Småland. *Current Swedish Archaeology* 1.

Jones, A, K, G. 1986. Fish Bone Survival in the Digestive System of the Pig, Dog and Man: Some Experiments. In Brinkhuizen, D. C. & Clason, A. T. (eds.), *Fish and Archaeology: Studies in Osteometry, Taphonomy, Seasonality and Fishing Methods.* BAR International Series 294. Oxford.

Jonsson, L. 1986a. Animal Bones from Bredasten – Preliminary Results. *Meddelanden från Lunds universitets historiska museum* 1985–1986.

Jonsson, L. 1986b. From Wild Boar to Domestic Pig – a Reassessment of Neolithic Swine of Northwestern Europe. *Striae* 24.

Jonsson, L. 1986b. Animal Bones from Bredasten: Preliminary Results. In Larsson, M., Bredasten: An Early Ertebölle Site with a Dwelling Structure in South Scania. *Meddelanden från Lunds Universitets Historiska Museum.* 1985–86.

Jonsson, L. 1988. The Vertebrate Faunal Remains from the Late Atlantic Settlement at Skateholm in Scania, South Sweden. In Larsson, L. (ed.), *The Skateholm Project* I. *Man and Environment.* Acta Regiae Societatis Humaniorum Litterarum LXXIX.

Juel Jensen, H. 1994. *Flint Tools and Plant Working: Hidden Traces of Stone Age Technology. A Use Wear Study of Some Danish Mesolithic and TRB implements.* Århus.

Juel Jensen, H. 2000. Slidsporsstudier – metoder til belysning af flintredskapers funktion. In Eriksen, V. B. (ed.), *En håndbog i systematiske analyser af flintinventarer.* Århus.

K —— **Kaliff, A. 1999.** *Arkeologi i Östergötland: Scener ur ett landskaps historia.* Occasional Papers in Archaeology 20. Uppsala.

Kaliff, A., Carlsson, T., Molin, F. & Sundberg, K. 1997. *Mörby. Östergötlands äldsta boplats.* RAÄ, Avdelningen för arkeologiska undersökningar, Rapport UV Linköping 1997:38. Linköping.

Karsten, P. 2001. *Dansarna från Bökeberg: Om jakt, ritualer och inlandsbosättningar vid jägarstenålderns slut.* Riksantikvarieämbetet Arkeologiska Undersökningar Skrifter 37. Stockholm: Riksantikvarieämbetet.

Karsten, P. & Knarrström, B. 1996. Norra Skåne – ett tidigmesolitiskt centrum. *Ale 4.*

Karsten, P. & Knarrström, B. 1998. Nya stenåldersfynd från norra Skåne: Den första kvartsboplatsen. *Ale 1998:1.*

Karsten, P. & Knarrström, B. (eds.) 2001. *Tågerup specialstudier.* Skånska spår – arkeologi längs Västkustbanan. Lund: Riksantikvarieämbetet, UV Syd.

Karsten, P. & Knarrström, B. 2003. *The Tågerup Excavations.* Skånska spår – arkeologi längs Västkustbanan. Lund: Riksantikvarieämbetet, UV Syd.

Kent, C. 1981. The Dog – Archaeologists' Best Friend or Worst Enemy: Spatial Distribution of Faunal Remains. *Journal of Field Archaeology 8.*

Kihlstedt, B. 1992. *Gladö industriområde.* RAÄ. UV Stockholm, Rapport 1992:45. Stockholm.

Kihlstedt, B. 1993. *Gladö bergtäkt: Arkeologisk utredning.* Riksantikvarieämbetet. UV Stockholm, Rapport 1993:62. Stockholm.

Kihlstedt, B. 1996. Boplatsbegreppet i antikvarisk praxis. In Bratt, P. (ed.), *Stenålder i Stockholms län: Två seminarier vid Stockholms läns museum.* Stockholm.

Kihlstedt, B. & Lindgren, C. 1999. Att vara beredd på det oväntade: Reflexioner utifrån tidigneolitiska fyndplatser. In Andersson, K., Lagerlöf, A. & Åkerlund, A. (eds.), *Forskaren i fält: En vänbok till Kristina Lamm.* Riksantikvarieämbetet Arkeologiska Undersökningar Skrifter 27. Stockholm.

Kihlstedt, K. & Wikell, R. Manuscript. Spår av stenålder längs Ostlänken. Working title. Riksantikvarieämbetet.

Kindgren, H. 1991. Kambrisk flinta och etniska grupper i Västergötlands senmesolitikum. In Browall, H., Persson, P. &, Sjögren, K.-G. (eds.), *Västsvenska stenåldersstudier.* Gotarc Series C. Arkeologiska Skrifter 8. Gothenburg.

Kindgren, H. & Schaller Åhrberg, E. 1999. From Sandarna to Lihult: Fredsjö's Enerklev Phase Revisited. In Boaz, J. (ed.), *The Mesolithic of Central Scandinavia.* Universitetets Oldsaksamlings Skrifter, Ny rekke 22. Oslo.

Knarrström, B. 2000a. *Flinta i sydvästra Skåne: En diakron studie av råmaterial, produktion och funktion med fokus på boplatsteknologi och metalltida flintutnyttjande.* Acta Archaeologica Lundensia, Series in 8°, 33. Stockholm: Almquist & Wiksell International.

Knarrström, B. 2000b. Tidigmesolitisk bosättning i sydvästra Småland: En komparativ studie över stenteknologi och regionala bosättningsmönster med utgångspunkt i en boplats vid Hamneda. In Lagerås, P. (ed.), *Arkeologi och paleoekologi i sydvästra Småland.* Riksantikvarieämbetet Arkeologiska Undersökningar Skrifter 34. Lund.

Knarrström, B. 2001. *Flint a Scanian hardware.* Skånska spår längs Västkustbanan. Lund: Riksantikvarieämbetet, UV Syd.

Knarrström, B. & Wrentner, R 1996. Diagnostik av plattformar. *Bulletin för arkeologisk forskning i Sydsverige 2/1997.*

Knutsson, H. 1995. *Slutvandrat? Aspekter på övergången från rörlig till bofast tillvaro.* Aun 20. Uppsala.

Knutsson, K. 1988. *Patterns of Tool Use: Scanning Electron Microscopy of Experimental Quartz Tools.* Aun 10. Uppsala.

Knutsson, K. 1995. Mesolithic Research in Sweden 1986–1990. In Buström, M. & Carlsson, A. (eds.), *Current Swedish Archaeology 3*. Stockholm.

Knutsson, K. 1998. Convention and Lithic Analyses. In Holm, L. & Knutsson, K. (eds.), *Proceedings from the Third Flint Alternatives Conference at Uppsala*. Occasional Papers in Archaeology 16. Uppsala.

Knutsson, K., Falkenström, P. & Lindberg, K.-F. 2003. Appropriation of the Past: Neolithisation in the Northern Scandinavian Perspective. In Larsson, L., Kindgren, H., Knutsson, K., Loeffler, D. & Åkerlund, A. (eds.), *Mesolithic on the Move: Papers Presented at the Sixth International Conference on the Mesolithic in Europe, Stockholm 2000*. Oxford: Oxbow Books.

Knutsson, K., Lindgren, C., Hallgren, F. & Björck, N. 1999. The Mesolithic in Eastern Central Sweden. In Boaz, J. (ed.), *The Mesolithic of Central Scandinavia*. Universitetets Oldsaksamlings Skrifter, Ny rekke 22. Oslo.

Knutsson, K. & Melchert, P. 1995. Teknologin, frakturbilden och redskapsanvändningen. In Apel, J. (ed.), *Skumparberget 1 och 2: En mesolitisk aktivitetsyta och tidigneolitiska trattbägarlokaler vid Skumparberget i Glanshammars socken, Örebro län, Närke. För- och slutundersöknings-rapport från Arkeologikonsult AB*.

Königsson, E. S., Lepiksaar, J. & Königsson, L.-K. 1971. Stenåldersboplatsen i Alby på Öland. *Fornvännen* 1971.

Kozlowski, J. 1975. *Cultural Differentiation of Europe from 10th to 5th Millennium B.C.* Warsaw.

Kozlowski, J. 2003. The Mesolithic: What do we Know and What do we Believe? In Larsson, L., Kindgren, H., Knutsson, K., Loeffler, D. & Åkerlund, A. (eds.), *Mesolithic on the Move: Papers Presented at the Sixth International Conference on the Mesolithic in Europe, Stockholm 2000*. Oxford: Oxbow Books.

L —— **Lannerbro, R. 1976.** *Implements and Rock Materials in the Prehistory of Upper Dalarna*. Early Norrland 4. Kungl. Vitterhets Historie och Antikvitets Akademien. Stockholm.

Lannerbro Norell, M. 1987. Pil- och spjutspetsar av sten från övre Dalarna. C-uppsats. Arkeologiska institutionen, Uppsala universitet.

Larsson, L. 1975. A Contribution to the Knowledge of Mesolithic Huts in Southern Scandinavia. *Meddelanden från Lunds Universitets Historiska Museum 1973–1974*.

Larsson, L. 1978a. *Ageröd 1:B–Ageröd 1:D. A Study of Early Atlantic Settlement in Scania*. Acta Archaeologica Lundensia, Series in 4°, 12. Lund.

Larsson, L. 1978b. Mesolithic Antler and Bone Artefacts from Central Scania. *Meddelande från Lunds universitets historiska museum 1977–1978*.

Larsson, L. 1980. Some Aspects of the Kongemose Culture of Southern Sweden. *Meddelanden från Lunds Universitets Historiska Museum 1979–1980*.

Larsson, L. 1982. *Segebro: En tidigatlantisk boplats vid Sege ås mynning*. Malmöfynd 4. Utgiven av Malmö museum. Malmö.

Larsson, L. 1983. *Ageröd V: An Atlantic Bog Site in Central Scania*. Acta Archaeologica Lundensia, Series in 8°, 12. Lund.

Larsson, L. 1984. The Skateholm Project: A Late Mesolitic Settlement and Cementery Complex at a Southern Swedish Bay. *Meddelanden från Lunds universitets historiska museum 1983–1984*.

Larsson, L. 1988. *Ett fångstsamhälle för 7000 år sedan: Boplatser och gravar vid Skateholm*. Lund.

Larsson, L. 1989. Ethnicity and Traditions in Mesolithic Mortuary Practices of Southern Scandinavia. In Shennan, S. J. (ed.), *Archaeological Approaches to Cultural Identity*. One World Archaeology 10. Southampton.

Larsson, L. 1990. The Mesolithic of Southern Scandinavia. *Journal of World Prehistory* 3.

Larsson, L. 1995. Man and Sea in Southern Scandinavia during the Late Mesolithic: The Role of Cemeteries in the View of Society. In Fischer, A. (ed.), *Man and Sea in the Mesolithic: Coastal Settlement above and below Present Sea Level. Proceedings of the International Symposium, Kalundborg, Denmark 1993.* Oxbow Monograph 53. Oxford.

Larsson, L. 1996. The Colonization of South Sweden During the Deglaciation. In Larsson, L. (ed.), *The Earliest Settlement of Scandinavia and its Relationship with Neighbouring Areas.* Acta Archaeologica Lundensia, Series in 8°, 24. Lund.

Larsson, L. 1999. From the Depth of the Sea: A Mesolithic Harpoon from the Baltic Sea. In Cziesla, E., Kersting, T. & Pratsch, S. (eds.), *Den Bogen spannen... Festschrift für Berhard Gramsch.* Beiträge zur Ur- und Frühgeschichte Mitteleuropas 21. Weisbach.

Larsson, L. 2001. Det senaste kvartsseklets stenåldersarkeologi i Skåne. In Bergenstråhle, I. & Hellström S. (eds.), *Stenåldersforskning i fokus: Inblickar och utblickar i sydskandinavisk stenåldersarkeologi.* Riksantikvarieämbetet Arkeologiska Undersökningar Skrifter 39/University of Lund, Institute of Archaeology Report Series 77. Lund.

Larsson, L. 2003. The Mesolithic of Sweden in Retrospective and Progressive Perspectives. In Larsson, L., Kindgren, H., Knutsson, K., Loeffler, D. & Åkerlund, A. (eds.), *Mesolithic on the Move: Papers Presented at the Sixth International Conference on the Mesolithic in Europe, Stockholm 2000.* Oxford: Oxbow Books.

Larsson, L. 2004. The Mesolithic Period in Southern Scandinavia: with Special Reference to Burials and Cemeteries. In Saville, A. (ed.), *Mesolithic Scotland and its Neighbours: The Early Holocene Prehistory of Scotland and its British and Irish Context and some Northern European Perspectives.* Edinburgh.

Larsson, L. 2005. Regional or Interregional Representation? A Slotted Bone Dagger from Offerdal, Jämtland. Manuscript.

Larsson, M. 1986. Bredasten – An Early Ertebølle Site with Dwelling Structure in South Scania. *Meddelanden från Lunds universitets historiska museum 1985–1986.*

Larsson, M. 1994. Stenåldersjägare vid Siljan: En atlantisk boplats vid Leksand. *Fornvännen* 89.

Larsson, M. 1996. *Högby: Arkeologisk slutundersökning 1. Mesolitiska och senneolitiska boplatser vid Högby i Östergötland: Bosättningsmönster och materiell kultur. Högby och Mjölby socknar, Mjölby kommun, Östergötland.* Riksantikvarieämbetet. Avdelningen för arkeologiska undersökningar. Rapport UV Linköping 1996:35. Linköping.

Larsson, M. 2003. Storlyckan. Investigation of an Early Mesolithic Site in Östergötland, East Middle Sweden. In Larsson, L., Kindgren, H., Knutsson, K., Loeffler, D. & Åkerlund, A. (eds.), *Mesolithic on the Move: Papers Presented at the Sixth International Conference on the Mesolithic in Europe, Stockholm 2000.* Oxford: Oxbow Books.

Larsson, M., Lindgren, C. & Nordqvist, B. 1997. Regionalitet under mesolitikum: Från senglacial tid till senatlantisk tid i Syd- och Mellansverige. In Larsson, M. & Olsson, E. (eds.), *Regionalt och interregionalt: Stenåldersundersökningar i Syd- och Mellansverige.* Riksantikvarieämbetet Arkeologiska Undersökningar 23. Stockholm.

Larsson, M. & Molin, F. 2000. A New World: Cultural Links and Spatial Disposition – The Early Mesolithic Landscape in Östergötland on the Basis of the Storlyckan Investigations. *Lund Archaeological Review* 6.

Larsson, M. & Olsson, E. (eds.). 1997. *Regionalt och interregionalt: Stenåldersundersökningar i Syd- och Mellansverige.* Riksantikvarieämbetet Arkeologiska Undersökningar Skrifter 23. Stockholm.

Lepiksaar, J. 1982. Djurrester från den tidigatlantiska boplatsen vid Segebro nära Malmö i Skåne (Sydsverige). In Larsson, L., *En tidigatlantisk boplats vid Sege ås mynning.* Malmöfynd 4. Malmö.

Lepiksaar, J. 1983. Animal Remains from the Atlantic Bog Site at Ageröd V in Central Scania. In Larsson, L., *Ageröd V, an Atlantic Bog Site in Central Scania*. Acta Archaeologica Lundensia, Series in 8°, 12. Lund.

Liljegren, R. 1982. *Paleoekologi och strandförskjutning i en Littorinavik vid Spjälkö i mellersta Blekinge*. Lund: Lunds universitet. Avdelning för kvartärgeologi.

Liljegren, R. & Welinder, S. 1976. Le Mésolithique dans le Nord-Ouest de l'Europe: L'apport de l'écologie dans un essai de répartition chronologique et spatiale. *Congrès Préhistorique de France: Compte rendu de la XXᵉ session Provence 1–7 juillet 1974*. Paris.

Liman, H. & Eriksson, J. 1986. *Natur, kultur – Miljöer i Östergötland: Naturvårdsplan och kultur-minnesprogram*. Länsstyrelsen i Östergötlands län 1983. Andra upplagan. Linköping.

Lindgren, C. & Nordqvist, B. 1997. Lihultyxor och trindyxor: Om yxor av basiska bergarter i östra och västra Sverige under mesolitikum. In Larsson, M. & Olsson, E. (eds.), *Regionalt och inter-regionalt: Stenåldersundersökningar i Syd- och Mellansverige*. Riksantikvarieämbetet Arkeologiska Undersökningar Skrifter 23. Stockholm.

Lindgren, C. 1991. En nyupptäckt stenåldersboplats i Östergötland. *Arkeologi i Sverige*, Ny följd 1. Stockholm: Riksantikvarieämbetet.

Lindgren, C. 1994. Ett bipolärt problem – om kvartsteknologi under mesolitikum. *Aktuell Arkeologi* IV. Stockholm Archaeological Reports 29. Stockholm.

Lindgren, C. 1996a. Fyndkoncentrationer och aktivitetsytor – metodval och tolkningsproblem. In Bratt, P. (ed.), *Stenålder i Stockholms län*. Stockholms läns museum. Stockholm.

Lindgren, C. 1996b. Kvarts som källmaterial – exempel från den mesolitiska boplatsen Hagtorp. *Tor* 28, 29–52.

Lindgren, C. 1997a. Mesolitikum i östra Mellansverige – en presentation av undersökningar under åren 1986–1993. In Larsson, M. and Olsson, E. (eds.), *Regionalt och interregionalt: Stenål-dersundersökningar i Syd- och Mellansverige*. Riksantikvarieämbetet Arkeologiska Undersök-ningar Skrifter 23. Stockholm.

Lindgren, C. 1997b. Östra Mellansverige. In the chapter Regionalitet under Mesolitikum – Från senglacial tid till senatlantisk tid i Syd- och Mellansverige, by M. Larsson, C. Lindgren & B. Nordqvist. In Larsson, M. and Olsson, E. (eds.), *Regionalt och interregionalt: Stenåldersunder-sökningar i Syd- och Mellansverige*. Riksantikvarieämbetet Arkeologiska Undersökningar Skrifter 23. Stockholm.

Lindgren, C. 1998. Shapes of Quartz and Shapes of Minds. In Holm, L. & Knutsson, K. (eds.), *Pro-ceedings from the Third Flint Alternatives Conference at Uppsala*. Occasional Papers in Archaeo-logy 16. Uppsala.

Lindgren, C. 2003. My Way or Your Way: On the Social Dimension of Technology as Seen in the Lithic Strategies in Eastern Middle Sweden during the Mesolithic. In Larsson, L., Kindgren, H., Knutsson, K., Loeffler, D. & Åkerlund, A. (eds.), *Mesolithic on the Move: Papers Presented at the Sixth International Conference on the Mesolithic in Europe, Stockholm 2000*. Oxford: Oxbow Books.

Lindgren, C. 2004. *Människor och kvarts: Sociala och teknologiska strategier under mesolitikum i östra Mellansverige*. Stockholm Studies in Archaeology 29. Riksantikvarieämbetet Arkeolo-giska Undersökningar Skrifter 54. Coast to Coast Books 11. Stockholm.

Lindgren, C. & Lindholm, P. 1998. *En mesolitisk boplats vid Jordbro Industriområde: Haningeleden 4. Arkeologisk förundersökning och undersökning av RAÄ 72, Österhaninge socken, Söder-manland*. Riksantikvarieämbetet, UV Stockholm, Rapport 1998:73. Stockholm.

Lindholm, K.-G. & Vogel, P. 1996. Omedelbarhetens landskap: En tvärkulturell undersökning av Jä-gare-Samlares kulturlandskap. CD-uppsats. Arkeologiska institutionen. Uppsala universitet. Uppsala.

Loeffler, D. 2005. *Contested Landscapes/Contested Heritage: History and Heritage in Sweden and their Archaeological Implications Concerning the Interpretation of the Norrlandian Past.* Archaeology and Environment 18. Umeå.

Löthman, L. 1993. Talrika stenåldersboplatser, järnframställningsplatser och gruvor i Västmanlands läns norra delar: 1989–1990-års inventeringsresultat. In Andrae, T., Sander, B., Trotzig, G., Selinge, K.-G., Forenius, S., Kyhlberg, O., Broberg, A. & Jensen, R. *Arkeologi i Sverige*, Ny följd 2. Stockholm: Riksantikvarieämbetet.

Lövgren, A.-K. 1998. Märgklyvning: Osteologisk analys av den mesolitiska lokalen Ringsjöholm. Photocopy. Arkeologiska institutionen, Lunds universitet.

Luho, V. 1956. Die Askolakultur: Die frühmesolithische Steinzeit in Finnland. *Finska fornminnesföreningens tidskrift 57.*

Luho, V. 1967. Die Suomosjärvi-kultur: Die mittel- und spätmesolithische Zeit in Finnland. *Finska fornminnesföreningens tidskrift 66.*

Lundqvist, G. 1965. Henrik Vilhelm Munthe. *Minnesteckning.* Levnadsteckning över Kungliga Svenska Vetenskapsakademiens ledamöter 9. Uppsala.

Lundqvist, J. 1998. Isavsmältning och israndlinjer i Sverige. In Andersen, S. & Pedersen, S. S. (eds.), *Israndlinier i Norden.* TemaNord 1998:584. Copenhagen: Nordisk Ministerråd.

Luthander, A. & Holm, J. 1999. Käglan som skärgård med kala kobbar och lugna vikar. *Blick för Bergslagen.*

Luthander, A. & Pettersson, M. 2002. Arkeologisk inventering i sydöstra Närke och västligaste Södermanland. In Åkerlund, A., Risberg, J., Hammar, D., Wikell, R., Luthander, A., Pettersson, M., Andersson, H. & Asplund, M., *Projektet "Människan i det tidiga landskapet": Inventeringar i höglänta skogsområden i nordvästra Södermanland, sydöstra Närke och nordöstra Östergötland.* Stockholm Archaeological Reports. Field Studies 8.

M —— **Magnell, O. 1995.** Människan och faunan kring Bökeberg III. In Cegielka, S., Eriksson, M., Ingvald, J., Magnell, O., Nilsson, K. & Nilsson, P., Jakten på det levande – En analys av det osteologiska materialet från den senmesolitiska boplatsen Bökeberg III, 148–170. Photocopy. Arkeologiska Institutionen, Lunds Universitet.

Mårtensson, J. 2001. Mesolitiskt trä. In Karsten, P & Knarrström, B. (eds.), *Tågerup specialstudier.* Skånska spår – arkeologi längs Västkustbanan. Lund: Riksantikvarieämbetet, UV Syd.

Mathiassen, T (ed.). 1948. *Danske oldsager* I. *Ældre stenalder.* Copenhagen: Nordisk forlag.

Mathiasson, S. & Dalhov, G. 1987. *Våra vilda djur.* Göteborg.

Møhl 1978. Aggersund-Bopladsen zoologiskt belyst: Svanejakt som årsag til bosættelse. *KUML.*

Molin, F. 2000. Mesolitikum i västra Östergötland – forskningsläge och aktuella problemområden. In *Vetenskaplig verksamhetsplan för UV Öst, arkeologiskt program 2000–2002.* Riksantikvarieämbetet. Avdelningen för arkeologiska undersökningar. Rapport UV Öst 2000:21. Linköping.

Molin, F. In prep. Trädgårdstorp: Mesolitiska huslämningar från Linköping i västra Östergötland.

Molin, F. & Larsson, M. 1999. *Mesolitikum vid Storlyckan – hyddlämning och fyndmaterial: Arkeologisk slutundersökning, RAÄ 275, Storlyckan, Väderstads socken, Mjölby kommun, Östergötland.* Riksantikvarieämbetet, Avdelningen för arkeologiska undersökningar, Rapport UV Linköping 1999:1. Linköping.

Montelius, O. 1871–73. Bronsåldern i norra och mellersta Sverige. *Antikvarisk Tidskrift för Sverige 3.*

Montelius, O. 1917. *Minnen från vår forntid* I. *Stenåldern och bronsålder.* Stockholm. Faksimiltryck. ARKEO-Förlaget, Gamleby 1994.

Moore, J. 2003. Enculturation through Fire: Beyond Hazelnuts and into the Forest. In Larsson, L., Kindgren, H., Knutsson, K., Loeffler, D. & Åkerlund, A. (eds.), *Mesolithic on the Move: Papers Presented at the Sixth International Conference on the Mesolithic in Europe, Stockholm 2000.* Oxford: Oxbow Books.

Munthe, H. 1940. *Om Nordens, främst Baltikums, senkvartära utveckling och stenåldersbebyggelse.* Stockholm.

N —— **Nerman, B. 1911.** Östergötlands stenålder. *Meddelande från Östergötlands fornminnesförening.*

Nerman, B. 1927. Ett bidrag till frågan om gånggriftstidens havsnivå vid Östergötland. *Fornvännen* 22.

Nerman, B. 1965. Knut Stjerna och hans seminarium för utforskningen av Sveriges stenålder. *Lychnos* 1963–1964.

Nilsson, E. 1953. *Om södra Sveriges senkvartära historia.* Meddelanden från Stockholms Högskolas Geologiska Institut 102. Stockholm.

Nilsson, E. 1968. *Södra Sveriges senkvartära historia: Geokronologi, issjöar och landhöjning.* Kungl. Svenska Vetenskapsakademiens Handlingar. Fjärde serien 12:1. Stockholm.

Nilsson, K. 1995. Bökeberg III – säsongsboplats/helårsboplats? In Jakten på det levande: En analys av det osteologiska materialet från den senmesolitiska boplatsen Bökeberg III. C-uppsats, Vt 1995. Arkeologiska institutionen vid Lunds Universitet. Lund.

Nilsson, P. 2004. *Detaljplan inom Kulla 1:1, Krokeks socken, Östergötland. Arkeologisk utredning, etapp 1.* RAÄ Rapport UV Öst 2004:59. Linköping.

Noe-Nygaard, N. 1977. Butchering and Marrow Fracturing as a Taphonomic Factor in Archaeological Deposits. *Paleobiology* 3.

Noe-Nygaard, N. 1988. δ^{13}C-values of Dog Bones Reveal the Nature of Changes in Man's Food Resources at the Mesolithic-Neolithic Transition, Denmark. *Isotope Geoscience* 73.

Noe-Nygaard, N. 1995. Ecological, Sedimentary and Geochemical Evolution of the Late-glacial to Postglacial Åmose Lacustrine Basin, Denmark. *Fossils and Strata* 37.

Nordén, A. 1932. Östergötlands äldsta stenåldersboplats. In *Stenåldersboplatser i Östergötland.* KVHAA 37. Stockholm.

Nordquist, P. 2001. *Hierarkiseringsprocesser: Om konstruktioner av social ojämlikhet i Skåne, 5500–1100 f.Kr.* Arkeologiska Institutionen, Umeå Universitet. Umeå.

Nordqvist, B. 1997. Västkusten. In the chapter Regionalitet under Mesolitikum – Från senglacial tid till senatlantisk tid i Syd- och Mellansverige, by M. Larsson, C. Lindgren & B. Nordqvist. In Larsson, M. and Olsson, E. (eds.), *Regionalt och interregionalt: Stenåldersundersökningar i Syd- och Mellansverige,* ed. M. Larsson & E. Olsson. Riksantikvarieämbetet Arkeologiska Undersökningar Skrifter 23. Stockholm.

Nordström, A. & Ferenius, J. 1984. *Huddinge forntid.* Huddinges historia 5. Huddinge.

Norrman, J. O. 1964. *Lake Vättern: Investigations on Shore and Bottom Morphology.* Meddelanden från Uppsala Universitets Geografiska Institution. Ser. A 194. Geografiska Annaler Häfte 1–2, 1964. Stockholm.

O —— **Olofsson, A. 1995.** *Kölskrapor, mikrospånkärnor och mikrospån: En studie med utgångspunkt i nordsvensk mikrospånteknik.* Arkeologiska studier vid Umeå universitet, 3. Umeå.

Olsson, E. 1992. The Grödinge Investigations – An Example of Interdisciplinary Study and Collaboration. *Laborativ arkeologi* 6. Stockholm.

Olsson, E. & Åkerlund, A. 1987. Stenåldersundersökningar i östra Mellansverige. In Andrae, T., Hasselmo, M. & Lamm, K. (eds.), *7000 år på 20 år: Arkeologiska undersökningar i Mellansverige.* Stockholm: Riksantikvarieämbetet.

Olsson, E. & Risberg, J. 1996. Archaeological Data and Models of Sea-level Change *c* 6000–3500 BP South of Stockholm, Eastern Sweden. In Robertsson, A.-M., Hackens, T., Hicks, S., Risberg, J. & Åkerlund, A. (eds.), *Landscapes and Life: Studies in Honour of Urve Miller*. PACT 50. Rixensart.

Olsson, E. & Runeson, H. 1999. *Högmo – en mesolitisk boplats i Gladöområdet*. RAÄ. UV Mitt, Rapport 1998:105. Stockholm.

P ___ **Pagoldh, M. 1992.** Smålands äldsta (?) boplats funnen långt inne i landet. *Populär Arkeologi* 1992:3.

Pagoldh, M. 1995. *Arkeologisk delundersökning av en ca 9000 år gammal stenåldersboplats i Anderstorp, Småland*. Jönköpings Läns Museum. Arkeologisk rapport 1995:15. Jönköping.

Pedersen, L. 7 000 Years of Fishing: Stationary Fishing Structures in the Mesolithic and Afterwards. In Fischer, A. (ed.), *Man and Sea in the Mesolithic: Coastal Settlement above and below Present Sea Level. Proceedings of the International Symposium, Kalundborg, Denmark 1993*. Oxbow Monograph 53. Oxford.

Persson, C. 1997. Mesolitikum i Jönköpings län. In Nordström, M. & Varenius, L. (eds.), *Det nära förflutna: Om arkeologi i Jönköpings län*. Jönköping.

Persson, C. & Svantesson, S.-I. 1972. The Highest Shore-line on Jakobsdalsberget i Kolmården, Sweden. *Geologiska Föreningens i Stockholm Förhandlingar* 94.

Petersen, E. Brinch. 1972. A Maglemose Hut from Sværdborg Bog. *Acta Archaeologica* 42.

Pettersson, M. 1999. *Stenåldern i Tyresta: De första människorna*. Tyresta-fakta 2. Solna.

Pettersson, M. & Wikell, R. 2004. The Outermost Shore: Site-location in Mesolithic Seascapes of Eastern Central Sweden. With a Case-study in a Burnt-off Forest Area in Tyresta National Park. In Knutsson, H. (ed.), *Coast to Coast – Arrival: Results and Reflections*. Coast to Coast Book 10. Uppsala.

R ___ **Rajala, E. & Westergren, E. 1990.** Tingby – a Mesolithic Site with the Remains of a House to the West of Kalmar, in the Province of Småland. *Meddelanden från Lunds universitets historiska museum* 1989–1990.

Regnell, M., Gaillard, M., Bartholin, T. S. & Karsten, P. 1995. Reconstruction of Environment and History of Plant Use During the Late Mesolithic (Ertebølle Culture) at the Inland Settlement of Bökeberg III, Southern Sweden. *Vegetation, History and Archaeobotany* 4.

Rex Svensson, K. 1988. *Hästefjorden under stenåldern. Fynden berättar*. Vänersborg: Älvsborgs länsmuseum.

Risberg, J. 1991. *Palaeoenvironment and Sea Level Changes during the Early Holocene on the Södertörn Peninsula, Södermanland, Eastern Sweden*. Kvartärgeologiska institutionen vid Stockholms universitet. Report 20. Stockholm.

Risberg, J. 2003. Landscape History of the Södertörn Peninsula, Eastern Sweden. In Larsson, L., Kindgren, H., Knutsson, K., Loeffler, D. & Åkerlund, A. (eds.), *Mesolithic on the Move: Papers Presented at the Sixth International Conference on the Mesolithic in Europe, Stockholm 2000*. Oxford: Oxbow Books.

Rolöf, M. 2005. *Stenålder i Fläskbergen: Boplats funnen vid arkeologisk utredning inför detaljplan för återvinningsstation (returpunkt) inom Lösings häradsallmänning: krokeks socken, Norrköpings kommun. Arkeologisk utredning, etapp 2*. RAÄ Rapport UV Öst 2005:9. Linköping.

Rosberg, A. & Sarnäs, P. 1992. Porfyr. *Populär Arkeologi* 1992:2, p. 34.

Rowley-Conwy, P. 1987. Animal Bones in Mesolithic Studies: Recent Progress and Hopes for the Future. In Rowley-Conwy, P., Zvelebil, M. & Blankholm, H. P. (eds.), *Mesolithic Northwest Europe: Recent Trends*. Sheffield.

Rowley-Conwy, P. 1998. Meat, Furs and Skins: Mesolithic Animal Bones from Ringkloster, A Seasonal Hunting Camp in Jutland. *Journal of Danish Archaeology* 12 (1994–95).

S ___ **Schierbeck, A. 1996.** *Arkeologisk utredning: Södertörns högskola.* RAÄ. UV Stockholm, Rapport 1996:125. Stockholm.

Schild, R. 1985. The Formation of Homogeneous Occupation Units in Open-Air Sandy Sites and its Significance for the Interpretation of Mesolithic Flint Assemblage. In Bonsall, C. (ed.), *The Mesolithic in Europe: Papers Presented at the Third International Symposium.* Edinburgh.

Schild, R. 1998. The Perils of Dating Open-air Sandy Sites of the North European Plain. In Zvelebil, M., Denell, R. & Domanska, L. (eds.), *Harvesting the Sea, Farming the Forest: The Emergence of Neolithic Societies in the Baltic Region.* Sheffield Archaeological Monographs 10. Sheffield: Sheffield Academic Press.

Schilling, H. 2001. Veje til en mesolitisk kulturhistorie. In Jensen. O. L, Sørensen, S. A. & Hansen, K. M. (eds.), *Danmarks jægerstenalder – status og perspektiver: Beretning fra symposiet "Status og perspektiver inden for dansk mesolitikum" afholdt i Vordingborg, september 1998.* Hørsholm.

Schnell, I. 1930. Södertörn under stenåldern. *Bidrag till Södermanlands äldre kulturhistoria* XXIV, 7–16. Utg. Av Södermanlands fornminnesförening. Strängnäs.

Selinge, K.-G. 1989. Det närvarande förflutna: 50 år med fornminnesinventeringen. *Riksantikvarie-ämbetets och Statens historiska museers årsbok* 1987–88.

Sigvallius, B. 1997. *Mörby: Fornlämning 168, Hogstad socken, Östergötland. Osteologisk under-sökning.* Stockholm: Statens Historiska Museum.

Sigvallius, B. 2004. Motala: Osteologisk undersökning av benmaterial från den mesolitiska boplatsen vid Motalaån. 2002 och 2003 års utgrävningar. Unpublished report.

Siiriäinen, A. 1969. *Über die Chronologie der steinzeitlichen Küstenwohnplätze Finnlands im Lichte der Uferverschienbung.* SM. Helsinki.

Siiriäinen, A. 1975. Quartz, Chert and Obsidian: A Comparison of Rawmaterials in Late Stone Age Aggregate in Kenya. *Finskt Museum.*

Siiriäinen, A. 1977. Problems of East Fennoscandia Mesolithic. *Finskt Museum* 84.

Skanser, L. 2004. *Stenåldersboplatser i Broddbo och en nyupptäckt boplats i Möklinta.* Västman-lands läns museum, rapport 2004:A57. Västerås.

Sørensen, M. 2003. Experiments with the "Tågerup Pressure Tool". In Karsten, P. & Knarrström, B. (eds.), *The Tågerup excavations.* Skånska spår – arkeologi längs Västkustbanan. Lund: Riksantikvarieämbetet, UV Syd.

Sørensen, S. 1996. *Kongemosekulturen i Sydskandinavien.* Færgegården.

Strömberg, M, 1986. Signs of Mesolithic Occupation in South-East Scania. *Meddelanden från Lunds universitets historiska museum* 1985–1986.

Strucke, U. 2003. Vedartsanalyser från Strandvägen 1, Motala, Motala kommun, Östergötland. In *Mesolitikum och yngre Järnålder på Strandvägen 1, Motala. Motala kommun Östergötland.* DAFF 2004:2. Riksantikvarieämbetet UV Öst. Linköping.

Stuiver, M. & Becker B. 1993. High-precision decadal calibration of the radiocarbon time scale, AD 1950–6000 BC. *Radiocarbon* 35.

Sundelin, U. 1919. Om en stenåldersboplats vid litorinagränsen i Östergötland. In Ambrosiani, S., Lindqvist, S. & Nerman, B. (eds.), *Studier tillägnade Oscar Almgren.* Stockholm. (Also published in *Rig* 120:3.)

T ___ **Thomas, J. 1993.** The Hermeneutics of Megalithic Space. In Tilley, C. (ed.), *Interpretative Archaeology*. Oxford.

Thomas, J. 1996. Neolithic Houses in Mainland Britain and Ireland: A Sceptical View. In Darvill, T. & Thomas, J. (eds.), *Neolithic Houses in Northwest Europe and Beyond*. Oxford.

Trotzig, G. 1993. Maltadokumentet. *Kulturmiljövård* 4/93.

V ___ **Vang Petersen, P. 1984.** Chronological and Regional Variation in the Late Mesolithic of Eastern Denmark. *Journal of Danish Archaeology* 3.

Verhart, L. 1990. Stone Age Bone and Antler Points as Indicators for "Social Territories" in the European Mesolithic. In Vermeersch, P. & Van Peer, P. (eds.), *Contributions to the Mesolithic in Europe*. Leuven.

Verhart, L. & Waansleben, M. 1997. Waste and Prestige: The Mesolithic–Neolithic Transition in the Netherlands from a Social Perspective. *Analecta Prehistorica Leidensia* 29.

Vretemark, M. 1996. Brända djurben från en mesolitisk-tidigneolitisk boplats i Östergötland. In Larsson, M., *Högby: Mesolitiska och senneolitiska boplatser vid Högby i Östergötland. Bosättningsmönster och materiell kultur. Arkeologisk slutundersökning, Mjölby och Högby socknar, Mjölby kommun, Östergötland*, Del 1, Appendix 1, p. 59. Riksantikvarieämbetet, Avdelningen för arkeologiska undersökningar, Rapport UV Linköping 1996:35. Linköping.

W ___ **Welinder, S. 1973a.** Mesolithic Sites with Flint in Eastern Middle Sweden. In Kozlowski, S. (ed.), *The Mesolithic in Europe*. Warsaw.

Welinder, S. 1973b. *The Pre-Pottery Stone Age of Eastern Middle Sweden: Sjövreten–Hagtorp–Östra Vrå–Överråda*. Antikvariskt Arkiv 48. Stockholm.

Welinder, S. 1975. Stenåldersproblem i Halland: Funderingar kring en boplats i Tönnersa, Eldsberga socken. *Halland: Årsbok för kulturhistoria och hembygdsvård i Hallands län* 58.

Welinder, S. 1977. *The Mesolithic Stone Age of Eastern Middle Sweden*. Antikvariskt arkiv 65. Stockholm: Kungliga Vitterhets Historie och Antikvitets Akademien.

Weniger, G. C. 1995. *Widerhakenspitzen des Magdalénien Westeuropas: Ein Vergleich mit ethnohistorischen Jägergruppen Nordamerikas*. Madrider Beiträge Band 20. Mainz.

Werthwein, G. 2000. Tillverkades mikroavslag med bipolär slagmetod? Fortsatt mikroteknologi under neolitikum? In Ersgård, L. (ed.), *Människors platser*. Riksantikvarieämbetet Arkeologiska Undersökningar Skrifter 31. Göteborg.

Westergren, E. & Hansson, A. 1987. Nya rön om stenåldern och bronsåldern i Kalmarbygden. *Kalmar län* 72.

Whittle, A. 1996. *Europe in the Neolithic: The Creation of New Worlds*. Cambridge.

Wikell, R. 2002. Arkeologi på hög nivå: Nya stenåldersfynd i Södermanlands skogar. In Åkerlund, A. (ed.), *Kulturell mångfald i Södermanland* 1. Nyköping.

Wikell, R. 2003. Sälknivar från Haninges stenålder. *Glimtar från Haningebygden* 2003:4.

Wikell, R. In prep. Pionjärer i västra Mälarmården.

Z ___ **Zvelebil, M. 1995.** A Final Word on "Man and Sea in the Mesolithic" – Good News for Women? In Fischer, A. (ed.), *Man and Sea in the Mesolithic: Coastal Settlement above and below Present Sea Level. Proceedings of the International Symposium, Kalundborg, Denmark 1993*. Oxbow

Previous publications in the series

1. Forntida svedjebruk. Om möjligheterna att spåra forntidens svedjebruk. G. Lindman. 1991.

2. Rescue and Research. Reflections of Society in Sweden 700–1700 A.D. L. Ersgård, M. Holmström och K. Lamm, eds. 1992.

3. Svedjebruket i Munkeröd. Ett exempel på periodiskt svedjebruk från yngre stenålder till medeltid i södra Bohuslän. G. Lindman. 1993.

4. Arkeologi i Attundaland. G. Andersson, A. Broberg, A. Ericsson, J. Hedlund & Ö. Hermodsson. 1994.

5. Stenskepp och Storhög. Rituell tradition och social organisation speglad i skeppssättningar från bronsålder och storhögar från järnålder. T. Artelius, R. Hernek & G. Ängeby. 1994.

6. Landscape of the monuments. A study of the passage tombs in the Cúil Irra region. S. Bergh. 1995.

7. Kring Stång. En kulturgeografisk utvärdering byggd på äldre lantmäteriakter och historiska kartöverlägg. H. Borna Ahlqvist & C. Tollin. 1994.

8. Teoretiska perspektiv på gravundersökningar i Södermanland. A. Eriksson och J. Runcis. 1994.

9. Det inneslutna rummet – om kultiska hägnader, fornborgar och befästa gårdar i Uppland från 1300 f Kr till Kristi födelse. M. Olausson. 1995.

10. Bålverket. Om samhällsförändring och motstånd med utgångspunkt från det tidigmedeltida Bulverket i Tingstäde träsk på Gotland. J. Rönnby. 1995.

11. Samhällsstruktur och förändring under bronsåldern. Rapport från ett seminarium 29–30 september 1994 på Norrköpings Stadsmuseum i samarbete med Riksantikvarieämbetet, UV Linköping. M. Larsson och A. Toll, red. 1995.

12. Om brunnar. Arkeologiska och botaniska studier på Håbolandet. I. Ullén, H. Ranheden, T. Eriksson & R. Engelmark. 1995.

13. Hus & Gård i det förurbana samhället – rapport från ett sektorsforskningsprojekt vid Riksantikvarieämbetet. Katalog. O. Kyhlberg & A. Vinberg, red. 1996.

14. Hus & Gård. Boplatser från mesolitikum till medeltid. Artikeldel. Hus och gård i det förurbana samhället. O. Kyhlberg & A.Vinberg, red. 1996.

15. Medeltida landsbygd. En arkeologisk utvärdering – Forskningsöversikt, problemområden, katalog. L. Ersgård & A-M. Hållans. 1996.

16. Living by the sea. Human responses to Shore Displacement in Eastern Middle Sweden during the Stone Age. A. Åkerlund. 1996.

17. Långfärd och återkomst – skeppet i bronsålderns gravar. T. Artelius. 1996.

18. Slöinge och Borg. Stormansgårdar i öst och väst. K. Lindeblad, L. Lundqvist, A-L. Nielsen. & L. Ersgård. 1996.

19. Religion från stenålder till medeltid. Artiklar baserade på Religionsarkeologiska nätverksgruppens konferens på Lövstadbruk den 1-3 december 1995. K. Engdahl & A. Kaliff, red. 1996.

20. Metodstudier & tolkningsmöjligheter. E. Hyenstrand, M. Jakobsson, A. Nilsson, H. Ranheden & J. Rönnby. 1997.

21. Det starka landskapet. En arkeologisk studie av Leksandsbygden i Dalarna från yngre järnålder till nyare tid. L. Ersgård. 1997.

22. Carpe Scaniam. Axplock ur Skånes förflutna. P. Karsten, red. 1997.

23. Regionalt och interregionalt. Stenåldersundersökningar i Syd- och Mellansverige. M. Larsson & E. Olsson, red. 1997.

24. Visions of the Past. Trends and Traditions in Swedish Medieval Archaeology. H. Andersson, P. Carelli & L. Ersgård, eds. 1997.

25. Spiralens öga. Tjugo artiklar kring aktuell bronsåldersforskning. M. Olausson, red. 1999.

26. Senpaleolitikum i Skåne – en studie av materiell kultur och ekonomi hos Sveriges första fångstfolk. M. Andersson & B. Knarrström. 1999.

27. Forskaren i fält. En vänbok till Kristina Lamm. K. Andersson, A. Lagerlöf & A. Åkerlund, red. 1999.

28. Olika perspektiv på en arkeologisk undersökning i västra Östergötland. A. Kaliff, red. 1999.

29. Odlingslandskap och uppdragsarkeologi. Artiklar från Nätverket för arkeologisk agrarhistoria. A. Ericsson, red. 1999.

30. Fragment av samtal. Tvärvetenskap med arkeologi och ortnamnsforskning i bohuslänska exempel. M. Lönn. 1999.

31. Människors platser. 13 arkeologiska studier från UV. Red. FoU-gruppen vid UV. 2000.

32. Porten till Skåne. Löddeköpinge under järnålder och medeltid. F. Svanberg & B. Söderberg, red. 2000.

33. En bok om Husbyar. M. Olausson, red. 2000.

34. Arkeologi och paleoekologi i sydvästra Småland. Tio artiklar från Hamnedaprojektet. Per Lagerås, red. 2000.

35. På gården. Rumslig organisation inom bostättningsytor och byggnader under bronsålder och äldre järnålder. J. Streiffert. 2001.

36. Bortglömda föreställningar. Begravningsritual och begravningsplats i halländsk yngre järnålder. T. Artelius. 2000.

37. Dansarna från Bökeberg. Om jakt, ritualer och inlandsbosättning vid jägarstenålderns slut. P. Karsten. 2001.

38. Vem behöver en by? Kyrkheddinge, struktur och strategi under tusen år. K. Schmidt Sabo, red. 2001.

39. Stenåldersforskning i fokus. Inblickar och utblickar i sydskandinavisk stenåldersarkeologi. I. Bergenstråhle & S. Hellerström, red. 2001.

40. Skånska regioner. Tusen år av kultur och samhälle i förändring. A. Carlie, red. 2002.

41. Bärnstensbarnen. Bilder, berättelser och betraktelser. J. Runcis. 2002.

42. Hällristarnas hem. Gårdsbebyggelse och struktur i Pryssgården under bronsålder. H. Borna-Ahlqvist. 2002.

43. Märkvärt, medeltida. Arkeologi ur en lång skånsk historia. M. Mogren, red. 2002.

44. Bronsyxan som ting och tanke i skandinavisk senneolitikum och äldre bronsålder. L. Karlenby. 2002.

45. Urban Diversity. Archaeology in the Swedish Province of Östergötland. R. Hedvall, red. 2002.

46. Arkeologi i Vadstena. Nya resultat med utgångspunkt i undersökningarna i stadsdelen Sanden. R. Hedvall, red. 2003.

47. I Tyskebacken. Hus, människor och industri i stormaktstidens Norrköping. P. Karlsson & G. Tagesson, red. 2003.

48. Åderförkalkning och portvinstår. Välfärdssjukdomar i det medeltida Åhus. C. Arcini. 2003.

49. Landningsplats Forntiden. Arkeologiska fördjupningsstudier kring yngre stenålder, järnålder och historisk tid, inom det område som tas i anspråk för den tredje landningsbanan vid Arlanda flygplats. J. Anund, red. 2003.

50. Mittens rike. Arkeologiska berättelser från Närke. L. Karlenby, red. 2003.

51. Järrestad. Huvudgård i centralbygd. B. Söderberg, red. 2003.

52. Stone Age Scania. Significant places dug and read by contract archaeology. M. Andersson, P. Karsten, B. Knarrström & M. Svensson. 2004.

53. Stadsbor och bönder. Materiell kultur och social status i Halland från medeltid till 1700-tal. C. Rosén. 2004.

54. Människor och kvarts. Sociala och teknologiska strategier under mesolitikum i östra Mellansverige. C. Lindgren. 2004.

55. Att föra gudarnas talan – figurinerna från Lunda. G. Andersson m.fl. 2004.

56. Gårdar från förr. Nordbohuslänsk bebyggelsehistoria utifrån arkeologiska undersökningar av tre medeltida gårdar. G. Lindman, red. 2004.

57. Forntida byggnadskult. Tradition och regionalitet i södra Skandinavien. A. Carlie. 2004.

58. Aktuella metodfrågor 1. M. Lönn, red. 2004.

59. Neolitiska nedslag – Arkeologiska uppslag. J. Holm, red. 2005.

60. Lionga. Kaupinga. Kulturhistoria och arkeologi i Linköpingsbygden. A. Kaliff & G. Tagesson, red. 2005.

61. Gravspråk som religiös strategi. Valsta och Skälby i Attundaland under vikingatid och tidig medeltid. G. Andersson. 2005.

62. Aristokratiskt rum och gränsöverskridande. Järrestad och sydöstra Skåne mellan region och rike, 600–1100. B. Söderberg. 2005

63. In the Wake of a Woman – The Pioneering of North-eastern Scania, Sweden 10000–5000 BC. The Årup Settlements. P. Karsten, ed. 2005.

64. Identities in Transition – Mesolithic Strategies in the Swedish Province of Östergötland. G. Gruber, ed. 2005.

65. Dealing With the Dead – Perspectives on Prehistoric Scandinavian Burial Ritual. T. Artelius & F. Svanberg, eds. 2005.

Since the end of the 1980s, the National Heritage Board has had an office in Linköping pursuing archaeological excavations in Östergötland. There are similar offices in four other places in Sweden. The main sphere of activity comprises preliminary archaeological studies, inquiries, and excavations occasioned by development work.

The results of the investigations are published by each office in its own series of reports. The excavation department also have a joint series for scholarly works and popular books.

Visit our website at www.raa.se/uv, where you will find the latest news on Swedish archaeology.